What is a Person?

In this book, John M. Rist offers an account of the concept of 'person' as it has developed in the West, and how it has become alien in a post-Christian culture. He begins by identifying the 'Mainline Tradition' about persons as it evolved from the time of Plato to the High Middle Ages, then turns to successive attacks on it in the seventeenth and eighteenth centuries, then proceeds to the 'Five Ways' in which the Tradition was savaged or distorted in the nineteenth century and beyond. He concludes by considering whether ideas from contemporary philosophical movements, those that combine a closer analysis of human nature with a more traditional metaphysical background may enable the Tradition to be restored. A timely book on a theme of universal significance, Rist ponders whether we persons matter, and how we have reached a position where we are not sure whether we do.

John M. Rist is an Emeritus Professor of the University of Toronto. Author of more than a dozen books and over a hundred articles on ancient philosophy, patristics and ethics, he is a Fellow of the Royal Society of Canada and an Aquinas Medalist of the American Catholic Philosophical Association.

What is a Person?

Realities, Constructs, Illusions

JOHN M. RIST
University of Toronto

CAMBRIDGE
UNIVERSITY PRESS

CAMBRIDGE
UNIVERSITY PRESS

University Printing House, Cambridge CB2 8BS, United Kingdom

One Liberty Plaza, 20th Floor, New York, NY 10006, USA

477 Williamstown Road, Port Melbourne, VIC 3207, Australia

314–321, 3rd Floor, Plot 3, Splendor Forum, Jasola District Centre,
New Delhi – 110025, India

79 Anson Road, #06–04/06, Singapore 079906

Cambridge University Press is part of the University of Cambridge.

It furthers the University's mission by disseminating knowledge in the pursuit of
education, learning, and research at the highest international levels of excellence.

www.cambridge.org
Information on this title: www.cambridge.org/9781108478076
DOI: 10.1017/9781108784160

First published 2020

Printed in the United Kingdom by TJ International Ltd, Padstow Cornwall

A catalogue record for this publication is available from the British Library.

Library of Congress Cataloging-in-Publication Data
NAMES: Rist, John M., author.
TITLE: What is a person? : realities, constructs, illusions / John M. Rist, University of Toronto.
DESCRIPTION: Cambridge, United Kingdom ; New York, NY, USA : Cambridge University
Press, 2020. | Includes bibliographical references and index.
IDENTIFIERS: LCCN 2019042097 (print) | LCCN 2019042098 (ebook) |
ISBN 9781108478076 (hardback) | ISBN 9781108746816 (paperback) |
ISBN 9781108784160 (epub)
SUBJECTS: LCSH: Personalism. | Philosophical anthropology. | Persons. | Agent (Philosophy)
CLASSIFICATION: LCC B828.5 .R57 2020 (print) | LCC B828.5 (ebook) | DDC 126–dc23
LC record available at https://lccn.loc.gov/2019042097
LC ebook record available at https://lccn.loc.gov/2019042098

ISBN 978-1-108-47807-6 Hardback

Contents

Acknowledgments

The immediate origins of this book lie in a course on persons I gave in the Graduate Faculty of Philosophy at the Catholic University of America, and I should like to thank Dean John McCarthy and his colleagues for giving me the opportunity to try out a few ideas I had been mulling over for some years – as well as for countless other acts of kindness. And I would also like to thank all the students in my course both for spotting weaknesses in what I said at that time and for enabling me to recognize various further holes in the argument which otherwise I would probably have missed. Special thanks are also due to Professors Robert Sokolowski and Arthur Madigan for various detailed and valuable criticisms of an earlier version of the written text. And finally, the structure I have produced has once again been scrutinized with the utmost care by Anna Rist who is well aware of how inferior it would have been without her patient assistance. On the more technical side I should like to thank the editorial staff of the Cambridge University Press, especially Beatrice Rehl, for their speedy and most obliging attention to the production of this book.

Cambridge, September 2019.

Introduction

> Nothing is more difficult than to realize that every man has a distinct soul,
> that every one of all the millions who live or have lived, is a whole and
> independent being in himself, as if there were no one else in the whole world
> but he ... We cannot understand that a multitude is a collection of
> immortal souls.
>
> Newman *PPS* IV 6 80–3

Despite the citation of Newman, this book will make no claims about the
immortality of the soul or of the person. Its subject is far less theological,
though overall not unreligious. What I want to try to answer is the more
elementary question of whether the concept of 'person', as developed over
time, adds anything (or should add anything) to our understanding of
what it is to be human: a question which has to underlie Newman's
challenging statement.

Although Newman understands that man has – not 'is' – a soul, he
might be taken to imply that a multitude of persons is a multitude of
souls. Presumably he prefers to speak of souls because the word 'soul', as
distinct from 'self' or 'person' – let alone 'ego' – has, after Christianity,
unavoidably religious connotations. In classical Greece, however, the
primary sense of *psyche* (which we translate as 'soul') relates to the
possession of *life*: humans have 'souls', corpses do not. But if we accept
that we are alive, we will ask what it is to be alive, and whether some
aspects of our life, some functions of our 'soul' (*psyche*), are more basic
than others. Then we might ask, as did the Greeks, whether we – or our
souls – are immortal and enquire into the relationship between our souls
and our bodies. And though I shall not discuss the question of

I

immortality, I cannot avoid – in a project about persons – asking whether there is a necessary and intelligibly enduring relationship between 'souls' and bodies.

Since in various respects these will seem to be *religious* questions, so those who *now* talk about souls may propose or assume some sort of religious understanding of the world, and attribute such an understanding to others. Hence, and bucking any residual taboo on 'religious talk', I shall also have to enquire whether 'soul' is an essential component of any intelligible account of human personhood: that is, whether we can be persons without in some sense 'having' souls. In the first part of the following study we shall find that those ancient and medieval thinkers who gradually built up the concept of the person included the soul within that account.

But if 'soul' is or became a term of religion as well as of psychology or anthropology, it by the same token belongs in a world in which there is a God or gods. And if the concepts of 'soul' and 'God' go together, we may wonder whether the concept of person – which had use in a world of souls and gods – has further authentic use in a world held to be bereft of both. Or at least, and more specifically, whether it can play the *same* role in a god-less and soul-less world as it did in earlier settings. And whether those who suppose – implicitly or explicitly – that talk of gods and souls is empty, even damaging to our self-understanding, can find some way of retaining the 'worth' that we earlier attributed to 'persons' equipped with souls: or whether they prefer (or should prefer) to discard it.

One corollary of that may seem of particular importance. It might be argued that in a god-less and soul-less world there is no true basis for moral obligation, since we live in a value-free universe – all values being human constructs – and that new-fangled ways of protecting persons (whoever they may be) cannot be intrinsically binding in that they can only be defended in conventional or at best prudential terms. And without God and soul other possible ideas or realities about persons may have to be rethought or abandoned too: spirit, for example, and any concept of the spiritual indicating not only religious but also aesthetic values more potent than the products of mere sentimentality.

If our liberal society is to be thought capable of justifying many of its basic assumptions philosophically, there are many threats it must defuse, including those just listed. If it cannot, then talk of persons and obligations to persons will seem merely descriptive and conventional, or – if axiological – arbitrary. Yet any satisfying answer to such challenges must be more than ideological. Hence I shall argue that if we have learned more about what it is to be a person than was apparent in the past, the mere discovery of new or newly recovered facts – as for example about the nature and origins of the person's incommunicable uniqueness – will, in and of itself, provide no further reason to attribute worth to persons: other, that is, than a man-made value which can be bestowed and cancelled, being ultimately dependent on the will of the powerful. If persons are to be *intrinsically* valuable, it may be the case that this is possible only if their worth depends on the existence of an extra-mental entity capable of conferring its own worth upon them. In any case, the distinction between descriptions of persons and evaluations of persons must be kept clear as we proceed.

What then is – or was – a person? How is he or she best identified? Just as a human individual? Or as some sort of bearer of qualities both physical and non-physical, to be denoted by two corresponding types of predicates (such as 'fat' or 'just'). Otherwise perhaps, as Boethius puts it, as 'an individual substance of a rational nature' (*Against Eutyches* 3)? If the last, then human beings are persons, but there may be other persons who are not human beings, perhaps angels: Boethius certainly believes that there are three 'persons' in God. That may help us understand why he and other Christians might think it more informative to call us 'persons' rather than just human rational individuals; because in some way we are like God.

Boethius sometimes (as at *Consolation* 5.4 and 5.5) says that human beings possess both 'reason' (apparently discursive reason) and 'intelligence' (presumably – like the Greek *nous* – the more 'divine' power of direct intuition). But what does identifying ourselves as persons – rather than merely as human rational animals, however richly 'rational' is understood – add to our understanding of our nature? Are there other more concrete 'structural' features common to all who should be designated 'persons', whether human or 'divine'? Is Boethius' account, however modified and explicated, specific enough? And again, what weight should we put on the fact that it was formulated in a 'religious', indeed in a Christian context: that is, in a world in which there were claimed to be both souls and a God?

In such a context there may exist an account of persons which is axiological rather than merely descriptive; even in contemporary non-religious circles it is often held that persons are not merely individuals, but individuals possessed of special value. However, if some humans (such as slaves or the unborn) have no (non-mercenary) value, they might not be persons; in particular, they might not be persons in the then necessary *legal* sense. Thus, there might (legally) be corporate persons, though a corporation is not a human individual, while some human individuals might not be (or not be legally recognized as) persons. In any case, we need to know the source – whether human or divine – of human 'worth' or 'value', and in whom it is (or could be) recognized, and why.

Boethius must have thought that all humans have, in God's eyes, some intrinsic worth, but he does not specify in what human 'dignity' – doubtless his preferred word – consists. Presumably as a Christian his account of it would have been stronger than what was traditionally Roman: namely that living beings are ranked both between species and within species such that in that hierarchical structure some human beings – even some free males – have more 'dignity' than others, and accordingly are more worthy of respect; this Cicero indicates in the *De Officiis* (1.109), where, as we shall see, discussing our various 'roles' (*personae*), he observes that the second *persona* indicates our social ranking within the human community. Such ranking, in non-Christian Roman jurisprudence, was legally recognized, albeit Roman law insisted that a real person was not only 'of an incommunicable nature' (*alteri incommunicabilis*) but also partaking 'of his own right' (*sui iuris*): that is, free to make his own decisions (as slaves, having no 'dignity', were not).

Despite his silence, such ambiguity could not have satisfied the Christian Boethius, since Paul (Galatians 2.6; cf. Deut. 10:17, Acts 10:34) teaches that God is no respecter of persons (*prosopa* = *personae*, as translated by Jerome); hence that in God's eyes *all* human beings possess equal 'dignity'. Nor, as we shall see, could it have satisfied Augustine who observes unambiguously that the 'dignity' of men as rational beings in God's image is bestowed by God's gift (*Sermon* 371.4).[1] For whereas the pagan Roman account of dignity implies hierarchic relationships within human society, the Christian version, though partially dependent on God's decree in *Genesis* that man is of higher order and dignity than other creatures, yet cannot be limited to that. For human dignity, as Augustine 'knows', is primarily determined by our creation in God's image – as by texts indicating that God is no respecter of persons – and

[1] For further Augustine references (*CD* 12.28; 22.24; *Spirit and Letter* 28.49) indicating that man's dignity is evidenced by his remaining even after the fall as a (distorted but real) image of God – but only by God's gift – see the extended discussion of Pera (2015: 86–109) and pages 47–49 below. Pera is right to emphasize the radical difference between Christian and Kantian accounts of human dignity, though he puts too much stress on part of the Christian account, at times almost seeming to suggest that man's dignity consists solely in his superiority to the lower creatures.

that therefore – one can infer – some portion of the respect due to God should also be shown to his image; hence eventually that since God expects us to respect his rights over us, so we must respect the rights we owe to one another as in his image.

Yet Boethius, Augustine and many others were often incoherent on the question of the 'dignity' and consequent due respect owed to many in their society – not least in the case of slaves. Signs of a more Christian approach, however, can be found elsewhere in late antiquity, not least among the Cappadocian Fathers. Especially powerful is the challenge of Gregory of Nyssa to any belief that monetary value can be put on a human being, on any instance, that is, of an image of God. So much for slavery, though Gregory's words had little immediate practical impact.

Two other areas, however, in which human dignity was manifestly degraded in ancient society were also subject to calls for reform: enforced prostitution (of males as of females) is roundly condemned both by Gregory and by his brother Basil. And before long laws were introduced to attempt to purify ancient society by suppressing it. As for the poor, their omnipresence (as the Gospels themselves had regularly lamented) was held to be a disgrace in a Christian society by the same Cappadocian preachers. Such calls for reform, however little immediately successful, were indicators that the Christian belief in human dignity could – eventually – become the source of major calls for more wide reformations of society.[2]

Hence, as noted, the problem arises whether without specifically religious (or perhaps in a 'Platonic' world metaphysical) claims it is possible to confirm and explicate inherent dignity and respect – hence, and in modern times, intrinsic rights – so that, as persons, we should not be treated only as means to an end, but as ends in our own right. That was Kant's hopeful non-religious formulation. If it is correct and defensible – despite Kant's failure adequately to defend it, which we shall inspect in

---

[2] For details on the Cappadocian defence of human dignity see recently Harper (2016). A certain foreshadowing of the idea that in some sense humans were born equal and that enforced sexual activity is contrary to the law of nature can be found in the work of the third century jurist Ulpian, but it is only a foreshadowing; thus as Honoré (2002: 85) puts it, 'All [humans] are [born] equal in that they possess dignity but, in contrast with modern thinking, the degree of dignity varies from person to person'. Honoré and others attribute this 'cosmopolitanism' – recalling Marcus Aurelius' 'Dear city of Zeus' and appropriate after the Constitutio Antoniniana (of 212) granted citizenship to all free inhabitants of the Empire – to Stoic influence. If so, that influence probably came more from ideas 'in the air' rather than specific Stoic sources.

due course – then even in a godless framework each person really is uniquely valuable in the same way as all other human individuals: that is, if and only if he or she is uniquely different from all those other human individuals. The question of whether such strictly 'secular' claims – for which Kant offered the most persuasive and compelling arguments – can do more than license a mere axiological whistling in the wind will be a recurring theme of the present study.

It is assumed by most of our Western theorizing contemporaries that persons are individualized members of the human species and not merely specimens of a human type; that each is unique and that all are equally valuable (however such value is to be measured) and therefore possessors of rights; or (as a legal positivist, equipped with no legitimate defense of intrinsic rights, would have to phrase it) 'worthy' of possessing them. Nor is being equally valuable normally construed as being equal in having no value at all, but as being an equal possessor of much, even of infinite and certainly of immeasurable value.

Yet if that is the case, there might seem something odd about treating some persons – say one's own family – as more important (to ourselves) than others. Should we distinguish (conceptually) between the absolute worth of all persons and the more variable worth which we are obliged to respect in our local situations? If we claim to love humanity, does that imply that we should never prefer one person to any other? If so, we not only seem to be talking 'academically' – in the worst sense of the word – but tending to neglect the *uniqueness* of individual persons in the very defense of their equally valuable status. Are we rather to conclude that as finite beings we are only in a position – in practice – to accept obligations to a limited number of our fellows? Perhaps our responsibility for others, and our concern with their value or worth, diminishes in accordance with certain inevitable modes of human society and human flourishing.

Here I should pause to clarify a terminological problem, perhaps already noticed by readers. Modern comments on human worth (at least since Hobbes who collapses 'worth' into 'value') normally treat of a man's 'value' – which suggests human evaluation; earlier writers normally prefer 'dignity' or 'worth'. I have tried to retain the distinction, but at times the demands of idiomatic English indicate that 'value' may have to be preferred where 'dignity' or 'worth' would be more appropriate. Nevertheless 'dignity' is better than 'value' in relation to the original Christian concept of man's being created in the image and likeness of God, since it indicates that human worth depends not on some later gift of God to humankind but on the fact that at our very creation as God's image we *ipso facto* participate in the divine dignity; hence we are worthy of a share of the respect due to God himself.

*

It might seem unnecessary to defend the historical approach I have adopted in the present essay. Unfortunately, that is not the case since authors who write sympathetically and systematically about persons often fail to understand that many of our apparent insights have in the past been far from self-evident; on the contrary, they are the result of hundreds of years of thought about human nature. Slavery offers an excellent test-case for this claim. Discussing it as a gross infringement of human rights and noting that ancient slave-owning societies tolerated a 'relationship that does violence to the personhood of those held as slaves', John Crosby writes:[3] 'We... marvel at the immaturity in the understanding of the person that ancient peoples had who simply took slavery for granted; we think it is as if they had hardly awakened to the personhood of human beings'.

Rejecting this as grotesque historical blindness, I shall argue that we can only understand many of our present intuitions about the 'personhood of human beings' by enquiring into the development of the concept of the person over long periods of time. In such an inquiry we should remember not only that ancient (and medieval) societies – including the Athens of Socrates, Plato and Aristotle – could never have developed as they did without slaves (as Aristotle himself pointed out), but that this-worldly slavery is not explicitly condemned even in the Gospels; nor, for that matter, by the great majority of ancient and medieval Christian and other thinkers of the highest rank. The 'personalist' approach, Christian or non-Christian, to slavery arose not from the *direct* words of the Scriptures but from extended reflection over centuries on their deeper implications as the concept of person was gradually worked out and became part of more extended philosophical investigation. And, importantly, as social and industrial substitutes for chattel slavery were developed.

Hence the present enquiry will proceed within clear chronological and spatial parameters. I shall pursue 'persons' first within Western culture

---

[3] Crosby (1996: 13).

from Socrates in the fifth century BC to Boethius in the fifth century AD,[4] and thence into the High Middle Ages. I shall call the account of persons that gradually emerged in this period the 'Mainline Tradition'. Thence I shall move through the early modern period and its precursors on to the present day, in the hope of casting further light on whether modern and contemporary challenges even to more developed versions of Boethius' summary can be met – and what we are left with if they cannot. I impose these limits not only because my competence does not extend beyond them but because the complex development of the concept of a person with which I am concerned took place – and perhaps could only have taken place – within our Western world where a remarkable – Christians should say providential – assimilation of Greco-Roman and Hebrew-Christian traditions was developed.[5] Parallel discussions of persons in the requisite sense might have occurred elsewhere, though a superficial trawl suggests this not to be the case. Which is not to deny that individual features of the concepts I shall examine may occur outside Western parameters.

I must constantly remind the reader, however, that in our Western tradition persons can be discussed descriptively within what are now taken to be the two distinct disciplines of philosophy and theology; but that there remains a serious unanswered question as to whether and how they can be discussed axiologically within strictly secular parameters. That question is of no mean contemporary importance since only in comparatively recent times have Western thinkers tried consciously to construct (rather than merely assume) an ethics and a theory of human value with no explicit or implicit reference to God.

What I have written is a very preliminary survey, largely limited to individual figures rather than examining radical changes in the *Zeitgeist*. Nevertheless, I can hardly insist too much on one 'world-historical' comment at the starting-point: that Mainline Tradition, the development of which I analyze in the first part of this book, was built, as already noted, on a combination of two sources: Graeco-Roman and Jewish-Christian. When we reach the beginnings of the modern age, we shall

[4] My limitation to Western writers means that I shall say little more about those Greek Fathers of the Church (Basil, Gregory of Nazienzen, Gregory of Nyssa) whose work on the delineation of the Divine Persons in the Trinity is of importance, but I shall subsume the effects of their theological work in my remarks especially about the contribution of Boethius: well versed in Greek theology between the Councils of Nicaea and Chalcedon.
[5] For an introduction to the question of how Christians came first to realize the need to take philosophy seriously see Rist (2007).

see that a number of those who contributed to the weakening and even (in the hopes of some) the destruction of that tradition, tried to remove the influence of one or other of those two foundational sources. Neo-pagans like Giordano Bruno – to say nothing as yet of Nietzsche and Heidegger – wanted to revert to the classical world, while many Protestants, starting with Luther himself, thought Greek ideas, especially in ethics, had corrupted Christianity and needed to be largely erased. That judgment of Luther's, of course, I believe to be false, since Christianity properly understood is no mere fideism and needs philosophical tools to explain itself theoretically.

Be that as it may, I also believe that if either of the two basic sources of the Mainline Tradition about persons be excised, that tradition must wither and die. I have not pursued that theme abstractly in this book, but my treatment of individual thinkers certainly must point towards it. It is no accident that those who have contributed most to emasculating the Mainline Tradition and so brought us into the post-Christian culture of our present Western world were Protestants by belief or culture: such were Grotius, Bacon, Hobbes, Locke, Shaftesbury, Mandeville, Hutcheson, Hume, Rousseau, Bentham, Kant, Fichte, Feuerbach, Hegel, Mill, Nietzsche – to name but a few and non-contemporary examples. Of course, there are early and still 'Catholic' exceptions: Machiavelli and Descartes in particular; and of course in many respects the latter-day history of Protantism belies the intentions of its sixteenth-century founders. Brad Gregory's *The Unintended Reformation* is a good place to look for confirmation of that judgment. It is perhaps particularly informative to compare the movement within and beyond American Protestantism from the hardline theocratic Puritanism of the founders of the Massachusetts Bay Colony, through the more liberal attitude to religious liberty defended in Rhode Island by Roger Williams, to the deism of Thomas Jefferson and in our own time to the post-Protestant, neo-Kantian and widely approved approach of John Rawls.

Despite the pre-emptive strike delivered in the previous paragraph, specialists on particular epochs may complain that their favourite lesser figures have passed unmentioned. If I offer no apology for my more cavalier procedure, it is because I want this book to enable the readers to see the broader acres of the forest through which I shall try to guide them and not to be lost among the trees, let alone the bushes and shrub. I have written this work because although 'persons' are often philosophically or theologically newsworthy, and excellent more or less systematic accounts of them exist – especially in their different ways those of

Sokolowski, Spaemann and Scruton – there are few adequately detailed historical accounts of how the concept of the person originated, how it was constantly modified, how it is open to further modification, how it disintegrated, and whether, to what extent, and under what wider cultural conditions, any version of it can still do useful philosophical work: in brief how over persons – as in other philosophical domains – we have found ourselves – I would argue for worse – where we are. Since understandings of what a 'person' is are now so varied, so vague and so disputed, it is unsurprising that those who employ the word – usually to advocate some mode of treating human beings well or ill – do not recognize that in their neglect of history they are often talking past one another.

Finally, I should draw attention to the fact that of the four parts of this book, the first is largely descriptive, purporting to explain how the basic features of the Mainline Tradition were identified and assembled. Though here there is much of philosophical interest – since the concept of person emerged as the result of attending to very specific philosophical challenges – this part of the book is substantially historical. The following three sections, however, are different; there I not only describe how the Mainline concept of the person was challenged or rejected – whether or not intentionally – but also offer my own views as to the strength and weakness of the various challenges it faced, as well as the metaphysical, moral and political implications if it has been found seriously wrongheaded. An essential part of my claim will be that many current beliefs about persons – widely, indeed now in the West almost universally, accepted uncritically – are none the better for that, and that embarrassingly unfashionable proposals, under increasing fire for more than five hundred years, are the only plausible alternative.

PART I

CONSTRUCTING THE 'MAINLINE TRADITION'

I

The First Foundations: Plato and Aristotle

> Universally Man is the father of man, but there is no Man, but Peleus is the
> father of Achilles and your father is the father of you.
>
> Aristotle, *Metaphysics* 1071a21ff

Aristotle tells us that apart from individual men there is no Man; that is, the word 'man' is used simply to designate the set of human beings all of whom share a common humanity. He implied that *particular* individuals (neither individuals in general nor individuality as such) are the cause of human individuals; the individuals who were my parents are the cause of the individual person who is me. Starting from that axiom, I shall try to answer four related questions:

1. How can we best understand *individual* persons?
2. What, if any, metaphysical and axiological implications are to be derived from such ever-improvable understanding?
3. Are there any coherent reasons to claim that each person is not only unique but further is possessed of intrinsic dignity?
4. If we all possess equal dignity, are our obligations to all members of the human race identical?

In the fifth century of the Christian era Boethius offered a summary definition of a person which gained much currency; it reveals, not least through his remarks about divine 'persons', that reflection on 'persons', however limited and fragmented, was by that time an established part of the philosophical and theological tradition in both Latin and Greek. Both Christians and pagans had participated in forming that tradition, though by the fifth century the two streams had coalesced. The concept of person, however, as understood by Boethius, is specifically Christian, with both descriptive and evaluative components, though the evaluative aspect is assumed rather than directly promoted. As already intimated, one of the most important questions to be raised in the present study will be whether – or to what degree – the account of the person offered in our Mainline Tradition, being both descriptive and evaluative, can be defended in a non-Christian – or at least a non-theistic – context.

In order to pose that question, I shall analyze the pagan and Christian features that contributed to the coalescing of ideas which we denote the concept of the person, and that not only with a view to contexts in which that concept can be reasonably debated but – if such contexts there be – whether 'person' can be applied informatively to every member of the human race; if not, where it is inapplicable. Whatever turn out to be the answers to these questions, I shall point to precursors even in the distant past to many of our present difficulties with proposals about persons. I shall further note that some of the material built into accounts of the person more or less excogitated by the end of the Middle Ages (by when the task was far from completed) can be recognized in earlier and apparently alien contexts and among writers whose understanding of 'persons' was far from what became the more or less standard (if implicit) set of ideas I identify as the developed 'Mainline Tradition'.

I shall only briefly go back to the earliest roots of our present society – passing over ancient Israel almost entirely and lingering momentarily on the Homeric poems, since one feature of the society revealed by Homer (whether historically or imaginatively) is of great importance for our present project. It is most clearly brought out in the thrashing meted out to Thersites by Odysseus in book two of the *Iliad* and in the regular slaughter (*androktasiai*) of those we would term 'cannon-fodder' – that is, ordinary, poorly-armed soldiers – which punctuate the highlighted personal duels between Greek and Trojan heroes.

Thersites is put down because he challenges his betters; rank and file soldiers are slaughtered to give a hero the chance to stand out and to put more notches on his spear. To the poet they have no other importance, suggesting that Greek society in its earlier form attributed no worth to mere human life – beyond that inferiors can be used by their betters; it assumes, that is, that worth depends not on human existence but on the attainment, whether by birth or 'virtue', of a recognizable excellence. Contrast that with the comments on creation in *Genesis*. Everything created, brought into existence – right up to Adam and Eve – is 'seen to be as good'.

That clarified, we leave Homer aside, not least because it was the self-imposed achievement of Plato to replace the original 'bible of the Greeks' by literary-philosophical dialogues to form the foundation of more sophisticated and philosophically defensible thought about the nature and character of human beings and their virtues. Whereas regarding ancient Israel, our developed concept of the person depends less on 'archaeological' excavation of the minds of the writers of Genesis, than on concentrated reflection by later generations of Christians on the texts handed down.

Plato, then, is our first, if perhaps unexpected, source; but before looking at some of his specific contribution we should turn to the command of the oracle at Delphi – taken seriously by both Plato himself and his master Socrates – that we should 'Know ourselves': exhortation pointing to that native capacity in human beings for self-awareness and self-reflection important in subsequent thought about persons. The influence of that oracular command did not wane with the end of antiquity but demanded observance throughout the Christian Middle Ages and beyond. For self-awareness and hence self-knowledge (in one later version called *suneidesis*) not only indicated to the Greeks a basic difference between humans and other animals – since to acquire self-knowledge requires reflection on one's character, motives and intentions – but in the modern period came to be seen as perhaps the only essential prerequisite for 'personal identity': hence of an understanding, however diminished, of the nature of the 'person'.

We turn, then, to Plato, but first identifying a little more of the wider intellectual context in which those aspects of his thought most relevant to our present project developed. Plato was a substance dualist, and like his master Socrates, a very religious man: human beings are the association of an immortal soul and a temporary physical body. Although Plato never tells us outright that *we* are to be identified with our souls, the probably spurious dialogue *Alcibiades* (attributed to him from the third century BC at least, and treated as a textbook by the Neoplatonists) certainly makes that claim.[1] Its unknown author seems to have supposed – not unreasonably – that such was Plato's fundamental position: not least, perhaps,

---

[1] Contrary to the currently official position that the *Alcibiades* is genuine – re-established by Denyer (2001) – Renaud and Tarrant (2015: 260–269) have argued more convincingly that it is probably a product of the third century BC. Academy of Polemo and Crantor.

because he could have seen no good reason to believe that the human soul could ever be naturally and permanently associated with a transient body. Perhaps our temporary situation is to be explained by some kind of fall – even a fall into bodies – as some Platonic dialogues might seem to suggest.

Substance dualism, as we shall see, generates problems about the blending, temporary or otherwise, of soul and body, and as later opponents realized, such problems already subsist in Plato himself. Despite such dualism, however, there are at least two aspects of Plato's thought of which later accounts of the person, of the real 'I' – no longer dependent on the view that we are simply to be identified with our souls – make considerable use. First there is the belief that our life is given meaning inasmuch as we can attain a moral and spiritual likeness to the gods if we direct our erotic powers – *eros* being far more than a mere search for pleasure, as its debased modern descendent is often held to be – towards the Form of the Good, the ultimate cause not only of all existence and all intelligibility, as Plato explains in book six of the *Republic*, but also of all worth. We – that is, our souls – are worthy in so far as we become good as the gods are good.

Those human beings who attain to such goodness – and insofar as they attain to it – are of perhaps infinite worth: a value superior to any value of the finite world, just as the Good itself is superior to that world in its nature and mode of existence. Our souls by nature love the Good, and love both recognizes and creates worth. We value what we love: intelligibly so if that object of love exists transcendentally rather than as some projection of our own desires and imaginings. If Plato made no claim that the Good loves us – which claim would generate a stronger worth for humans – at least he accepted a revised version of the older Greek belief that good men are loved by the *gods*: the gods, of course, being for Plato – at least for most of his life – lower in the ontological hierarchy than the (impersonal) Good itself.

Yet there is a difficulty here. There are a number of passages in Plato, not least in the *Symposium*, where – in accordance with traditional ideas to which I have already drawn attention – he suggests (albeit not consistently) that whatever worth godlike individuals have lies not in their mere existence as human beings but in their possession of moral qualities.[2] It is not, that is, human beings but various godlike qualities that are valuable as such and confer worth on their human subjects. It would of course

[2] For an excellent discussion see Chappell (2004).

follow that those humans devoid of such qualities would have less or even no worth; that, in line with the standard social norms of his time, would help explain why in the *Republic* Plato is prepared to endorse not only abortion but in the case of the 'unfit' infanticide. Hence, we must recognize that theories of human worth – even those which invoke 'transcendent' and realist metaphysics – are far from identical; hence – and remembering that the concept of 'person' is absent from Plato – that not all of those whom *we* might want to recognize as persons are for him necessarily persons at all.

There is a further significant complication: as already noted, the highest principles in Plato's world – the Forms – are impersonal, while the goal for the wise man is not to obtain 'likeness to Form', but likeness to god, and Plato's gods are, to an extent and especially in the *Phaedrus*, individualized. Problems arise because the relationship between gods – and thus human souls at their best – and Forms remains uncertain. The gods – deriving as they do from cleaned-up traditional religion rather than new metaphysical speculation – are not mere metaphysical powers. In the *Timaeus* Plato speaks of the demiurge as the 'father' of the informed universe – and his language is not to be dismissed as mere metaphor: nonetheless, the ambiguity indicates him to be uncertain as to the nature and metaphysical status of individual divine (and therefore also human) souls. Yet we find in Plato more than a glimmer of what we would think of as our 'personal' nature – not least in his portrait of Socrates.

Apart from the existence of objective transcendent worth-bestowing objects of love – whether gods or Forms – we have already introduced a second feature of Plato's thought which was to form an essential part of the growing recognition of what was eventually to be denoted a 'person': the thesis (shared and developed by the Neoplatonists) that the soul is passionate/erotic, even as Socrates is erotic. And if the soul is by nature erotic, it is always intentionally so, never inert, self-satisfied or merely self-aware (as Descartes and others have supposed), but always *willing* and *loving* to think, to intend and consequentially to act. The soul is not only our life – as the word *psyche* already tells us – but our living (and loving) *thought* and cannot be some inert substrate independent of its proper activities. Its first 'inclination', dependent on our capacity to be inspired, is towards the Good, and its attainment of its desire is not only psychologically satisfying but also creative. As the medievals were to express it, *bonum est diffusivum sui*; the good is diffusive of itself, whether in procreation or in other 'higher' forms of creativity.

*

Noting Plato's claim that to be properly human we must partake in
something transcendent, reflect on our own nature and love the Good
to which we are naturally directed, we turn to Aristotle whose principal
contribution to the Mainline Tradition is of a more formal order, indicating the direction in which a *definition* of the individual – hence eventually
of the person – may be found. His starting point is different from Plato's.
For Aristotle we are certainly not 'just' souls; rather we are an inseparable
conjunction of souls and bodies: our souls are the forms of our living
bodies, equipped as these bodies are with the organs adapted to nutrition,
reproduction, perception and thought.

The soul as the form of the body is the 'combination' recognized as a
human individual, but in a well-known passage of the *Metaphysics*
(Z 1035b34ff.) – the implications of which proved troublesome for the
understanding of individuality in the Middle Ages – Aristotle argues that
of the individual there is no definition. Individuals are logically unknowable, but each can be recognized either by sense perception or by some
sort of mental grasp. That is a challenging claim about human capacities,
hence about human nature. If true, it implies that we cannot 'capture' the
nature of individual members of the human race (even – perhaps – of
members of any other set of beings) though we can identify them, know
about them and refer to them in particular and presumably uniquely
individualized ways insofar as they are members of a group. Yet in so
referring we should not forget that the whole is greater than the sum of its
parts. As Plato had pointed out in the *Theaetetus*, a hundred pieces of
wood do not, indeed could not, of themselves, make a wagon. Nevertheless, as Aristotle understands 'definitions', these tell us about the 'essence'
of Socrates only in so far as he is a man, since that essence or nature is
somehow common to all individuals within the existing set. The question
is therefore left open whether (or rather in what sense, to what purpose, to
what degree and with what significance) the essence of (say) Plato differs –
and can be understood to differ – from the essence of Socrates.[3]

---

[3] This was recognized by Wojtyla (1978), who thinks that Aristotle tends to 'reduce man to
the world'. This, he implies, 'diminishes his particularity', though Aristotle's intent – as
distinct from his effect on the Aristotelian tradition – seems to have been merely to argue
that metaphysics can do little to elucidate the character of each *individual* human being. It
is only by observation of and reflection on individual characteristics and their origins that
we can advance our knowledge of the nature of human individuality – though not
necessarily of human worth. In the present study I shall substantially follow (and defend)
the comment of Guardini (1965: 115) that 'antiquity did not have a true concept of the

Aristotle does not ignore individuation,[4] in that he tries to explain how within a set it is the (already 'particularly' informed) matter which is the cause of the plurality of the members (*materia quantitate designata*, as it was later spelled out). That, however, as such, tells us less than we should like to know about what it is to be an individual. It accounts for numerical differences within the human set, and perhaps for the fact that individuals are also different qualitatively, but on the nature and origin, let alone the importance, of that qualitative difference Aristotle in the *Metaphysics* leaves the details to our individual judgment – albeit assisted to a degree by materials to be found in his other writings – limiting himself to the suggestion that what is one in number but composed of variable constituents cannot be known 'philosophically'.[5]

That the individual cannot be so 'known', however, does not entail that its uniqueness might not point to something of great, perhaps even of immeasurable significance. Nor does the claim that something is strictly 'unknowable' license one to say that we know nothing *about* it. Elsewhere, especially in the *Nicomachean Ethics,* Aristotle tells us quite a lot about what individual human beings – for better or worse – may or may not *do,* are capable of doing or ought to do, though little specific about what (let alone why) they *are.* Yet if he is serious about what we *should* do, that must imply a good deal about what we naturally *are* and *should*

---

person – indeed one does not find it outside of revelation'. Yet I shall also argue that though it was revelation which proposed (implicitly or explicitly) a hopefully defensible account of the dignity of all human individuals as persons, substantive further truths about that individuality have been recognized by the addition of important non-Aristotelian data (both pagan and Christian) to the Aristotelian claim that human individuals – hence *a fortiori* persons – cannot be understood in terms of strict substance dualism. The historical approach to personal differences favoured by Augustine (and others) will be among those additions of particular (if often unrecognized) importance.

[4] See especially Anscombe (1953), Albritton (1957), Woods (1968), Lloyd (1970), Whiting (1986).

[5] So, carefully, Halper (2005: 138). Halper (251) offers good reasons to conclude that for Aristotle both 'form' and 'matter' play important roles in the process of individuation. But how did Aristotle (as distinct from his followers) understand what he calls form and matter? For beneath the words lies the more basic problem that form and matter can be distinguished conceptually but perhaps cannot be separated actually, being conceptual devices intended to refer to the same metaphysically indivisible thing under different aspects: thus, we speak of *my* leg, *my* character, *my* behaviour, *my* brain, etc. The tendency to turn conceptual distinctions between form and matter into real distinctions in the nature of objects in the world (like the attempt to play off 'intellect' and 'will') was to dominate and bedevil philosophy for centuries, and often still does. This is not the place to examine Aristotle's own view in more detail, but I incline to think he would rebuke many of his followers for confusing concepts with realities and distinctions with distinct realities.

be. Nevertheless, though well aware of the moral importance of habits and their dependence on education, Aristotle is reticent as to the metaphysical and moral significance of cultural and personal histories.

Yet the opening pages of the *Politics* shed a certain light on what Aristotle thinks about the social roles of individual human beings, as about the notional 'obligation' to which we are all, he believes, subject. He asserts (1.1253b25ff.) as self-evident that the *polis* is prior to its individual members, and whatever else is implied by 'prior', it is clear that there will be circumstances in which the immediate goods of the individual (such as the preservation of his or her own life) should be subordinated to the good of the community which may demand that he or she be prepared to die – as in battle or in childbirth or as felon – on its behalf. The commitment to a political community entails that sort of subordination of individual goods to the common good, and in the case of military service and giving birth not only that without such possible self-sacrifice the *polis* cannot survive, but that the well-being of the individual citizen can only be achieved by his or her acceptance of such civic duties. Agreeing with Plato, Aristotle holds that such are not only an obligation but the fulfillment of our very nature as human beings, for if a man cannot live socially, he is in fact 'a beast or a god'. Later, 'persons' too will emerge as some sort of community animal.

But human social life is of a very specific kind; there are other social creatures (such as bees and ants) which differ from us in that their instincts commit them to behaviours analogous to those to which we may commit ourselves only after reflection. Human obligations, that is, are specifically human in so far as we have the rational power to think and speak. Nevertheless, the ability to describe the world is not the sole indicator of our humanity – though some modern Aristotelians seem to misread him in that sense. To omit it, however, is to omit an essential ingredient of each human being, albeit by having some natural and 'immortalizing' goal (*N.E.* 10.1177b33), we are revealed as *more* than social, proposition-forming animals whose choices depend on reflection on our formulated propositions.

Insofar as an Aristotelian citizen must be prepared to fight in the army (thus theoretically if well-trained becoming a useful unit in a larger organization), his worth depends not only on his individuality but – as an individual – on his capacity to contribute to the common good. If this claim can be justified on grounds other than those of universal self-interest, it may prove more important than is often supposed – not least for the future concept of the person. Nevertheless if – to flourish and to have worth – we must have wider obligations, we cannot but ask how wide those obligations will be and how wide the group (do we need to bother about those outside the *polis*?) to which we are obligated. Those questions can only be approached when prior questions have been answered: what, if anything, is the nature and worth of the individual *qua* individual, and on what does that worth depend? In the *Nicomachean Ethics* Aristotle writes of 'immortalizing ourselves as much as possible'. If we do that – and what does immortality mean in this context? – we become better. Yet again what does it mean – beyond what is conventional – for an individual to become better?

Much evidence from Greek society points to ideas about the common good similar to Aristotle's. Thus, women are often said to bear children 'for the city': an expectation less instrumentally crass than it might seem to us, for our own contemporary states – especially but not only in Europe – confront all kinds of difficulties both socio-economic and ideological precisely because there are insufficient births to ensure their survival at least in their current and received form.

Aristotle would deny that cultures arise by contract, though he knows they can be rationalized as existing by contract. Though contract-theory was discussed in his day – being promoted, for example, by Socrates' interlocutors in the second book of Plato's *Republic* – Aristotle largely ignores it, thinking of human society rather as natural. Yet his claims about the common good in no way commit him to defend a separate *morality* for the individual human being and for the state: such as would advocate the advancing of special *moral* rules in politics as *raisons d'état*. Nor do they imply that individuals derive their *entire* value (as distinct from many of their opportunities for excellence) from the society in which they live. Yet whatever Aristotle's position on the structure of individual human differences and their importance, his discussion did little to promote debate about the possible worth of the human individual – as distinct from his or her virtue and natural capacities. His individual is best described not with reference to his dignity or worth but ontologically as a soul acting as the form of a body equipped with organs.

2

From Stoic Individuals and *Personae* to
Christian Persons

God, according to Paul echoing the Old Testament, is no respecter of persons, but regards all human beings, whatever their status in human society, as of equal and unique worth since created in his own image and likeness. That hardly sounds culturally Greek. And although the *concept* of the person is implicit rather than explicit in the New Testament, the influence of the New Testament on Christianity constantly reasserted itself over subsequent centuries; indeed is still doing so; nevertheless, it took many hundreds of years before enough Christians took seriously the implicitly mandated Christian attitude to a variety of ancient *institutions*, such as slavery and the subordination of women. The ancients generally tended to assume that institutions (even 'structures of sin') are more or less unchanging, indeed unchangeable; what mattered was the moral reform of the individual. Hence, on the wider and more fundamental question of the nature of the 'person', there were features of New Testament Christianity noted rather inadequately at first, but which more recent centuries have recognized cannot be ignored if anything like an adequately Christian account of the person is to be developed and defended.

The New Testament proposes two distinctions particularly relevant to our present inquiry: the first is that between flesh and spirit, as in 'The spirit is willing, but the flesh is weak'; here 'spirit' seems to denote the moral and what we would still call the spiritual aspects of human nature. To that there were pagan parallels; late Stoics, such as Epictetus, used the word *prohairesis* to denote the moral as distinct from the physical character of human beings.

The second New Testament distinction is related to the first, being between soul and spirit, where 'soul' often approximates to its common pagan sense: the principle of life, perhaps the life of the body. This becomes peculiarly important in later times, as we shall see; for when in the early modern period we find 'soul' being replaced by 'mind' or 'self' – either of which may be reduced to epiphenomena of the body – the concept of spirit more or less drops out of philosophical debate (except among those who talk pantheistically about an Absolute Spirit), but, as we shall see, it is disastrous for any Christian concept of the person for it to be allowed to disappear altogether from theological and philosophical discourse. For 'spirit' can be deployed to concentrate our attention on those aspects of the soul which might otherwise be airbrushed out if soul is reduced to mind or self – or seen merely, in Aristotelian terms, as the form of the living body. Aristotle's idea that intellect comes to us (somehow: *Generation of Animals* 2.736b27–29) 'from outside' may indicate that he was aware of the difficulty.

*

In post-biblical Christian thought the word *persona* in a theological sense can be found at least as early as the second century when Tertullian applies it to the Persons of the Trinity (*Against Praxeas* 27), probably to indicate their different roles, especially the different roles of the Person of Christ. (Thus the masks worn by actors [*personae*] indicate different roles played by actors on the stage).[1] Tertullian also finds the word suitable for indicating some kind of *combination* in which at least two substances are united in a new relationship, the whole forming a 'person': thus Christ is a 'Person' in two senses; as one of the Trinity and as a combination of human and divine natures. For Tertullian, Christ is not (as sometimes for our contemporary theologians) merely a relation: 'Trinity' denotes a relationship between substances (understood on largely Stoic principles). In the case of the Trinity that relationship is unique.

I shall not comment further on Tertullian's heroically incomplete account of the Trinity, except to repeat that he uses the concept of *persona* primarily with reference to God. Yet the nature of a human *persona* is dependent on the divine *persona* of Christ, and one can assume – though Tertullian does not say so explicitly – that the dignity of each human being will depend on the fact that as *personae* we are like

---

[1] Interesting comment can be found in Tassi (1993).

to God, being created in His image. Our dignity (hence worth) must depend, on this account, on claims about the existence of that God from whom that worth depends. That is, our worth is defensible in a universe governed by God, and it follows that any claim that we have dignity or worth in a non-theistic universe requires a different defence. That fact was in the past usually *assumed* by Christians and *ignored* by those agnostics and atheists who spoke of human dignity. Now, however, Christians too often forget it, and when thinking about 'rights' (for example) rely on unsubstantiated claims made from outside theistic circles.

In his *De Anima* (27.2) Tertullian asserts that in human beings there is a binding together (*coniunctio*) of body and soul – indeed a *concretio* – with which latter 'relational' term he seems to refer to the Stoic notion of a complete blending of substances (*krasis di'holou*), as of wine with water: an option which goes some way – though not far enough – toward showing that a human being is a unitary reality significantly distinct from the parts of which it is composed. That understanding, however, was easier for Tertullian than for most later Christians, for since he holds both soul and body to be material substances, he avoids any problem about 'blending' the material with the immaterial; God too is a material substance. Later Christians rejected this Stoic 'total mix', preferring in the case of God – and sometimes of humans – to speak of a different kind of structure: an 'unconfused unity' (*asugchutos henosis*), or some parallel term in Latin to accompany the basic word *persona* (in Greek *prosopon* or later *hupostasis*). But the connection of 'persons' with various sorts of combinations or associations persisted, as did the concomitant difficulties – even if only linguistic – about their being but imperfect unities of two substances. We have already identified some such idea of combination, and some of its difficulties, in Aristotle.

We have noted that Tertullian's thought is influenced by Stoicism – not least because he considers that Stoic-style 'materialist' (better, 'vitalist') accounts of the soul can more readily represent its relationship with the body than any blend of the material with the immaterial – albeit his 'vitalism' implies that some sorts of matter can think; moreover, if the soul is material the survival of the resurrected body after death can be more effectively defended against pagans prepared to take seriously only the possible immortality of the *soul*. In any case, in Tertullian's view, without an adequate account of soul-body unity – that is, of the overall unity of the human 'person' – no account of the resurrected individual as required by Christian teaching, is possible. As we shall see, concern about the possibility of Resurrection was still operative – and still associated with the *post mortem* fate of 'persons' – as late as the very different seventeenth century world of John Locke (who also wondered whether matter might think – as do some of his successors).

In sum, there are two distinct aspects of Tertullian's view of human *personae*: one with far-reaching implications for the possibility of human dignity, the other purely descriptive. The word 'person' may indicate either (or both) a *'whole'* formed from some kind of (physical or metaphysical) blend, mixture or association, or it can point (theologically) to the intrinsic worth of each particular and unique 'personal' subject. In what follows – and not only with Tertullian but with all Christian and post-Christian thinkers – we must keep both claims in mind.

Tertullian's notion of *personae* as *roles* – and functions – also reminds us of Stoicism, but before looking at a version of Stoicism which he might have found especially attractive – that of Panaetius, certainly available to him, as to us, through Cicero – we need to note an important and potentially fundamental change in Greek philosophical thinking as in the Hellenistic age the Stoics succeeded the Platonists (and the less influential Aristotelians) as the dominant school. That change can be recognized if (*inter alia*) we compare the Stoic theory of categories with Aristotle's earlier version. According to Seneca (*Ep.* 58.15) at least 'some Stoics' point out – as Aristotle does not – that before looking at individual categories of being, we need to ask whether a substance subject to categorial scrutiny actually exists. Giants and Centaurs, they say, do not, but we speak of them.

It is true that both Plato (*Tim.* 52b) and Aristotle (*Posterior Analytics* 2.92b7ff.) have things to say from time to say about non-existent items; however, their interest in them – not least their logical interest – is limited. But Stoic logic deals with possible as well as actual worlds, so that before we try to describe what a substance is, they bid us ask (at least at times), 'Does it actually exist?' Nevertheless, Stoics paid but limited attention to existence in and of itself, ignoring questions later so prominent such as why there is something rather than nothing or whether plain existence – not least human existence – is good and has (in the human case) inestimable worth as such.[2] Yet although they offered no reflection on its possible

---

[2] This last is important since it has been argued that Stoic accounts of natural law and of some sort of basic equality of all human beings could justify calling them advocates of human rights (so Hadot 1992: 331; Banateanu 2001: 147; Long [more restrainedly] 2006a: 357–359). Bett (2012), however, carefully notes that although one might claim that the Stoics provide a small part of the material needed for more contemporary rights claims, the drift of their thought would point strongly otherwise. And none of these writers

goodness – a basic axiom of the Mainline Tradition (as indeed of Christian thought in general) – their attention to existence might be thought by others to imply important consequences for an understanding of the worth of persons. For, as we shall see, the eventual abandonment (as by Pufendorf) of claims about the goodness of existence as such might in principle have correspondingly deleterious effects: we might the more easily revert to the ancient view that not existence but particular qualities give humans their value or worth.

And there is a further, related, group of Stoic ideas which certainly did have an indirect impact on the Mainline Tradition. For, as we shall see, Stoic accounts of self-care seem to have been very influential on Augustine's account of the 'person', though in Stoicism itself the word *persona* is normally less indicative of those we would call persons than (especially in Epictetus) is the term 'human being' (*anthropos*).[3] All *anthropoi*, the Stoics held, are born equal; none is born a slave. Slavery is a human convention.[4] Yet such equality of birth does not point the Stoics to equality of dignity, let alone the possession of rights; dignity depends on one's moral achievements, and is equally achievable by slave and free alike. In line with what we have noted about the significance of human existence as such, it in no way generates even a basic human right. We are all equal as humans in that we possess moral capability; we are far from equal, therefore far from of equal worth, when we fail to live up to it. Stoic slaves are 'human beings', but in terms of dignity, so what!

Nevertheless, Stoic *personae* do contribute to our story and a version of Stoicism which Tertullian might have found attractive when thinking about *personae* as roles was propounded by Panaetius. The best evidence for it is available in the first book of Cicero's *De Officiis* (98–121),[5] where we learn of a theory, seemingly derived from Panaetius, according to which we are all presented as 'masked' in some way by four *personae*: four different 'hats', as we might less precisely express it, which indicate the differing roles each of us plays throughout life. By reflecting on these four *personae*, we understand both our common and our individual human situations. By interpreting them honestly and in the proper order,

seems clear that a possible degree of human *equality* provides scant support for the notion of equal *dignity*; on the contrary for the Stoics dignity (as normal in ancient thought), depends on moral worth: for the Stoics, that is, in being a sage.
[3] See recently Long (2006a: 337).   [4] For Stoic views of slavery see Manning (1986).
[5] For discussion of the influence of Panaetius on the *De Officiis* see especially Gill (1988 and 1994); and, most helpfully, Vimercati (2014: especially 158–164). See also Vimercati's comments (158) on Panaetian self-knowledge as presented by Plutarch.

we acquire the longed-for (Delphic) self-knowledge – identifying increasingly detailed and precise aspects of our individual character and personal setting: hence recognizing how each of us, in different ways, can function well and live the 'good' life. Cicero is, of course, aware that the overall individual – the 'actor' behind the masks – can already in earlier Latin be called a *persona*.[6]

And how do we view that good life? When we understand our nature and the possibilities within which we live, we can decide to live accordingly. But why should we so decide? Presumably it makes sense to do so. But, if we do so decide, is that decision merely the result of our recognizing that we shall ensure some kind of contentment by not 'kicking against the pricks'? Is our decision, that is, no 'moral' decision, but a resignation to fate? Or in the providential world of the Stoics are the two somehow identical?

Even if we are capable of recognizing the 'sensible' and rational course for each of us, why does it matter whether we decide to adopt it? Would we not be 'freer' if we declined to do so? Or would we be better if we accepted the 'rational' course for moral reasons – not just because like the dog tied behind Seneca's cart, we know we shall be dragged along in any case, regardless of what we choose? For if we are to be merely 'rational', would being a person simply mean possessing the ability to be consciously – if in the longer run – self-serving? The Stoics, as providentialists, have some sort of answer to such questions.

Panaetius' first and 'outer' *persona* indicates that, in virtue of our common nature (*communis* – or *universa* – *natura*) as members of the human race and as imposed by Nature itself, we can achieve the requisite self-control and self-direction that will point us toward peace of mind. If we could not do that, we would not be human beings. The second *persona* reveals our individual character (*propria natura*) and aptitudes[7] given by Nature (within the parameters of what is possible for human beings), since human capacities and talents differ in each individual and need to be honestly assessed. That has significant ethical consequences, as is revealed by Seneca (*De Beneficiis* 4.27) when he expounds the Stoic view that ordinary people have all the vices potentially, but that some are more prone to particular vices than others. And that points to the need, later

---

[6] For helpful discussion see Nédoncelle (1948).

[7] Panaetius seems to have used the word *aphormai* (in an untraditional Stoic sense) to indicate our aptitudes (so Clement of Alexandria, *Stromateis* 2.21 [= Panaetius fr. A82, cf. B3, Vimercati (Milan, 2002)] and Plutarch, *Tr. An.*13, 473A (= B16 Vimercati).

examined by Augustine, to recognize not only vices (or virtues) in general but one's own particular weaknesses.

That done, we are in a position accurately to survey our third *persona* (*De Officiis* 1.32.115), which indicates the social rank and class in which we find ourselves and which will limit our possible achievements. Under-standing of this *persona* will discourage our aiming at what is impossible and depriving ourselves of the chance of peace of mind. According to Panaetius (if Cicero records him accurately), this third *persona* is imposed by some chance or 'time', being presumably a reference to our personal historical circumstances: a theme, as we shall see, important in later discussions of persons. Finally, a fourth *persona* will indicate the particu-lar profession or job which we estimate (we can hope correctly) we can perform in our special and individual circumstances: thus, we may have the right talent and live in the right kind of society to be able to choose to be a doctor, a soldier, or a politician. Whatever profession we choose (wisely or not), we 'assume by our own decision' (*iudicio nostro accom-odamus*), by an act of our 'will' (*voluntate*).

Here, if anywhere, according to Panaetius, there remains some possi-bility that we humans are not wholly determined: that it is a core part of our basic humanity to be able to make decisions each in his or her own way with an informed grasp of our particular situation. All this points to the necessity for 'persons' to understand what they are in their unique portion of space and time. And the expanded account of free will which Panaetius' version of Stoic *personae* offers could only have been the more attractive to Christians like Tertullian, concerned as they were to show that 'free' human actions are intelligibly rewarded or punished by God.

When we have understood what our various *personae* reveal, we have the possibility of choosing to live the best life available as individuals in a specific place and time. Our individual needs and opportunities are dis-tinct and important: in the providential world of the Stoics they *matter*. We are not just members of the set of human beings, but each of us has a specific role to play in an individual situation. That 'matters' both for ourselves and then even cosmically, since as members of the human race – fragments of the divine – we cooperate in achieving the common good of a providentially ordained universe. For Panaetius, the uniqueness of our individual roles is enhanced – contrary to 'classical' Stoic teaching – in that we live not in an unending sequence of identical worlds, each of which comes to be and passes away in a universal conflagration, but in a world which is eternal, and within which each individual is allotted a single, non-repeatable time-line. And as a Stoic, Panaetius will have to invoke the standard Stoic answer to the question as to how that time-line can be understood in terms of a diachronically continuous personal identity.

For a forerunner of our contemporary disagreement about possible 'persons' had arisen in debates between Stoics and Sceptics, which debates need to be set against a wider background of Stoic thought. The Stoics criticized both Plato and Aristotle for paying too little attention to individual differences between members of a set: even each grain of sand, they argue, is significantly different from every other, and so much the more are such differences important in the case of human individuals who, as we have seen, need to identify themselves very precisely if they are to have a chance of living the good life. In that spirit, therefore, the Stoics argue that we must recognize – and formulate within a theory of categories – not only the common qualities of individuals within a set, but also their individual qualities. Despite Aristotle's hesitation, the Stoics believe that the sage (and as far as possible others) must attend philosophically to knowledge of individual differences – and account for them.

*

Modern disputes about human nature often revolve around whether all first-person statements ('I think this is green' – or 'pleasant') can be reduced without remainder to third-person descriptions. 'This person (or Person One, if the situation needs to be expressed numerically or statistically) thinks that this is green', or 'pleasant', where 'I' is airbrushed out of an objective and 'scientifically' intelligible world. If we go down that road, we may infer from the fact that we do not 'know' scientifically who or what we are, either that 'we' do not exist or that our individuality does not matter, or that it does not matter whether 'we' exist. What would matter (though in some unclear sense of 'matter') would be whatever can be accurately, impersonally, reported of us: thus 'Person One thinks that this is green'.

If that is the case, then everything can (and should) be described naturalistically, statements about 'values', whether moral or aesthetic, becoming comments on what we want, what our community happens to accept or what after looking at various psychological and sociological analyses we suppose will give us the most comfortable life or a life which seems to provide the greatest opportunity to exercise the specific talents we desire to exercise. Such an account points to a limited prospectus for human beings: namely how most agreeably to fill in the time before we die – which may be when we choose to die – or before we perhaps become someone else.

In these recent debates there seem – strictly materialist or mechanistic explanations apart – to be three models of the person on offer: something roughly Aristotelian, whereby I am, as we have seen, a particular subject and object formed from human matter in a particular way. We call this a sketch – and Aristotle's version may be incomplete – of an adequate hylomorphic account; or I may be that debased form of a Platonic mind which is the 'Cartesian' ego: an arid substance which somehow 'owns' my body and its experiences and 'affections', physical or psychological: whether I am fat, unjust, feel good, want this, etc.; or I may be a set of sequential selves, like the famous 'ship of Theseus' dredged up from antiquity by Hobbes[8] – though ships may be sequential in significantly different ways from human beings, who are allowed personal identity (or not), as Locke and his followers thought, by their possession of memories or chains of memory – and deprived of it by their loss. We shall return to all these options in later parts of this discussion.

Yet various – and often preferable – alternative accounts of human beings existed in earlier times; we have already been introduced to aspects of the Aristotelian hylomorphic option and to the Platonic 'two-substance' account. These options eventually formed parts of the material from which a more complete concept of the person began to be put together as the Mainline Tradition. Eventually (most persuasively with Augustine in his *Confessions*) it began to be recognized (though rarely made explicit) that 'first-person' statements are peculiarly informative about the human condition and *cannot* be reduced to their 'scientific' equivalents without loss. Such developments began to take their place in the world of Stoic individuals plundered for Christian use by Tertullian.

Plato tells us in the *Theaetetus* (152e) that Epicharmus (a Syracusan writer of comedy who lived in the early fifth century BC) can be bracketed with Heraclitus as one of those who think – in his case for comic purposes – that physical objects are in constant flux, never remaining the same. He appears to allude to an incident in one of Epicharmus' plays when a man declines to pay his debt because he is now not the same person who incurred it. At this point, however, the lender gets angry and

---

[8] See Plutarch, *Vita Thesei* 23; cf. *De sera numinis vindicta* 559b.

strikes his debtor, and when the other complains, tells him that he is not the same person as he who struck the blow.[9]

This is tomfoolery, but the underlying idea is that everything that lives (if not simply everything) is constantly changing. First presented as comedy by Epicharmus, when turned into the subject of serious philosophical debate the thesis became known as the Growing Argument (*Auxanomenos logos*). Since antiquity it has been associated with the Pythagoreans, but despite the allusion by Plato to its paradoxical character it was only logically investigated in the third century BC, when it was revived by the Sceptic Arcesilaus as part of an attempt to demonstrate, against the Stoics, that there can be no knowledge by anyone of anything, not least of ourselves. Were that to be case, talk of persons would become largely empty – and for Arcesilaus there could be no Stoic sage.

Arcesilaus' point was that if a human being – and for present purposes we can limit our comments to human beings – is a (rather Humean) bundle of qualities, when some of these qualities change, we cannot say that the entity has grown (or diminished) but that it has been destroyed and another entity has taken its place. Since such generation and destruction might seem to entail that we could have no knowledge of the object changing – in the spirit of Heraclitus' saying that you can't step into the same river twice (narrowed by others to once) – it was incumbent on the Stoics, if they wished to insist that one can have knowledge of changing particulars, to show that beneath the ongoing change there is always something stable (not necessarily inert) which acts as the bearer – the underlying substance – of the shifting qualities. In the case of human beings they identified that underlying substance as the rational soul, as the soul *simpliciter* in the case of non-rational animals, and as 'nature' in the case of plants.

Although Aristotle knows nothing of the 'Growing Argument', some believe that he could have handled it successfully,[10] fitting it into his account of the essences of things. Yet how he would do so – the problem being closely related both to his account of individuation and to the

---

[9] The tale has been reconstructed in recent years – and its philosophical sequel has aroused considerable debate, being first examined by Sedley (1982). Further discussion can be found in Lewis (1995) and Irwin (1996). For Seneca' concept of the individual as a self-concerned subject whose self-concern persists throughout his life see Long's comments on *Letter* 121.16 (2006b: 372): 'I am the same individual as I was as an infant, a boy and a young man'.

[10] So Sedley (1992: note 4) citing Anscombe (1953).

nature (whether static or dynamic) of essences[11] – is not entirely transparent, albeit since the soul is an 'act' (*energeia*) and not merely a disposition (*hexis*) and so always intentional, it is certainly not inert. Yet more than non-inertness is required to defeat the Growing Argument; we must show the individual human being as dynamic and yet capable of retaining a fundamental and substantial *continuity*.

Aristotle may have had the resources to explain qualitative differences in individuals adequately by deploying the dynamic individual soul plus the distinctive matter from which each is formed – even if his insistence that we cannot know individuals philosophically would inhibit him from doing so perspicaciously. Yet, as we have observed, he made no very obvious attempt to explain qualitative as distinct from quantitative difference. Perhaps the task seemed unimportant, impossible, or outside philosophy – or perhaps he just never got around to thinking about it. Among the scholastics, as we shall see, this Aristotelian ambiguity, if not error, persisted, though Duns Scotus suspected that a clearer reformulation of the hylomorphic theory is necessary: *forms* of individuals – not mere material differentiation – are required to account for the unique 'this-ness' (*haecceitas*) of particulars: for a difference, that is, not merely numerical but qualitative.

*

Having glanced at Panaetius' account of *personae*, we are positioned to return to another plausibly related part of Stoicism: the four categories that they propose[12] and which I shall discuss with reference to human individuals. The first category indicates whatever lump of matter underlies each human being; the second (*pace* Plato and Aristotle) refers to qualified particulars (*poioi*) and has two aspects: a common quality (*koinōs poion*) and an individual quality (*idiōs poion*). These indicate the two ways our substance is characterized, so how we are generated by Nature as uniquely ourselves. Whereas each substance is subject to constant change, our peculiarly qualified 'self' is synchronically and

---

[11] For a modern treatment, which attempts to retain the essence of an individual while allowing it to develop as that same individual see Oderberg (2005). Oderberg offers a modern rendering of an important theme of the present study that a *person* cannot be identified with his soul (if the soul is the substantial form that bestows a rational nature on the body). See also Oderberg's *Real Essentialism* (2007). For precursors in Aquinas see Cory (2014), but Aquinas cannot helpfully be inspected without prior reference, as Cory knows, to his appropriation of Augustine's *De Trinitate* – to which I shall attend below.
[12] Evidence is to be found especially in Simplicius, *In Cat.* 66.32–67.2 = LS 27 F.

diachronically stable. The Growing Argument can thus be dismissed as irrelevant to our 'selves' since these – identified as our material and substantial souls – are unchanging. We are always the same 'person', and our 'qualities' being put together reveal what can be identified as a combination of Panaetius' first and second *personae*: the 'masks' under which we initially present ourselves in self-scrutiny.

The last two Stoic 'categories' need little further comment here. They are connected to Panaetius' last two *personae*. Thus, the *persona* which indicates our status or class in society is related to what the Stoics call the category of 'things in some condition', while the final *persona*, indicating the job or vocation we may wisely (or unwisely) choose, would be connected to 'things in some condition relative to something else'.

The Stoic explanation of personal uniqueness was in part ideologically self-serving: the sage must be infallible, but if any two qualified individuals are exactly the same, he could not distinguish them and at best would have to suspend judgment! Epistemology apart, however, Stoic metaphysics demands that human individuals be uniquely distinct, the soul remaining the source of their essential diachronic identity. Without that latter principle, the Growing Argument would make the continuing identity of the individual impossible. The Stoic material soul seems intended to perform the same unifying function as its Aristotelian immaterial analogue, though, and not least because of pressure from Arcesilaus and the Sceptics, the Stoics are more specific about the individual's uniqueness. That specificity points to – and will support – important features of later Christian accounts of persons.

Stoic theorizing thus enables the uniqueness of the individual to be defended; while their monistic psychology (perhaps more obviously than Aristotle's) seems to protect them from Hume's criticism of Descartes that we never meet a 'static' or 'inert' self, but always see ourselves engaged in some activity: thinking, remembering, imagining, etc. Nevertheless, the Stoic solution to the Growing Argument does nothing to enable us to infer the peculiar *worth* (unless to a specimen-collector) of the individual from its uniqueness. If individual human beings are to be considered intrinsically valuable, their worth will depend not on their uniqueness but on the nature of the humanity which that uniqueness reveals uniquely in each individual case.

In this regard the Stoics do better than the historical Aristotle. For despite its material nature, the Stoic soul – and therefore the Stoic qualified individual – has somewhat more chance of being uniquely valuable, possessed of unique worth. That is because the Stoics are providentialists, which the historical Aristotle – in contrast, that is, to the 'Aristotle' of the Greek and Arabic commentators and their Scholastic successors – is not. For the Stoics, each of us is a different and unique fragment (*apospasma*) of God. That, therefore, we might appear uniquely 'dignified' as such must be a theoretical possibility, though there is no evidence that the Stoics developed it explicitly. Indeed though humans, identified as soul-fragments, are as a group 'higher', more advanced, than animals and plants – let alone than 'brute' matter – yet since almost all of us are 'fools' rather than sages, our dignity (*pace* – in our own evaluation – in relation to lower beings) might appear largely forfeit: because we fail to lead the right kind of life. That locates the Stoics in a world similar in some ways to that of Plato – also a providentialist and for whom we are all immortal souls, but, as we have seen, only 'godlike' – that is somehow of worth – insofar as we long to live good, 'divine' lives and not simply insofar as we live at all.

And Plato accepted reincarnation, except for those noble spirits who can escape from the cycle of births and deaths. In its implications for human individuals that too might seem not too far from the Stoic belief in an endless series of worlds. The original Stoic version – 'corrected' by Panaetius and a few others – is that our individual lives will be repeated in each cycle; however, if that is so, it is hard to see why virtue matters, unless in terms of what a pantheist God *wants* – or even compels – us to do. For it obviously to matter, we would have to posit a certain capacity permanently to escape from the eternal cycle – this Plato thought possible for some and Panaetius necessary for all – if a providentialist divinity is to sustain a limited intrinsic value for uniquely distinct 'fragments' as such. But if that deity is pantheist, as for the Stoics, its capacity to bestow any 'semi-autonomous' worth would seem to be limited.

3

Mixtures: Plotinus, Porphyry, Nemesius

Once the Stoics had drawn attention to the qualitative uniqueness of individuals, and attributed it to differences in form, the problem of the nature of that form might expectably have been discussed within a non-pantheist, but still providentialist and specifically Platonist world view. That brings us to Plotinus, who took up the question of individuality, albeit hesitantly, even incoherently, and without apparent awareness of the full significance of the issues involved. His chief 'anthropological' concern was to defend Plato's two-substance account of the soul–body relationship and to fend off Aristotelian and Stoic attacks on it. His attempt to do that – though apparently convincing the young Augustine – can hardly be called an unqualified success.[1]

If my analysis of certain relevant features of Stoic thought is at all correct, although consideration of the worth of unique human individuals lurks beneath the surface of Stoic replies to the Sceptics on personal identity, their basic concerns were epistemological and descriptive. Nevertheless, however the problem of the uniqueness of the individual developed, once it had reached the philosophical table, it would have to be either dismissed, determined or forgotten. Since, as we have observed, Plotinus saw himself as defending Plato against attacks of Stoic or Aristotelian provenance, he would have felt obliged to attend to Stoic ideas about individuals if he detected any implication that Plato's account of the individual as the representation or mirroring of a Form in the Receptacle

[1] Some of the material in the next section will involve reconsideration of themes discussed earlier (Rist 1963, 1973, 1982, 1988, 1998). More recent treatments of individuals in Plotinus can be found in Aubry (2008) and Tornau (2009).

(as in the *Timaeus*) is defective. I have argued elsewhere that his account of particulars is too 'etherialized'[2] – certainly, I would now add, too etherialized for a Stoic – and that he portrays the brute materiality of individual particulars inadequately. I must now further ask why he came to believe that the introduction of Forms of individuals might be a necessary supplement to what he thought he had learned about individuals from the *Timaeus*, and whether his solution still leaves basic problems about 'persons' largely untouched.

In *Ennead* 5.7 Plotinus asks whether there are forms of individuals, in particular of individual human beings, thus strongly suggesting that he was aware of Stoic views on individuality. He argues that although some individual differences may derive from the inability of the form (as of Man) to master the relevant matter, not all of them can be so explained. That leaves open the possibility that we must posit a form of, say, Pythagoras as well as a form of Man.[3] There are, however, at least two obvious difficulties. If we allow that Pythagoras may be a reincarnation of some previous person P (this Plotinus, presumably out of deference to the Platonic tradition, is sometimes inclined to accept), then we should not need forms of every individual human being, but only of those souls which subsist in each re-incarnated line: the 'real person' P is represented by Pythagoras,[1] Pythagoras[2] (or whatever the actual name of Pythagoras[2] happens to be: perhaps Euphorbus!), Pythagoras,[3] etc. But perhaps Plotinus only pays lip-service to reincarnation.

Similarly, if Plotinus thought, as did 'orthodox' Stoics, that we live in a series of recurring universes, where later versions would be exact copies of our own, then the number of individuals would be limited by the number of people (or lines of people) who live within each recurring universe. Nevertheless, there would remain a certain number of possible forms of individuals, and these 'forms' would be – or rather would generate – individual souls (as the Stoics, in their own 'materialist' way, had also claimed), viewed *inter alia*, as causes of the unity of each individual *qua* individual. Plotinus never realized, however – or else dismissed – what

---

[2] Rist (1993, 1996).

[3] Significantly Plotinus would not ask whether there is a form of Xanthippe as well as a form of Socrates. That would be because he probably follows Plato's apparent view that sexual differentiation is purely bodily. That would imply that the possibility of a form of Xanthippe would raise no special difficulties since her real self/soul is male/asexual; for further discussion of sexual differentiation in the Platonic tradition (and its comparative unimportance in debates about individuality until recent times) see Rist (2008: 16–78, especially 29–33).

Panaetius had glimpsed and what Augustine was later to see clearly: that if history is circular rather than linear, the significance of human life is correspondingly diminished.

Whatever we do with Plotinus' account of reincarnation, we must certainly ask how his proposals about individual forms cohere with his over-etherealized account of the human body. Apart from the differences caused by the inability of the individual form to master the particular matter (and it is not entirely clear what sort of differences Plotinus would discount in that way), all other differences would have to be accounted for by the difference of form, and that would seem to imply that they would be differences in character rather than in (say) height or weight. Several men, says Plotinus, will vary 'not only because of their matter but because of countless individual differences', and such differences – or what they add up to – are important: it would matter that an excellent Socrates is significantly different from an excellent Plato. If we leave reincarnation and recycled universes aside, this implies that Plotinus accepts the uniqueness and perhaps also by implication the unique *worth* of each individual. That in turn might require that the number of forms is potentially infinite, as he himself warns us (5.7.1.25), and we know that his pupil Amelius held this to be the case (Syrianus, *In Met.* 147.1ff.).

Plotinus does not specify whether individual differences – even individual material differences – are *bound together* into the 'combination'[4] of matter and qualities which makes even the 'empirical' bodily individual unique, but the fact that we are our souls would seem both to make that inevitable and to imply that the soul would do (or be) the binding, thus in effect securing for each of us during our incarnate lives diachronic as well as synchronic unity. For since it is a Plotinian axiom that an 'unfallen' part of the soul persists, the problem of diachronic unity with which the Sceptics baited the Stoics disappears, and *we* would exist individually as empirically recognizable and distinct human beings as well as – more fundamentally – partly undescended souls.

Yet although in *Ennead* 1.1 Plotinus raises the possibility that the 'we' (*to hemeis*: the phrase is perhaps the closest antiquity came to signifying directly something like the modern 'self') might be distinct from the soul, he concludes that such a distinction is only helpful in descriptions of our 'empirical' life in the body; our true 'we' (when we are released from our temporary bodily condition) must be identified as the soul alone. Thus

---

[4] *sumphoresis*, *Ennead* 6.3.8: a concept dismissed by Epicurus (*Letter to Herodotus*, D.L.10.68–69).

although, as we shall see, he is at rare times prepared to use 'mixture' language in the case of our 'empirical' self, the view that we are ultimately our souls – originally specified, as we noted, in the pseudo-Platonic *Alcibiades* – eliminates any possibility that we are ultimately 'persons' in the sense of some Stoic-style 'mixture' – however explained – of soul and body. We are our souls, and the soul/body association – the 'presence' of the soul to the body – is the result of ephemeral activity by the soul in 'constructing' an ephemeral body.

Yet for Plotinus, while we are *embodied* souls (though not 'persons'), we are also each a definite 'empirical' unity with individual power to rise above or sink below our normal level. His pupil Porphyry – sometimes thought to have been the first of the pagan philosophers of late antiquity to take the problem of the *precise* relationship between soul and body seriously – tried to explain that relationship and its implications more formally. He tells us (*Life of Plotinus* 13) that on one occasion he encouraged Plotinus to discuss it for three whole days, and it is believed that in his *Mixed Questions* (and in passing elsewhere) he investigated it in his own name. He does not, however, claim that Plotinus was unaware of it before he issued this challenge; indeed, as editor of the *Enneads* he would know that such was far from the case.

For Plotinus treats of the soul–body relationship from the beginning of his 'literary' career (4.7, chronologically no.2) to 1.1 (chronologically no.53) where he does suggest that there may be a 'mixture' (*migma*) of soul and body which experiences pleasure and pain. Earlier, however, in 4.3.22 (chronologically no.27) he had suggested that the soul may be present to the body just as (immaterial) light is present to the air but 'mixed' with none of it. That is intended to indicate at least that a *Stoic* total interpenetration is ruled out – as it is also in *Ennead* 4.7.8[2] and 2.7 (no.37). In any case, whatever kind of 'mixture' Plotinus had in mind when thinking of the relationship between soul and body, the technical language of 'unconfused unity' that we find later in Nemesius, the Christian bishop of Emesa (and some say also in Porphyry), is absent from him. What Plotinus wants to show is that since the soul is immaterial and the body material, no theory of mixture (Stoic or other) which discounts immateriality could pertain: a claim which was to be an essential feature of subsequent Mainline accounts of the person.

Although Plotinus' role in the development of the concept of the person – despite forms of individuals – is rather limited and even in some respects retrograde, it would be misleading to leave unnoticed various metaphysical moves by which he brought more clarity to related problems bequeathed him by Plato. Thus he solved Plato's problem of the relationship between gods and forms by adapting Aristotle's psychology to Platonic purposes. The forms are now substantive objects in the divine Mind – rather like predecessors of medieval 'transcendentals' – and that extension of the scope of life gave him the opportunity to develop, if hesitantly, Plato's tendency to see the universe as constructed by a 'father-Demiurge' who is more than a metaphysical metaphor. And Plotinus' highest principle, the One, is identified as living and loving: indeed (in *Ennead* 6.8.15) as 'love of itself'. Had he pursued the implications of that, his perfect (or 'individual') soul might also have resulted less impersonal and more individualized, thus perhaps possessed of greater worth as such – not merely as more qualitatively perfectible.

*

Porphyry's treatment of the relationship between soul and body must be determined largely from citations in later writers, since the book on *Mixed Questions* in which he discussed it has disappeared. Yet there is an important text from his *Isagoge* (7.19ff.) which offers a clue. It tells us that each individual is a 'collection (*athroisma*) of properties[5] which can never be the same for another'. That would derive from a combination of the language of the *Theaetetus* (157b) with Plato's account of individuals in the *Timaeus* (49e ff.) and refer to our empirical self – and might fail to evade the difficulties Plotinus runs into over the 'etherealization' of our materiality. In any case, as a two-substance theorist, Porphyry thought of the 'collection' as held together temporarily by a soul which abandons it at death. That is standard 'Platonism' and while Porphyry's account of the 'collection' of properties indicates that he was aware of problems about personal uniqueness, it sheds no new light on Plotinus' views on forms of individuals; indeed, it might suggest that Porphyry had no time for such new-fangled forms.[6]

---

[5] The term *athroisma* had already been picked up, notably by Alcinoos; see especially Shrenk (1991). For Alcinoos, his 'bundle' indicates what we *perceive* in individuals of a certain kind, such as, for example, fire or honey; we do not perceive matter as such (whatever view Alcinoos took of that). On the 'bundle' problem more broadly see Sorabji (1988: 44–59).

[6] Chiaradonna (2000) notes the influence of Stoic ideas of individuation on Porphyry's account, adding that Porphyry and later Neoplatonists often preferred the word *sundrome* for the individuated collection of qualities. He also argues that Porphyry's account of matter is two-sided, one side depending on Plotinus, the other on his desire to combine a platonizing view of matter with that preferred by 'Aristotle'.

Porphyry's attitude to the relationship between the soul and the collection of qualities which together form our empirical selves is echoed in a passage of Bishop Nemesius, whose work and intentions will prove perhaps surprisingly important in our history. It has often been assumed that Porphyry's *Mixed Questions* is the source of *all* the material in sections 3.129–139 (Morani) of Nemesius' *On the Nature of Man*, though Nemesius only cites Porphyry by name at 3.139: that is, after he has discussed different types of 'blending', of which one is supposed to indicate the exact relationship between the soul and the body. That might suggest that, apart from Porphyry, Nemesius has a second and probably Christian, source for his treatment of the soul–body problem, and in particular for his unexpected concept of an 'unconfused unity' (*asugchutos henosis*).

Nor is there reason to assume that this second source offered exactly the same account of soul–body relations as Porphyry. Nor is there even evidence that Porphyry himself – in contrast to some *later* pagan Neoplatonists – used the phrase *asugchutos henosis*, let alone that he applied it to the controverted relationship between souls and bodies. I have argued elsewhere that in non-Christian writers – at least those available to Nemesius – *asugchutos henosis* refers only to relationships between two incorporeals (as soul and soul, soul and Form).[7] If that is right, then a second and historically significant source for Nemesius is certain.

To judge by his fierce attack on Origen (3.144), Nemesius was writing in about 400 AD. He mentions four possible ways of explaining the 'mixture' of soul and body, three of which plainly reflect Stoic distinctions: that there is complete fusion between body and soul; that they are merely juxtaposed; that they blend like wine in water: this last we saw as the interpretation of Tertullian. Finally, there is what Nemesius takes to be a non-Stoic option and this he adopts: namely that there is an unconfused and incorruptible unity (*asugchutos kai adiaphthoros henosis*) of soul and body. That view, which might suggest that each person possesses material and non-material attributes and that the two should not be confused or reduced to one another, he attributes to 'Ammonius the

---

[7] The most influential treatment of the relationship between Porphyry and Nemesius is that of Dörrie (1959). More detailed objections to Dörrie's view that Porphyry is Nemesius' sole source (and to his account of *asugchutos henosis* in Nemesius) are to be found in Rist (1988). Debate continues. thus, Motta hesitates (2010); contrast (as yet without hesitation) Motta (2004: 125).

teacher of Plotinus' – about whom he himself seems to have been confused.[8]

'Ammonius the teacher of Plotinus' wrote nothing, but by Nemesius' time material attributed to him (perhaps originally by a Christian writer named Theodotus) was in circulation. Nemesius seems to have used this material before turning to Porphyry, perhaps to confirm it. Yet in his direct citation from Porphyry the significant word *asugchutos* apparently used by 'Ammonius' does not occur. The intended concept just possibly might be similar, albeit our discussion has suggested it is not; yet it is apparently so taken, probably erroneously, by Nemesius. The important point is that this second source is either an otherwise more or less unknown Christian Theodotus or the *Christian* Ammonius himself.

Unfortunately – and with one important exception – Nemesius' remarks about the 'unconfused unity' shed little further light on how the new possibility should be interpreted. The exception appears in his attempt to rewrite what he supposed to be Aristotle's account of *entelecheia* (he believes that for Aristotle the soul is a quality, not a substance) in order to apply *entelecheia* to his own understanding of the immaterial and substantial soul and its relationship with the body: this, however, seems itself virtually Aristotelian! Porphyry may have done something

---

[8] The situation is complicated by recent disputes not only about how many Ammonii (or ps.-Ammonii) there were, but about the related question of how many Origens. Relevant information is provided by Eusebius (*Ecclesiastical History* 6.19.7–10) and by Porphyry in his *Life of Plotinus*. Most scholars would now agree that there are two Origens (one Christian and one pagan). The pagan Origen and his writings are discussed by Porphyry in the *Life of Plotinus* and there is no reason to think that Porphyry confused him with his Christian namesake, whom he abused elsewhere – as is recorded by Eusebius. The question of the Ammonii is more complicated. Eusebius quotes Porphyry as saying (probably wrongly) that an (originally Christian) Ammonius turned pagan; that mistake would derive from the fact that he assumed there was only one Ammonius, namely the by then pagan teacher of Plotinus. We can begin to sort out the muddle if we recognize there must have been a second and ever-Christian Ammonius. Eusebius (rightly) 'knows' that 'Ammonius' (the teacher of the Christian Origen) was always Christian, thus indicating that he is not thinking of the teacher of Plotinus. But if that is right, then when Nemesius speaks of 'Ammonius the teacher of Plotinus', he too, like Porphyry, is wrongly assuming only one Ammonius, but is right in thinking that his own source, if named Ammonius, must be Christian.

Porphyry does not identify an 'unconfused mixture' of body and soul, nor does Nemesius attribute it to him. That language – at least as applied to soul and body – comes not from the teacher of Plotinus (nor of course from Plotinus himself) but from what is elsewhere attributed [e.g. by Theodotus: see Rist (1988: 408)] to the *Christian* Ammonius who is not Porphyry's source. We should perhaps distinguish the two Ammonii as 'Ammonius Sakkas', the teacher of Plotinus, and plain Ammonius, the Christian teacher of Origen and probable originator of the 'unconfused unity of soul and body'.

similar, though without using the phrase *asugchutos henosis*. Insisting that the soul is somehow related to the collection of qualities which is the body, he probably followed Plotinus' distinction between the 'activity' of the soul in itself insofar as it exists and the activity of its radiation: like sunlight in the air, as Nemesius puts it – thus also directly or indirectly echoing *Ennead* 4.3.22, a passage we have noticed. Such radiation is perhaps intended to explain how soul bundles the bodily qualities together, thus ensuring they are a genuine collected unity and not a mere heap.

We conclude that although Nemesius' conclusions about how to describe the soul–body relationship may look superficially similar to those of Porphyry, they do not entail that he followed Porphyry in introducing an *asugchutos henosis*. His comments on the presence of the soul to the body are part of his misguided attempt to rewrite the supposedly Aristotelian account of *entelecheia* and to indicate that the soul is a separate substance. In further (if weak) support of his theory's being derived partly from a Christian 'Ammonius' and partly from Plotinus independently of Porphyry – though, as we have seen, the jargon of 'unconfused' is not Plotinian – we may notice that (and like Plotinus) he describes (3.135) how the body is 'in' the soul, not the soul 'in' the body in the sense of 'contained in'. Plotinus, however, goes further, suggesting that if the body is 'in' the soul we must recognize the implication that it is caused 'by' the soul:[9] a thesis which Nemesius as a Christian cannot accept, implying as it does that the soul is the real 'I' and its presence to the body almost fortuitous. On that Porphyry is even stronger than Plotinus: *omne corpus est fugiendum*. For him, if we are to be 'persons', those persons are unambiguously souls.

*

Before approaching Augustine – as so often a pivotal figure – it will be helpful to summarize those principal ideas thus far identified that were eventually to be incorporated into a consciously adopted account of the 'person': of his structure and of his unity. After Plato's groundbreaking proposals about *eros*, self-awareness and an immaterial world, we found Aristotle rejecting substance-dualism but leaving the question of qualitative differences between individuals largely unbroached in the *Metaphysics*, though more of his thoughts on the subject can be discovered in his ethical and political writings. The Stoics, or at least Panaetius, offered a theory of four *personae* intended to help those seeking the happy life to evaluate their own characters realistically. That tells us that we must take

---

[9] Arnou (1967: especially 167–172).

individual differences seriously both theoretically in metaphysics and practically in aiming to lead the good life. And since the Stoics are providentialists, their position must have included some sort of understanding (if only implicit) that the individual is not only unique but of some limited and unique worth.

If we all have worth, and we know that we cannot help everyone even if we want to, how do we fix our priorities, as is obviously necessary? The Stoic answer is given in their theory of *oikeiosis*[10] – a formalized version of the obvious truth that by nature we are inclined to love primarily our nearest and closest. After that our obligations widen and diminish until in theory – normally only in theory – they embrace the whole human race. At that point we – like the Stoics – shall need to avoid the 'utilitarian' temptation to treat all human beings as units equally deserving of our immediate support: which lack of priorities leads either to inaction or to a hypocritical 'love' of humanity.

Plotinus, also a providentialist and following the Stoic lead, asks whether we need forms of individuals to explain the metaphysics of individuality. Since he decides in the affirmative, he must also have supposed that each human being, having a 'model' in the intelligible world, has a certain worth: albeit, in the last resort, 'we' are our souls alone. Yet despite their two-substance account of the relationship between soul and body, both Plotinus and Porphyry found it necessary to improve traditional Platonist accounts of the relationship in earthly life between the enduring soul – the 'I' – and the mortal body: not least in regard to our capacity to rise above or fall below our normal spiritual level.

Returning finally to the Christians, we recall that Tertullian used the Stoic theory of total blending to explain how material souls are linked to material bodies in a unity which he dubs quite specifically (and in accordance with earlier ordinary Latin usage) a *persona*. That solution, however, could only be unacceptable to Nemesius; for him the soul must be immaterial, hence a different version of the soul–body 'mixture' is required. He refers to it – in this probably following a congenial Christian source – as an 'unconfused unity'; this enables him not only to allow for the worth of the human being as an image of God, but to show that we display a special kind of unity of soul and body, comparable in its own way to the unity of the human and divine natures in Christ. He introduces this suggestion, however, by way of his 'anthropology' – in contrast to Tertullian who thinks of 'persons' in the first instance in the context of theological debate about the Trinity.

---

[10] The best study is still perhaps Pembroke (1996). See also Vimercati (2007).

4

Augustine's *Personae*: Theology, Metaphysics, History

> You are now a great man; you have restored the ancient church; and what is
> a mark of even greater glory, all heretics detest you.
>
> Jerome

Our next stop is Augustine, a thinker who, as he himself says, recognizes
that he should obey the old command of the Delphic Oracle that tells him
to know himself. Indeed, from near the beginning of his literary career, in
the *Soliloquies*, he said that he only wanted to know about God and the
soul – doubtless especially his own soul, and doubtless assuming a connection between the two subjects. He sees the Delphic command in terms
of a version of Meno's Paradox (*De Trinitate* 10.9.12): I want to know
what I am, because I do not know myself, but how, if I do not know
myself, could I understand that I have come to know myself. I seem both
to know myself and not to know myself.

Augustine makes no formal distinction between philosophy and theology; hence he is never tempted to try to find 'purely philosophical'
solutions to questions of man's worth. As for human nature, that is in
part accessible to philosophical enquiry, but is ultimately unintelligible
and descriptively incomplete unless the 'philosophy' is, as it were, topped
up by what we would call 'theology': that is, claims about the soul, God
and the creation of mankind. Such claims are 'endemic' in Augustine's
writings, and all his comments about man and his destiny, however
perceptive, are ultimately only intelligible under that theistic light. Thus,
in the context of the Christian doctrine that God created the world out of
nothing, he was among the first – if not the first – to write a full-scale

44

treatise on the origin of the soul (*De Anima et eius Origine*).[1] Christians since Justin in the second-century had claimed that, in contrast to the view of many Greek thinkers, the soul is not naturally immortal; it is created immortal by God's grace. Augustine's treatise on its origin spells out some of the implications of that basic belief.

Let us begin by recognizing two significant features of all Augustine's philosophical-theological writing: first, that where on several occasions (especially at *City of God* 11.26 and *De Trinitate* 15.12.21) he offers proofs of his own existence, these are proofs not simply of the existence of his *soul*, but of *himself*. They tell him something about himself, i.e. that he is, that he exists. But do they tell him more, and if so how much more, about *what* he exists *as?* Even in the *De Trinitate* – and here we may find a distant echo of his early view that he is his soul – it remains uncertain whether he is *fully* aware of the difference between his argument (i.e. that I think therefore I am) and the very different version which would read, my soul thinks, therefore I am (or it is). That uncertainty might become toxic among later thinkers influenced by it and open the way for Descartes and others to revert to the view that since I am my soul (or my immaterial mind), I am not in some sense also my body. That, however, is not Augustine's mature position. He came to think that as a 'person' he is relational, and that to understand himself he would have to understand the relationship between his material body and his immaterial soul.

I leave further examination of such intellectual development aside, to move immediately to the fact that Augustine starts not with 'there is thinking' but with 'I think'.[2] Typically, he will say that 'I think therefore I am', and that must be understood to entail that I am in some sense an agent. I do not just think that I think or about thinking (like, it seems, Aristotle's God), though I may perform those activities. I think about *myself* as doing *something*: in his most widely cited example thinking that I am making a mistake about something.

---

[1] Noted by O'Donovan (1984: 54).

[2] Augustine follows Plotinus in assuming that where there is a thought there must be a thinker (thought would otherwise be unintelligible), and he assumes that each person will call that thinker an 'I'. So, the 'I' names an agent, though Augustine does not say that explicitly. As we shall see, Thomas Aquinas comes to adopt a very similar position, but can deploy more sophisticated philosophical tools – in part derived from Aristotle – to explain it in detail. For the context of Plotinus' arguments that thought-objects must entail a thinker (whether human or divine) see especially Armstrong (1960) – and on the possibility of self-knowledge, O'Meara (2010: 1. 316 [with reference to *Enneads* 5.3 and 5.5]).

Augustine also thinks he knows that *I* as agent know I exist because I can think – with what he traditionally calls my 'soul'. But although he knows (in an awareness brought to consciousness when he thinks about it) that he exists, yet, as he regularly tells us, he does not know more than a rather limited number of basic facts *about* himself: overall he does not know what he is in that he cannot understand why he thinks what he thinks, or why he does what he does, or – strikingly – what he will be *like* tomorrow.[3] He knows that (assuming he is still alive) he will be able to *act* tomorrow, but he does not know what sort of person, morally and spiritually, he will be; he will have ideas *about* that but they may be proven wrong. He is aware of himself; he knows that he is an existent agent named Augustinus who can think about what he is and does, but his inner nature is mysterious even to himself, especially in that he recognizes that he is strangely frail morally and spiritually. Without the Scriptures, however, he would have little idea as to *why* he is frail. He thinks that in some sense he is like God, but defectively; that though created in and as God's image, his inadequacy is revealed not least in his ability 'freely' to err; that is, to fall short in desiring and pursuing the good. That in turn confirms that he is a mystery to himself (*Confessions* 10.9.15) and intelligible only by reference to largely revealed truths.

Hence in the *De Trinitate* (and elsewhere), discussion of the Persons of God (and of God's agency) and the nature of the human person (and hence human agency) cannot be separated. In the case of human beings Augustine recognizes a triadic structure: memory, intelligence and love (sometimes unhappily called *voluntas*, then mistranslated as 'will'). But these characteristics or aspects of our nature – as of God's nature – are not 'possessions' owned by some underlying substrate; mysteriously, while all being realities in their own right, they are united as the 'person' who also exists in his or her own right. Just as one God exists perfectly in three Persons, so we as persons exist (though incompletely and imperfectly) in three capacities, each of which, since it entails the others, might even also be called a person. We may wonder whether any of this depends on Cicero's account of Panaetius – as we wondered in our account of Tertullian.

At *De Trinitate* 9.4, Augustine concludes a long discussion by observing that 'love and knowledge are not contained in the mind as in an [underlying] subject (*subiectum*), but these also exist substantially, as does

---

[3] See Rist (2000).

the mind itself'.⁴ That might seem to suggest (again) that it is only our mind (or soul) which is the true 'us': the platonizing view which Augustine has discarded even though it might intelligibly reveal us as immaterial images of the immaterial Persons of God. Yet that is inadequate because Augustine has come to think that something must be said directly about that model of a divine person which is the human body.

Now, however, we are getting ahead of ourselves. Before looking at such wider considerations we should turn to a famous passage of *Letter* 137 to Volusianus, written in 411, where for the first time Augustine identifies a *persona* as a 'mixture' of soul and body.⁵ And although, as we have noted, in his earlier career he had accepted the platonizing (Plotinian) view that we are our souls, in his later years the theme of *Letter* 137 recurs frequently: at *Letter* 169.2.8 (AD 415) soul plus body makes a person, while the Word plus a man makes the particular Second Divine Person. In the *Commentary on John's Gospel* (19.15) a soul plus a body is not two *personae* but one man. At *De Trinitate* 13.5.22 one *persona* contains two substances. Interesting too is a passage of the *City of God* (19.3.4), where following Varro Augustine raises the question whether man is a soul, a body, or the two 'together':⁶ the last option has by this time become his own.

We should not assume, however, that the *personae* of *Letter* 137 come from nowhere: from the beginning of his literary career Augustine had been commenting on self-care and self-scrutiny, observing not only that he exists but what that implies for himself and other human beings – at the same time making use of various themes of earlier thought, largely pagan and Stoic, about care of the self and examination of conscience: not least, as we have noticed, in the writings of Seneca who represents a long tradition on this subject. Although Augustine had not read some other

---

⁴ The importance of the passage (cf. 15,26.42) is recognized by De Libera (2008: 204–205). It is treated in much more detail in De Libera (2007: 257–269). De Libera argues persuasively that Augustine is rejecting an 'Aristotelian' view, perhaps not held by Aristotle (and which De Libera calls 'attributivism'), to which Augustine himself subscribed earlier (as in *De immortalitate animae*).

⁵ *Letter* 137 is not, of course, the first time Augustine has used the *word persona*. Of earlier uses one of the more interesting is at *Against Faustus* 23.8 where the *persona* of a male is said to be more honorable than that of a female: this might refer to legal status.

⁶ Inevitably (in the spirit of Dörrie's pan-Porphyrianism), Fortin (1959: 111–128) appeals to Porphyry's (albeit apparently non-existent) introduction of *asugchutos henosis* rather than to Varro or some later Christian source (Tertullian?) to account for Augustine's thinking about the mixture which is a *persona*. Yet in Augustine the equivalent of the Greek *asugchutos henosis* is absent.

practitioners of the art of self-care, such as Epictetus and Marcus Aurelius, he certainly knew of the tradition.[7] And he knew how that tradition depended on the command of the Delphic Oracle to 'Know thyself'.

By introducing the term *persona* Augustine is able finally to free himself, at least in theory, from the temptation to which he had yielded in his earlier days – and which he found so strongly represented in Plotinus – that in the last analysis the 'I' is to be identified with the soul. By now he regards this as bad anthropology, but his formal acknowledgement of that is instructive. Just as people knew the difference between wetness and water before Aristotle described one as a quality and the other as a substance, so Augustine, as far back as the *Soliloquies*, was treating of the 'I' in ways which might seem to indicate what he later spoke of as a *persona* though without as yet so naming it: that is, the soul–body complex with its various capacities.

Personae for Augustine are not always *obvious* 'mixtures'; their 'complexity' may be indicated, as in the case of divine Persons, solely by their *relational* nature, the substantial Persons of the Trinity being distinct only in their relationships to one another (*De Trinitate* 7.3.7, 15.2.11, etc.; *City of God* 9.13).[8] In the case of human beings, however, we recognize in *Letter* 137 that while the Trinitarian character of the soul is obviously in the background, the word *persona* indicates both a relational 'mixture' of soul and body *and* that this relationship results in 'something single and individual' (*De Trinitate* 7.3.11), and *further* (by implication) that the 'original' and perfect nature of each individual will have been compromised by his or her genetic and personal histories after the Fall.

That 'compromise', however, in no way excludes (as later would often be supposed) any of our 'capacities' from being persons in the strict sense, albeit in differing ways they all are defective. Each 'I', as one *persona*, possesses powers of memory, understanding and love, though it is not identical with any one of these powers (15.6.42, cf. 4.5.30). Nor am

---

[7] For recent discussion see Stock (2017: especially 98–115) and earlier (e.g. Hadot 1995).

[8] *Pace* Ratzinger (1990), Augustine does not mean to suggest that the Persons of the Trinity are pure relations; they are substances in relation to one another. Pure relations would in fact be non-existent, which is presumably not what Ratzinger wants to attribute to Augustine, nor to Aquinas, to whom he also seems to attribute this bizarre concept; nor indeed to God. The strange thesis attributed to Augustine is discussed at length on page 444 of Ratzinger's article where we read that 'the person *exists* [my italics] only as relation'; presumably Ratzinger should (following Aristotle) have written that the person is of its essence relational. The same confusion reappears in the same issue of *Communio* in a paper by Connor where the influence of the Hegelianism of W. Kasper is all too visible (see Connor 1990).

I either my soul or my body, and neither of these is a 'person' (*IoEv.* 19.15). The *persona*, as a whole, both transcends its 'parts' – as at *Against Faustus* 23.8, where 'human being' transcends 'male' and 'female' – and is also fully represented by each of them.

What is important philosophically in this approach is that there is no underlying substrate or 'possessor' of those mutually-entailing realities. Any theory of human nature which uses possession-language is thus shown to be at least potentially misleading. In addition, Augustine has greatly enriched the concept of the person – and his challenging approach suggests that human persons can only be understood – only even begin to be understood – in a *Christian* theological context. Christian trinitarianism, he believes, is at least intelligible, though that does not make it necessarily true. If untrue, however, then the term 'person', as he uses it and as was to become a major part of the Mainline Tradition, has lost most of its evaluative force.

As relational 'persons', unique and individual, we are a 'mixture' of soul and body, but now Augustine, like Nemesius, needs to comment on what kind of mixture is in question. And like Nemesius he cannot do that: as he says in the *City of God* (22.24), it is a 'miraculous combination', while in the letter to Volusianus he merely notes that the 'mixture', the union of soul with body, can be compared with the union of God and man in the Person of Christ. We notice again, however, that the phrase 'unconfused union' deployed by Nemesius and supposed by some to depend on Porphyry, is absent in Augustine.[9]

Although Augustine cannot explain the 'miraculous combination', he came to identify one of its most important features, a feature which reveals how close is the bond between souls and bodies, albeit souls are never reduced to bodies nor vice versa. After about 407 (that is some five years before his letter to Volusianus), and often citing Paul's letter to the Ephesians (5.29: 'no one hates his own flesh'), Augustine began to think of 'a kind of conjugal union of flesh and spirit' (*On the Usefulness of Fasting* 4.5), of a 'sweet marriage bond' (*dulce consortium*) of body and soul (*Letter* 140), and later, at *City of God* 13.6, that the pains of death arise because the soul is torn unnaturally (*contra naturam*) from its

---

[9] Even if Porphyry is the underlying source for Nemesius, as argued by Fortin (1959: 111–128) and O'Daly (1987: 43), he could hardly be the immediate source for Augustine. And if Nemesius found 'unconfused unity' not in Porphyry but in Ammonius or some other Greek Christian writer, it would be even less likely to appear in the work of the bishop of Hippo. It appears to be as yet outside the Latin tradition, certainly when referring to the soul–body 'mix'.

embrace with the flesh. Before the fall, Augustine means, our souls and bodies were in loving harmony, and we as persons long for that state to be restored (*Sermon* 344.4):

You do not want to die. You would like to pass over from this life to another in such a way that you would not rise again as a dead man, but alive and changed for the better. That is what you would like. This is the nature of human feeling. Somehow the soul itself wishes and desires it... No one hates his own flesh.

In Augustine's eyes, the marriage imagery is appropriate not least in that it indicates a hierarchical relationship: 'The mind has a natural appetite for ruling the body' (*Literal Commentary on Genesis* 12.35.68), and after death 'my flesh shall be my friend throughout eternity' (*Sermon* 155.14.15), when that natural appetite is accepted by the body. In their union of friendship and marriage we realize how firmly bonded are the soul and body as one 'person'; hence Augustine's final position is that we are a single thinking and loving person, compounded in some strange and (to him) inexplicable way, of soul and body: a person so conceived as the image and likeness of God as to possess infinite value. In such a now Christian world many of the prerequisites of a useful concept of the person are in place.

Nevertheless, even granted the necessary existence of God, Augustine, as we have seen, finds the nature that we are as 'persons' hard to fathom philosophically. His analysis of the term *persona* reveals that he is 'looking for' a hylomorphic explanation of the soul–body 'mix' but cannot light upon it. He had too readily accepted Plotinus' 'demolition' of Aristotelian psychology, so finds it difficult to be entirely rid of the 'we are our souls' thesis – at times concealed beneath the Pauline distinction between the 'inner' and the 'outer' man – even long after he had formally renounced it. Nevertheless, his extended and developing analysis of the dogma that we are created *as* (as well as according to) God's image enables him to propose a more sophisticated interpretation of our divine likeness than had his (Latin) predecessors, thus to account better for our *dignity* as persons, and to relieve serious and long-standing tensions in the Platonic/Plotinian account of the participation of the sensible world – especially the human soul–body world – in its intelligible counterpart.

One of those tensions can be approached as follows: Plato uses both participation language and image-copy language to describe the relationship between the good things we see around us and the Good itself. Aristotle found such mixed phraseology inexplicable, not least because Plato insisted rightly on both the logical and the ontological distinction between the two 'worlds'. But Plato's Good, as we have noted, is impersonal – as, if less so in some respects, is the One of Plotinus – while Augustine's claim that we are the image of God implies that we, as persons, are images of a *personal* God: specifically – and even to a degree in his earlier writings – that we are the image of the incarnate Christ. In contrast to his Latin predecessors like Tertullian and Hilary of Poitiers, he holds that Christ's being the image of the Father – as all 'Nicene' Christians agreed – need not entail that we are only 'according' to God's image; for we too *are* also God's image, even though that image, which participates in the divine, needs purification and ultimately adoption: a task beyond its own powers.[10]

Augustine taught that there are degrees of imaging, but also that human participation in God can only be better achieved by our imitation of Christ who is fully God and fully man. Christ as the perfect man is the image *of* God, and the image *as* God in the Trinity. We can participate in God as more or less perfect images insofar as we participate in Christ as the perfect human being. Hence for Augustine the dignity of mankind is – again – explicable if and only if we are participating images of God. Unfortunately, the corollary – as we have noted – is that if there were no God, the so-called person, though describable more or less accurately, would have no intrinsic worth. That helps to explain why those who have attempted to account for persons without reference to our being in God's image, have felt compelled to find some other explanation (other, that is, than convenience) to justify believing human beings (or at least some human beings) to possess worth at all.

So far so good, but there is a second source of tension. In his early writings, as we have noticed, Augustine accepted the Platonic/Plotinian/ Porphyrian claim that we are our souls – soul being more or less understood as 'inner man'. Later, although there is some kind of unity of soul and body, it might still seem hard – not least in the light of his Trinitarian account of the soul – to understand how the *body*, clearly subordinate to the soul, could also be in God's image, as might appear to be required if the person is a unity. Yet although Augustine never resolves the 'soul–body' problem, he did advance towards a resolution of the 'divine' nature of the body, which, as a Christian, he must accept in light of the

---

[10] For a recent valuable account of Augustine's early theory of man as image (with welcome treatment of his Latin predecessors) see Boersma (2016: especially 159–223, 257–259). See also Teske (1990), Meconi (1996), Gioia (2008), Cameron (2012) and – earlier – Markus (1964).

Incarnation and the bodily Resurrection of Christ. His proposal, when eventually it arrived, was striking. Since we are not just our souls; our bodies too must, even in their corporeality, be understand as somehow images of God. As he puts it in the *De Trinitate* (14.18.24):[11]

> In this respect, too [with regard to the body] we will be like God, but only like the Son, who alone in the Trinity took a body in which he died and rose again, carrying it up to the heavens. For this too is said to be the image of the Son of God in which like him we shall have an immortal body conformed in this respect not to the image of the Father or the Holy Spirit but only of the Son, because of him alone we read and receive on most wholesome faith that 'the word became flesh' (John 1:14).

Nothing in that, of course, contradicts a further part of the picture: that the flesh of Adam, as of his descendants, taken on by Christ, was already created in the image of God.

Nevertheless, given that the body is also in the image of the divine Son, we may wonder whether Augustine is thinking of bodies female as well as male. Presumably he is, since in his mature thought he always insists that women as well as men are created in the image and likeness of God. Yet ambiguity remains: it seems that Augustine accepted the 'Platonic' view that sexual difference is physical only, though that does not imply that physical sexuality leaves the activities of the soul unaffected. In one of Augustine's references to Perpetua's dream of her coming martyrdom in the amphitheatre at Carthage (*Sermon* 281.2), he tells us that although she remained physiologically female her 'inner human' (*interiorem hominem*) became male: meaning that in her heroism she revealed and lived up to the 'masculinity' of her rational soul. It appears not to cross Augustine's mind that if her 'inner humanity' were female she might still act heroically. That being so, although he comes to hold that the bodies of all human beings – male and female alike – are in the image of Christ, he still assumes that the soul (or at least its 'higher' aspects) is male, both in males and female alike. If that is correct, he would see no more need than did Plotinus to propose that, though individual souls are unique, there is some specifically female uniqueness in about half of them.[12]

*

[11] Since in earlier accounts of Augustine's view of sexual difference (Rist 1994: 112–121 and 2008: 68–78) I neglected this important text from the *De Trinitate* on the image of God in the body, my comments below should be seen as something of a corrective. For more on the 'earthier' aspects of the body see Cavadini (2005), Hunter (2011).

[12] Burnell (2005: 44–49) denies that Augustine thought that all souls are 'male' (that is, undifferentiated by sexuality), but his arguments are unconvincing, being essentially *ex silentio*. Thus, noting that 'the human flesh itself ... shows sexual differentiation to be

A fundamental derivative from the body's being an ineradicable part of the person is that we are subject to the vicissitudes of history. It is one of Augustine's chief claims to philosophical fame in his mature account of persons that he is aware not only that they must be understood (metaphysically and theologically) as a mixture of soul and body, but also in terms of their history precisely as individuals.[13] That history can be studied biographically or autobiographically (as Augustine studied his own person and own history in the *Confessions*), but also culturally (as he studied the theological history of the human race in the *City of God*). Indeed, and the more so in light of his view that we all existed in our 'common life' in Adam (on which more anon), that 'cultural history' also forms a part of our individual biography.

In this concrete connection, we need to consider further facts about the word *persona* and the persons (or Persons) it names. As we have seen, the theological use of the term goes back at least to Tertullian and persisted in Latin writers discussing the Trinity. In Greek, however, although the equivalent of *persona* – that is, *prosopon* – existed, the Persons of the Trinity are normally called, as at the Council of Constantinople (AD 389), *hupostaseis*. That word literally refers to the subject-term which indicates what underlies the 'species': thus, one being, three *hupostaseis*, each of whom is 'personal'. Hence the Father exists, the Son exists, and the Spirit exists; they 'exist' individually and together.

But although there can be no objection to using both *persona* and *hupostasis* of the Trinity, the two terms indicate rather different approaches: *persona* suggests an actor, an 'acting person', an agent: it is thus in a sense a rather historical-sounding word, perhaps better indicating God's activity so far as it can be recognized in human history. *Hupostasis*, on the other hand, is more metaphysical, indicating the metaphysical 'Godhead' of the divine Persons. It is also more likely to be (mis)interpreted as indicating some sort of underlying inertness. *Persona*, on the other hand, cannot be misread in that way, and is thus more readily applicable to human as well as divine subjects with no fear of it seeming to be an underlying 'I know not what', and thus liable to an

---

basic' he continues: 'This does not imply that differentiation is restricted to the flesh'. True enough, but it does not rule it out either, and other passages point to non-differentiation being Augustine's view. See Rist (2008) for more detail, not least (page 76) on Perpetua.
[13] For a more detailed account see Rist (2012).

'Humean' critique. None of this, of course, precludes the careful use of *hupostasis* for human persons; indeed, medieval thinkers and not least Aquinas (as we shall see), regularly used the Latin verbal equivalent, *suppositum*, to denote individuals within the species Man (*homo*). Thus Socrates (a *suppositum*) is a man.

*

One of the strangest and most fascinating features of Augustine's account of human nature, as already noted, is that we live a 'double' life: a common life insofar as we are members of the human race (all related, *we* might say, through that mitochondrial Eve who apparently existed some 200,000 years ago): one in Adam and thus sharing in Adam's original sin as a kind of faulty genetic inheritance; but having a personal and individual life (*propria vita*) in our ordinary existence from birth (or *we* should say 'from conception') until death.[14] While we might reasonably surmise, as suggested above, that in making this distinction Augustine was influenced not only by Trinitarian speculation but also by the various *personae* of Panaetius, he gives no clue as to that; nevertheless, it is not implausible that since he knew of Panaetius' views through Cicero (and probably others), Panaetian *personae* have left their mark on his thinking.

According to Panaetius, as we have seen, we have a 'common' or 'universal' *nature* and an individual (*propria*) *nature*: our common humanity plus our individual characteristics and situation in space and time. For Augustine, we have our common *life* in Adam and personal *life* as our individual selves. That combination is part of what makes us *personae*. However, if Augustine was influenced on this subject by ideas ultimately derived from Panaetius or some other Stoic, he has 'historicized' them, his two lives deriving not from metaphysical or psychological analysis, but from theological reflection on what he takes to be a historical event in the Garden of Eden.

Augustine's two 'lives' deserve further comment and they might invite an updated interpretation. In his day Christians were divided about the creation of the human soul. Most thought it was created at birth (though they should have placed it at conception). Some, and especially Augustine, were doubtful: if that were the case (as he told Jerome in *Letter* 166), how do we account for our inheriting the sin of Adam? For 'creationism'

---

[14] For an introduction to the double life see Rist (1994: 121–129).

would seem to imply that original sin is purely bodily, while Augustine's view is that all sin is imposed on the body by the soul. Yet perhaps both accounts are in some sense correct and perhaps Augustine's own theory of the two lives can explain how that can be the case.

At conception our personal life begins, but we are not procreated from scratch; we inherit a genetic structure from our parents who thus pass on to us something of our common humanity as well as the occasion of our individual existence. And that inherited humanity is, according to Augustine's theory of original sin, seriously flawed. Hence if we take his account of our two lives seriously and explain how each life comes to be present at conception, we seem to be able to explain that we are a new creation (or better: procreation) as individuals, but also a renewed creation in so far as we are members of the human race – represented by the genetic structures of our parents. And those structures carry with them the weakness and 'sin' which we have inherited 'from Adam'. Even in the womb we are nurtured in our sins (*Confessions* 1.7.12),[15] hence though individually differentiated (1.6.8–9) the new soul (because of its inheritance) is not a perfect soul, and since our procreation is unique in time and space, our virtues and vices will be potentially different. In the *Confessions* Augustine notes that while one of his own vices was sexual excess, his friend Alypius was not troubled that way – but *he* had the bloodlust of the amphitheatre. The theme of varying vices, as we have noted, was treated by Seneca and the Stoics and I shall return to it in its wider metaphysical context in considering the work of Edith Stein.

In sum, Augustine's eventual sketch of the unique and valuable psychological and social make-up of each individual is a very substantial advance on what had appeared before – despite his failure to identify some adequate (more or less Aristotelian) meta-psychological structure on which to ground his perceptions and Scriptural reflections. Even so, the radically historical aspects of his claims about understanding persons and their worth proved difficult to comprehend even in Christian circles; many were to find supposedly good 'Aristotelian' reasons to water them down or relegate them to the back-burner. Yet Augustine's ambition of combining personal and 'racial' history with metaphysical analysis ultimately was not forgotten. He knew that (in modern language) human beings – persons – are both objective realities and subjective historical structures.

---

[15] For comment on the individuality of infants see Burnell (2005: 50–53).

5

The Definition: Boethius and Richard of Saint Victor

There is no place for philosophy in the councils of kings.

Thomas More, *Utopia*

Augustine believes that human worth is explicable only given the existence of a beneficent God – plus, of course, a related account of the soul – but his failure to account for the miraculous combination of soul and body left much room for further Christian thought about persons. That leaves us wondering what further progress would be made on the lines he indicated. It is therefore time to return to the semi-Aristotelian Platonist Boethius, who like Augustine suffers from the inability to understand what he is (*Consolation* 1.P.2.13; 1.P.6.40–42, etc.). The resulting definition that a person is an individual substance of a rational nature reveals in the word 'substance' an Aristotelian metaphysics more technical than the language regularly used by Augustine: that man is a mortal rational animal (*On the Trinity* 7.3.7; *City of God* 9.13). Yet the *Consolation's* platonizing Lady Philosophy might find this definition excessively abbreviated, even to the point of being misleading, and Boethius, specifically talking 'philosophy' rather than 'theology', to have lost sight of the immortality of the soul – hence of the key to our God-created nature in his own image. Nor does Boethius attend to Augustine's emphasis on history, thus setting an unfortunate precedent for subsequent ages.

Though an attempt at a formal definition is a big step forward – it matters greatly that 'by moving the goalposts' it becomes the new centre of philosophical reflection – the contribution of Boethius to our topic might seem rather disappointing. His treatment of 'person' in that

small-scale polemic *Against Nestorius and Eutyches* is largely theological.[1] Unlike Nemesius, his concern is not primarily with the human
person – despite his definition of this as an individual substance of a
rational nature – but is virtually restricted to explaining how Nestorius
and Eutyches are confused because they want in theology to treat 'nature'
and 'person' as equivalents. Hence Nestorius argued that if Christ exists
in two natures, he must exist in two persons, while Eutyches (and the
'monophysites', as his followers came to be called) argued that since
Christ is only one person, he must have only one nature. Both these
'heretics' have ignored the fact that the word 'person' (or its Greek
equivalent *prosopon*) had since Tertullian always been used by Christians
to refer to some *unified combination*; thus, the Persons of the Trinity are
united relationally, and the Person of Christ is a singular combination of
human and divine natures, while human 'persons' (as in Augustine) are a
combination of soul and body.

Unlike Augustine and even to some extent Nemesius, Boethius writes
in a notably Aristotelian idiom. He emphasizes that persons must be
Aristotelian 'substances' because they really exist as individuals –
although (in the case of Christ, but doubtless also of human beings) they
are a *coniunctio* as well as a unity (*unificatio*). As we should expect,
however, the strict and specific language of 'unconfused and incorruptible
union' offered by Nemesius is absent, as it was from Augustine's account
of the 'miraculous combination'. Boethius is familiar with much of the
post-Nicene theology of Basil, Gregory of Nazianzen and Gregory of
Nyssa – and so with the Greek *prosopon*'s equivalence in theology to
what the Latins called a *persona*, as also with '*hypostasis*' as representing
what he himself saw as an Aristotelian unity or primary substance. Yet in
his more strictly theological texts, he deploys a less technical terminology,
saying that the 'conjunction' which is Christ is a great and unprecedented
miracle, unique and never to be repeated, the two natures remaining
'distinct' but forming a single 'person'. Seemingly, and despite any possible influence of the Council of Chalcedon, the Latin tradition on the
divine nature is not yet fully acclimatized to Nemesius' more technical

---

[1] For discussion see Koterski (who oddly neglects Tertullian) (2004: 203–224). Koterski
(211) claims (without references) that the 'Cappadocians' took the concept of *prosopon* to
indicate a 'center of agency'. At least it is clear that their term *hypostasis* (=*prosopon*) is no
mere (Aristotelian?) substrate, and that Boethius rightly recognizes it as a type of substance
possessed of a nature. For more on the character of Boethius' theological writings see
Daley (1984).

language nor familiar with much of the Stoic and Neoplatonic debates which contributed to its development.

Nor *a fortiori* does Boethius speak of *human* nature as 'unconfused'. Indeed, even in Greek-speaking thinkers after Chalcedon the term *asugchutos* will become almost entirely restricted to God, leaving in abeyance its possible application and exegesis in the peculiarly human 'combination' and unity of soul and body as 'persons'. According to Lampe's Patristic Lexicon, the word is applied to human beings only by Theodoret of Cirrha and – in a probably ninth-century text presumably depending from Nemesius – by a monk, Meletius (*PG* 64, 1296c.ff.).

There are further questions to be asked, however, about Boethius' more Aristotelian treatment of human beings: how, for example, are we to interpret the phrase 'of rational nature' in the light of Boethius' tendency only rarely to add 'intuitional' to 'rational'? Is 'rational' to be explained in richly Platonic mode, or in the weakened but still recognizably similar Aristotelian version, or even in a more modern and aridly Cartesian sense? In other words, what in Boethius is the relationship between the mind and the emotions; for our individuality, as Augustine well knew, depends to no small extent on the relationship between our thoughts, desires and loves? In asking such questions we must look not at what the medieval commentators made of Boethius' 'rationality' but at the view, insofar as we can recover it, of Boethius himself. And though the material is scanty, it is probably reasonable to rule out any Cartesian mental aridity. And there is a second question – which by now we should recognize as basic, and later to become more so – as to the relationship between 'mind' and the presumably broader term 'soul'?

Boethius does not allow his Aristotelian metaphysic of individual substance to erase the Christian doctrine, now clearly established in the West by Augustine, that human beings are not only some sort of *combination* of soul and body but that this combination exists relationally (however difficult it may be to establish how that 'works' philosophically). What he ignores (at least explicitly) is that Augustine saw the person – the soul–body combination – as active *subject*. Hence, as was increasingly recognized both in the Middle Ages themselves and among our contemporaries (some of whom will be discussed below), his definition, though useful, is misleading because incomplete Even if, as has been suggested[2] – and leaving the Aristotelian John of Damascus aside – the

---

[2] As, for example, by Koterski (2004: 211).

Cappadocians to some extent developed the concept of the subject, the clearer view of Augustine will only be recovered in the thirteenth century, and even then still kept largely separate from more formal discussions of 'persons'. Boethius' definition may be one of the factors which together with his rather 'narrow' Aristotelianism – contributed to that strange divorce. That in turn shows how easy it is for the elements thus far assembled to construct a Mainline Tradition about persons to fall apart.

*

After Boethius, the multiple *sources* of the Mainline Tradition get lost – making it easier to forget some pieces of the concept that needed to be kept together. What we find in the Middle Ages is first analysis and commentary on Boethius' definition, accompanied to a greater or less degree by the assimilation of his ideas into a wider Augustinian and particularly Aristotelian framework. Then a gradual deconstruction begins with Scotus. That process was accelerated in the early modern period in their different ways by Descartes and Hobbes; then – as it gathered force – by Locke. As for the high medieval period itself, by the early thirteenth century a clear but un-Augustinian distinction had been attempted – and in part established – between the subject-matters of philosophy and theology, while a semi-platonized version of Aristotelian metaphysics gradually displaced the purer 'Platonism' of earlier centuries as study shifted from the Cathedral Schools to the new universities or the *studia* of religious orders.

One of the results of this change was that specific concern with 'persons' – even among those termed 'theologians' – was more and more focused on description and especially on explanations of their plurality rather than on their 'theological' status in light of their uniqueness and of the immortality of each human soul journeying through its individual history. And generally as the Middle Ages wore on, questions of theology, especially of salvation, tended to become separated from questions of philosophical psychology, hence of ethics and broader philosophical reflection; so the worth to be attributed to persons, deriving above all from theological claims – as Augustine so well understood – tended to be taken for granted as interest focused on more immediately 'philosophical' disputes.

As the medieval period faded, this descriptive rather than normative emphasis continued in increasingly secular debates accompanied by the arrival of purely secular rights-theories. And if we ignore the theology, that change might seem justified. As Marcello Pera put it, in Humean mode, in his discussion of the relationship between accounts of the person and human rights, 'From ontology alone we cannot derive values' (*Dal solo ambito ontologico non si derivano valori*).[3] That said, it is striking that among various definitions of person cited by the careful Aquinas we find one of striking theological – and axiological – significance: a person is 'an hypostasis distinguished by a feature pertaining to its dignity (*hypostasis proprietate distincta ad dignitatem pertinente).*[4]

*

One of the most interesting, influential, indeed prophetic early medieval developments in the discussion of the person is to be found in the *De Trinitate* (4.23–24) of Richard of Saint Victor. Richard glosses Boethius by defining a person as 'a sole self-standing existent in a certain singular mode of rational existence' (*existens per se solum iuxta singularem quondam rationalis existentiae modum*), the emphasis being not just on persons as substances but also as 'primary substances' in that they actually exist. He adds, echoing the old Roman jurists without further comment, that this 'existence' is *incommunicabilis* – apparently meaning that there is a something about the experience of each existent human being that cannot be conveyed to any other (he might have added even entirely to each person himself). To the question 'What is it like to be Person X?', no complete answer can be given.

Richard thus emphasizes the sheer distinctiveness of every person as well as the fact that persons exist in a certain way, that is as 'rational': to be noted is the approximately Aristotelian approach – though without *specific* mention of a 'substance' – half-intended by Nemesius, desiderate in Augustine and broached by Boethius. There is again, however, no recognition of the Augustinian turn to history and biography or autobiography – or to the concept of the person as an active subject. Instead we find a more impersonal approach: persons are simply identified as individual and distinctive members of the human set, with 'rationality' their most significant feature. As with Boethius, that demands further explication of 'rationality' – not least with reference to self-knowledge and self-incommunicability.

Emphasis on the person as a rational substance underestimates one of the original building blocks on which the concept of a person had thus far

---

[3] Pera (2015: 92).   [4] *ST*, I.29, 3, a.2. I owe this reference to Crosby (1996: 66).

been constructed: the union of two 'substances', however explained, namely soul and body. In the high Middle Ages while the Aristotelian account of that blend predominated – the soul being seen as the form of the body – continuing difficulties about the nature of the mixing or forming left the door ajar for the abandonment by Descartes of the form/body immediacy ('maritally' explained in Augustine), and the return, as we shall see, to an inferior version of the Platonic view of an immaterial soul using the material body while remaining external to it. And too restrictedly Aristotelian explanations of persons pointed toward abandonment of the Mainline Tradition altogether when Aristotelianism itself began to be called in question. And as we shall also see, its anticipated demise was supposed (and is often still supposed) to eliminate many theological claims about persons in the context of 'God and the soul' even though these had originally been developed quite independently of the Aristotelian ontology later brought in to underpin them.

6

Toward a Synthesis: Thomas Aquinas

If it is true Aquinas would have said it.

Etienne Gilson

After Richard of St Victor, it is reasonably safe to leave aside other medieval thinkers and move directly to Thomas Aquinas, whose treatment of persons, according to Spaemann, follows on in sequence from Richard's but exhibits greater 'perspicuity and clarity'.[1] This, though true, may underestimate the importance of a change in the historical context of the two authors, for Richard was still living in a largely 'pre-Aristotelian', patristically determined world where human persons, as images and likenesses of God, were subjects of reflection with primary reference to the divine Persons. It is no accident that Richard, in the footsteps of Augustine, attended to persons in works principally devoted to Trinitarian theology while Boethius, though offering an Aristotelian-sounding definition of the person, published it in a rather technical treatise against Trinitarian heresies,

When a more full-blooded 'Aristotle' arrived, much more detailed attention was paid to new, predominantly descriptive psychological theorizing: about human cognition, self-awareness and especially intentionality. Not least in light of the gradual eclipse of Augustinian theories about divine illumination, theological ideas about man's being in the divine image – though in the background and almost inevitably reappearing in discussions of the views of Augustine and Boethius on the

---

[1] Spaemann (2012: 31).

Trinity – stimulated less serious reflection, often yielding pride of place to more specifically analytic and 'humanistic' concerns. There was rather little *development* of thought about man as God's image in the Middle Ages.[2] On the more positive side, however, Aquinas' Aristotle is to a degree removed from the more localized background of Aristotle's own moral thinking. Whereas Aristotle thought of those human beings with whom he was principally concerned as free inhabitants of city-states, Aquinas looked on them as 'persons', as members of the human community as a whole, however individual groups of them happened to be governed. Hence less pressure to see the virtues as those conventionally recognized in any particular human society.

What might seem more immediately surprising (and misleading) about Aquinas' approach to 'persons' (now identified as 'supposits') is that he has rather little to say specifically about them. One might suppose that because when discussing 'persons' he is wearing his philosophical rather than his theological hat, he is less concerned about human worth, more concerned as to how they fit into his much wider metaphysical construction. Aquinas certainly distinguishes the roles of the theologian and the philosopher, remarking that 'the theologian considers sin chiefly insofar as it is an offence against God, but the moral philosopher considers it chiefly insofar as it is contrary to reason' (*ST* 1-2ae, q. 71, a.6, ad 5). Nevertheless, he always tries to maintain the connection between his analysis of human characteristics and his account of them as aspects of man's nature as an image of God. Thus, he writes (*ST* I.IIae, preface):

Since, as Damascene says, a human being is said to be made in the image of God, insofar as by 'image' is meant something with understanding, free in its judgement and with power in itself ... it remains for us to consider God's image ... A human being, insofar as he is also the source of his actions, i.e. having free will and power over his own actions ...

The implication of that is that in reflection on the human person it becomes impossible to separate the theological/evaluative from the philosophical/supposedly descriptive.

Aquinas identifies persons/supposits – with Augustine (*De Trinitate* 15.6.42, as we have seen) – as 'individual singulars', possessors of natures, self-conscious sources of their own actions, indeed as the most perfect beings in all nature (*ST* I, q.29, a.3). His formal recognition that a

[2] For a survey of Thomas' Aristotelian rephrasing of Augustine's account of the image of God see O'Callaghan (2007).

person is the *possessor* of a nature, that is of a human nature, and not
merely an example of it, is perhaps his principal contribution to the
Mainline Tradition; yet we do not *own* our various characteristics, we
are those characteristics; nor are we merely units within the species –
though as we shall see, Aquinas is not as explicit as he might be in his
explanation of why human individuals, persons, are not just members of a
set, but unique subjects; though persons have a nature, each of us is a
human being in a significantly different way from all others.

One of the more complete statements of Aquinas' position (*ST* I. q.29,
a.1) runs as follows (I use the translation of the English Dominicans):

In a more special and perfect way, the particular and the individual are found in
the rational substances which have dominion over their own actions; and which
are not only made to act like others, but which can act of themselves: for actions
belong to singulars. Therefore, also the individuals of the rational nature have a
special name even among other substances; and this name is 'person'.

Emphatic though this is about the special characteristics of persons, a
number of basic features of Augustinian 'personalism' which will better
reveal the uniqueness and incommunicability (even somehow to ourselves) of our individual personal experiences – such as his emphasis on
biography and cultural history – have disappeared in Aquinas' more
abstract treatment which is largely ontological rather than meta-ethical
or theological.[3] Metaphysics in its neo-Aristotelian guise has reassumed
independence of history – and sometimes in accordance with the medieval
attempt to separate instruction in philosophy and theology – from theology too: a pair of separations which were to blight philosophy, non-
Christian as well as Christian, over large parts of succeeding centuries.

Nevertheless, as Thomists rightly point out, Aquinas often assembles
and organizes many of those characteristics of persons we have been
examining in contexts where persons as such are not under immediate
consideration: a fact which has seriously misled many of his readers
especially in one important respect: that of his treatment of the person
as active subject or agent. Thus we can reasonably follow Finnis,[4] for

---

[3] The index to Wippel's book (2000) on Aquinas has no entry for 'image of God' (perhaps
unsurprisingly since on his own admission Wippel is distinguishing Aquinas' metaphysical
from his theological thought, and as far as possible discussing the former rather than the
latter); more informative is that Wippel finds Aquinas has little to say about persons except
in terms of their relationship (as 'supposits') to their nature (pages 238–253). A more
recent study (West 2007) adds little of interest on the human person.

[4] Finnis (2005: especially 250–252). For Aquinas' comments see (e.g.) *In III Sent.*, ad.2, q.2,
a.3, sol.1; *In I Sent.*, ad.34, q.1, a.1 c; *ST* I, q.29, a.1.

example, in noting how Aquinas recognizes four features of a 'what-is-it' which enable us to recognize it as a personal 'who-is-it', though strangely Aquinas denies the relationality of human (but not of divine) persons (*ST* I, q.29, a.4c), thus underestimating those social aspects of the person which are essential features of his or her proper development and of which many of his predecessors were well enough aware. For persons are relational right from the moment of conception: in the first place to the mother.

Finnis' four features of Thomistic persons are as follows: the objective nature (or species) of each person; his or her cognitive capacities, broadly understood to include self-awareness; his choices and deliberative actions which form his 'subsisting' character; and finally his skills, which include the use of language. This amounts to an approximately Aristotelian summary of those metaphysical and psychological features of persons which had been earlier identified; Aquinas, though, largely following (while Aristotelianizing) Augustine, has substantially clarified the notions of agency and self-awareness, thus showing that he too could have dismissed Hume's powerful attack on what Descartes thought of as the self. The Thomistic soul is not inert, nor is it a self in the Cartesian sense; like its Augustinian predecessor, it is always in act.[5] With the help of Avicenna and other more recent thinkers, Aquinas is able to offer an enriched account of Augustine's concept of the active person, the first of whose acts is the 'act of existence' by which it is distinguished from a mere nature or essence.

The question of agency is too important to be passed over in haste. De Libera[6] has pointed to a substantial number of passages of Aquinas where he says that 'actions belong to *supposits*', i.e. persons do things (including thinking). And they belong not as qualities, but as descriptions of an agent's activities. Hence if I am that agent, they are *my* activities, just as in Augustine (who lacks the technical Aristotelian vocabulary) thinking is an act of an agent such that if I am the agent, then I am thinking. The axiom that thinking without a thinker is impossible, as Augustine learned

---

[5] It is important, however, as we shall see when we examine aspects of the semi-phenomenological Thomism of Wojtyla, that the context of 'act' should not be reduced to that of action. For details of Aquinas' account of the person 'in act', see especially Cory (2012, 2014). Cory acknowledges her indebtedness to the massive erudition of De Libera (2007), who demonstrates that the concept of the active subject is no early modern discovery. However, he gives Augustine too little credit on this score (as my present account reveals). See also De Libera (2008).

[6] De Libera (2008: 210).

from Plotinus, is fleshed out by Aquinas. Or as Cory puts it (102), 'the notion of subject-as-agent hinged on an increasingly prevalent view of accidental being as a determination or mode (not a quality) of a substance'. In brief, for Aquinas, although events can be perceived apart from their causes, actions cannot be perceived apart from their agents. Or again persons can be perceived, even by themselves, only in their acts (broadly understood), and thus only partially: hence the obscurity of my knowledge of myself.

Nevertheless, despite this sophisticated development of Augustinian ideas about agency, the connection, established in Patristic times, between persons and image-theory still held. As persons, each of us is an image of the divine Persons, and our *dignity* depends on that image-relationship. If God were to be removed from the equation, then some different way of accounting for human worth would need to be identified. To Aquinas such a possibility would have looked irrelevant, and even when Scotus raised the possibility that God is not part of the equation with his *Etsi Deus non daretur*, it was only as a theoretical possibility; the revised reality which would ensue on this was barely recognized, let alone seriously explored.

*

With Aquinas, we approach the end of the first part of our story. Within his work, though not as a clearly recognizable whole, are to be found many, though not all, of the elements of that powerful concept of the person which we have called the 'Mainline Tradition'.[7] In that tradition the word 'person' indicates a complex and easily forgotten set of facts about human nature. If these facts are assembled, the concept of a person can begin to do useful philosophical work. But though the nature of persons can be identified when the various elements of the relationship between soul and body are enunciated, their timeless *worth* and *dignity* can still be recognized only if human beings are created in the image and likeness of God. But that image is of the whole person; every element must

---

[7] Some elements of persons more recently emphasized are of course absent, and there is no point in pretending that they are present. Thus, there is nothing about rights in Aquinas, though a Thomist (as an Augustinian) can easily build an account of them into Thomas' traditional comments about the dignity and worth of each person. And after Descartes far more stress was placed on self-awareness, seen as the ability to 'transcend oneself'. That sort of transcendence should not, of course, be confused with the transcendence of a Platonic Form or of God.

be recognized as important if persons are to be recognized for what they are – each with his own worth.

It follows, as we shall see, that if one element, such as consciousness, or some particular set of skills, or even the soul itself – the nature of which remained frequently fuzzy in both ancient and medieval times – is regarded as overwhelmingly significant or as in itself definitive of persons (or, as later, of personal identity), then its disappearance will cause some of the supposed images of God to be deprived of the dignity they would otherwise possess. And of course, if no God, then no dignity as his image. Then we could identity persons but attach value to them only if we choose (for whatever perhaps non-compelling reason) to do so. Indeed, the word 'person' would have become only a shorthand form of reference to the set of psycho-physical characteristics which we determine make up a real (as distinct from an approximate) human being.

*

But at least two gaps, and wider than we have yet indicated, remain open in Aquinas' project.[8] The first derives from his following closely Aristotle's assertion that philosophy can tell us nothing about individuals, but that we recognize them by the senses or the mind; perhaps here is to be found the basic explanation of his comparatively limited specific discussion of 'supposits'. Aquinas neglects Augustine's intuition that there are 'non-philosophical' ways of learning about individuals in their uniqueness: by way of biography and autobiography – and history, their cultural analogue. Such investigations might challenge traditional assumptions about the relationship between soul and mind, even the self-conscious mind, thus subverting older ideas about what it is to be – or perhaps to have – a soul.

The second gap is more strictly philosophical, and equally basic. It relates to the idea, shared by Aquinas with many other medieval thinkers, that the cause of individuality is material. There is certainly reason to believe that the presence of different matter in different individuals can

---

[8] In fact, there are more than two, but I limit myself here to comment on those which had already been to some degree filled in earlier thought. Further holes are partly a side-effect of Boethius' definition, for Boethius might seem to give the impression that humans are only distinct in their rationality (narrowly understood). That rationality, however, more broadly understood, not least through the power of imagination, has substantial (and specifically human) effects on the emotions and feelings. We shall return to this especially when considering writers of the eighteenth century.

account for their *plurality*. But, as we have seen, individuality is more than plurality: this was a worry for both the Stoics and Plotinus and is part of the explanation of why Plotinus determined that there may exist forms of individuals, at least of human individuals. To suggest that material difference is the cause of individuality is to neglect the fact that the 'matter' of each individual person is already a unique combination of matter and form; it is not, though Aquinas may at least give this impression, the combination of specific form and *prime* matter (which can only exist in abstraction).

Let us look at this a little further, noting in passing – while deferring it for a later chapter – that when a new human being is conceived, it is not a matter of the combination of 'any old' sperm and ovum which produces the new person, but the combination of sperm and ovum of particular characteristics, with the resultant effect of the radically different DNA of each newly conceived being – not to speak of the fact that some of the new persons will have the chromosome structure of males, others of females. Thus the generation of a new human person – not merely of another member of the human species – requires the imposition from the start of a unique formal element. To be in-formed, that is, is *more* than to become a member of the human species. As we shall see, this major weakness in Aquinas' account was a very proper concern of Edith Stein when she found herself following in the footsteps of Aquinas' early critic, Duns Scotus.

Aquinas' account of the person thus turns out to be incomplete in ways which have only become clear in recent times, though more attention to Augustine's more concrete approach might have rendered some of them visible earlier. Thus the Mainline Tradition, though much elaborated, was still incomplete on Thomas' death and we must enquire whether later thinkers (intentionally or not) enable us to fill in the gaps when some more or less completed parts of his synthesis (or their implications) are challenged: as about whether immature humans are potential persons or persons with potential, or whether varieties of damaged human being have ceased to be persons, or if not, why not.

Such difficulties, lurking beneath the surface of Aquinas' work or dependent on misinterpretations of it, will thus require further consideration. And in that reflection we shall find that an enriched Mainline Tradition will owe something to what is revealed not only (as for Augustine) by biography and cultural history but by a new respect for the spotlight shed by literature and other arts more generally representing a wider humanity through the humanity of specifically identifiable individuals with whom we can identify and so learn about ourselves. That being so, some of Aquinas' modern philosophical successors, though losing sight of much of the merit of his basic account of persons, may have much to contribute to the Mainline Tradition. Nevertheless, the relationship between the soul – however well understood naturalistically – and the *worth* of the person will in and of itself not be changed by the addition merely of new *information* about the capacities either of the soul itself or of the mind. Nor, as we shall see, is asking what a person *is*, to be identified, as some have come to suppose, as an enquiry into the related but more limited question – already broached by the ancient Stoics and Sceptics – about continuing personal identity through time.

7

Between Two Worlds: Duns Scotus

Particulars are recognized by the mind or by perception.

Aristotle, *Metaphysics* 1036a6

Up to this point we have been tracing, in broad outline, the development of a concept of the human person as a unique and uniquely dignified individual composite of body and soul. And we have attended to the Christian thesis that man is created in the image and likeness of God, recognizing it as the justification of that intrinsic dignity which we all share, whatever our social 'estate'. In the second part of this study I shall argue that in the early modern period what I have called the Mainline Tradition was widely, if with some hesitation, abandoned: not least because beliefs about God and the soul – essential preconditions for its further development – were being discarded. We shall have to ask whether that discarding implied that earlier beliefs about human dignity could intelligibly be retained – or whether alternative justifications of our status and worth were perhaps identified, bearing in mind that even if alternatives fail to preserve our intrinsic worth, it does not follow that the Mainline Tradition is fit for that purpose.

By the time we reach John Locke, we shall find that the whole debate has entered on a period of radical change, with thinkers instead of building further on foundations in the Mainline Tradition emphasizing a variety of new and very different problems, among which was not least one that had appeared prominently in classical antiquity, albeit in a world innocent of mechanistic accounts of the universe. That resurrected question was: Does our personal identity continues through time? The answer to that will inevitably affect – though the effects may not be immediately noticed – not only the account of persons themselves, but whether it matters whether we (or perhaps only some of us) are accounted persons.

The revised debate about identity reflects a radical change of direction. Instead of asking the Christian questions 'What is a person?' and 'What does it mean that we are created persons in God's image?' some began to ask: What kind of human item, if any, has any specific sort of personal identity? That introduces the possibility that some humans have no personal identity – however defined (though consciousness becomes the most common feature recognized as supplying the criterion). And if these lack personal identity, they may appear to lack (or to have lost) human dignity and so – in the coming more modern parlance – any human rights. Thus they need not be treated as persons in the traditional sense; they are just individuals, even though human: inadequate or worthless leftovers of the human species, 'scientifically' not significantly different from individuals of any other set or species – so to be treated or mistreated similarly. And if some humans do not matter – and we cannot agree as to what gives humans that personal identity which is the root of their mattering – perhaps no humans matter, unless to themselves.

*

Between the Mainline Tradition in the Thomistic form (still today in some places promoted, but with too little acknowledgement of the development required) and the early modern world, we meet the figure of the Franciscan Duns Scotus who Janus-like seems in several rather complex ways to bridge the gap between two philosophical universes. While a number of Scotus' challenges – about the univocity of being, about human and divine voluntarism, about his more explicit separation of morality from salvation and his mitigation of the effects of original sin – show the author as a significant forerunner of the post-medieval world, his approach to the long-recognized problem of individuality and its causes indicates a path by which the Mainline Tradition might have been enriched.

In Patristic times the Fathers (especially Augustine) had emphasized the uniqueness of each historically developing individual within the human set. In the Middle Ages too individuation was widely debated – now in an Aristotelian context – and the view of Aquinas came to predominate: matter, he argued, designated by quantity, is the cause of individuation, understood as the plurality of unique individuals within the more specific category of persons.[1]

Scotus offers a detailed analysis of earlier accounts of individuation (all of which he finds unsatisfactory) and in various places indicates his own. Yet although he thinks that to treat simply of a general *human* nature fails to capture the ineradicable and basic differences between one person (one *supposit*) and another, his own proposals, though based on the right questions, are at the least incomplete. His terminology varies, but in the late *Quaestiones* (especially book 7, q.13) he regularly refers to an 'individual form' (*forma individualis*) to account for that uniqueness of persons for which he was to be promoted by Gerard Manley Hopkins (not least in his poem 'Felix Randall'): that 'this-ness' (*haecceitas*) which indicates, say, the difference between Socrates and Plato. Discussing the passage from Aristotle's *Metaphysics* that appears at the head of this chapter, he notes that our minds and sensations enable us to recognize an individual thing with reference to its common nature; they enable us to see that Socrates is a man. Yet there remains a problem about how we can *understand*, as distinct from how we can *recognize*, what it is to be Socrates and what it is to be like Socrates and – at least by implication – whether it is important that Socrates is unique, even if he is.

In treating of individuation Scotus develops a lot of technical language, referring to the individual form which indicates the presence of a common human nature in each person as its 'contracted being', leaving the relationship between this 'contracted being' and the common nature rephrased rather than understood. According to Noone, Scotus' solution is that there is a formal distinction between the 'common nature and the individuating difference' but that they are really identical (*Ord.* 2, d.3, qq.5–6). This, though focusing on the right problem, does little to help with how we should learn to understand the differences between individuals, ignoring, that is, the need for an historical account of each person in his or her place and time. Scotus' failure to resolve his problem – rather than merely better to clarify its nature – probably occurs because his overriding concern was less with individuation *per se* than with understanding how differences between particulars, including between human beings, impinge on more general metaphysical (rather than 'personal') problems about the relationship between individuals and universals.

[1] See Gracia (1988, 1996), Noone (2003: especially 112–122), Tullius (2013).

Predictably, he was no more interested than was Plotinus (or indeed Augustine) in whether there are specifically female souls/forms to account for the femaleness of women.

Nevertheless, in positing, in addition to a common nature, a form to generate individual this-ness, Scotus puts the question of how to understand the relationship between the two 'forms' clearly on the philosophical table. For what *is* the relationship between our common nature, indicating our membership in our species, and our this-ness? As we have seen, Augustine, in his doctrine of our two lives – common and individual – had suggested a partial answer, but Scotus does not turn to that. Rather, to resolve the problem, he proposes a 'formal distinction' between the two forms, thus seeming to suggest – if not to imply – that the individual person is informed not by one form but by two. Without further exposition, that risks making his essence as a unitary being unintelligible.

Although this, as we shall see, is not an insoluble problem in the Aristotelian terms to which Scotus was accustomed, Scotus left it unresolved. Hence, although in general philosophy his influence remained strong, and even in some places predominant, for several centuries, and although *haecceitas* emphasizes the uniqueness of persons – and thus might have afforded a link between the theological account of persons as unique images of God and the philosophical necessity to do justice to the fact that a person is more than a human unit – in the shorter term Scotus added less than one might have hoped to the Mainline Tradition. Of course, and despite the fact that he deploys Richard of St Victor's more developed version of Boethius' definition of persons – thus again emphasizing incommunicability[2] – we must also remember that *haecceitas* – however explained 'naturalistically' – cannot in and of itself explain why that very uniqueness and incommunicability gives persons *dignity* – even if it does.

*

Haecceitas, if developed, could have made a real difference to the Mainline Tradition, yet it was a second and more surprising proposal of Scotus' that turned out to be in principle and in indirect effect the more attractive to his immediate successors: less, however, for further developing the concept of person in the Mainline Tradition than for dismantling 'person'

---

[2] See *The Examined Report of the Paris Lecture: Reportatio I-A, vol. 2*, ed. A. B. Wolter and O. V. Bychkov (St Bonaventure, NY, 2008) d.25, q.1-2, 41.

as a term of evaluation and moving it out of a theistic and into an increasingly godless world-view. For Scotus revived and reconstructed a distinction of Anselm's between two 'affections' of the human will: to the advantageous (*commodum*), whether among sensibles or intelligibles, and to the just (*iustum*).[3] The former affection, he thought, is determined by its objects, and it is in virtue of our ability to correct it with the aid of our desire for justice – albeit understood not 'cosmically' but coterminous with the good of our own human species – that we can be considered radically free. Such freedom is the essential mark of our creation in the image of God and, seen as the ability always to choose otherwise, remains an essential feature even of the saints in heaven who without it, he thinks, would not be human beings.

This is not the place to comment in detail on such a claim: merely to observe that Scotus' proposal about our 'affections' introduces a new, basic and corrosive feature into any potential concept of a person – though presumably Scotus did not see it like that. For although he is traditional enough to retain a mitigated version of the doctrine of original sin, his emphasis on the metaphysical importance of choice in any account of human nature is prophetic, pointing to a new, secularizing and value-free world from which all traces of the theological account of man as ordered not to autonomous choice but to goodness have been – it is hoped – erased.[4] Emphasis on the capacity to choose as the basic feature of a human and personal nature tends to remove that person from the world of transcendent reality, pointing rather to a world where our nature is less discovered than constructed – and from which those who have lost (or as yet failed to develop) the capacity to choose can be dismissed as non-persons.

And there is a second and related pointer to the future – also destructive of the Mainline Tradition – to be found in Scotus' writings. Scotus thought that he could defend morality – hence by implication, the intrinsic worth of human beings as rational moral agents – even were God not to exist in a world where choice is the specifically human capacity and where a happiness which is not salvation is possible without God's grace. But is he right to suggest this comparative irrelevance of God to human worth

---

[3] See further Rist (2014: 143, 153) on the more limited effects of original sin.

[4] Scotus' account of choice was developed by William of Ockham into an unambiguous liberty of indifference – indicating that the 'secularizing' direction I have indicated in Scotus was almost immediately canonized, supposedly to sustain God's absolute power and help explain moral obligation as intelligible only in terms of obedience to God's commands.

or even to happiness (whatever in the circumstances that could be)? What would really follow if there is no God? Not least – and especially not least for Scotus – what would become of moral obligation?

It has recently been argued that before Scotus there is no recognition of a specifically moral 'ought'. The adverb 'specifically', however, is important: with God in the equation such an 'ought' is assumed; with the prospect of atheism – with no divine commands to represent, induce or confirm objective morality (not, note, necessarily to 'invent' it) – some quite different explanation is needed if such morality is to gain purchase. If we see Scotus' work in the light of such questions, then like Boethius, but in a mode more toxic for the Mainline Tradition, he becomes indeed a hinge-figure.

In sum: to set *haecceitas* on the one hand and on the other Scotus' account of freedom together with the possibility of godless morality is to show Scotus with one foot in a potentially enlarged version of the older world of the Mainline Tradition, the other in a coming world where that tradition is to be ever more vigorously dismantled.

PART II

NO GOD, NO SOUL: WHAT PERSON?

8

Virtue, 'Virtue', Rights

As we move from Scotus into what is more normally thought of as the early modern period, we will notice five destructive approaches to the Mainline Tradition – often originally developed in more or less separate interests. The first tends to subordinate the search for virtue to the supposedly more basic search for human rights; the second minimizes or eliminates the effects of original sin; the third replaces the concept of soul, with its Christian implications, by that of mind or 'self'; the fourth limits or eliminates the role of God in human affairs; the fifth moves from discovering and respecting nature's 'laws' to denying final causes and seeking to master the physical universe.

The first and fourth of these approaches can already be recognized in Hugo Grotius (1563–1645). The third is developed in a line of succession which follows both John Locke in his concern less with persons than with 'personal identity', and the followers of Descartes who want to ease God out of at least the moral picture as being radically unknowable in his voluntarist essence: hence to argue that we – as purely immaterial *minds* – must understand ourselves and our possible virtues by strictly psychological reflection on our empirical nature without being too inhibited by earlier theological accounts of the soul–body complex as the (fallen) image and likeness of God. The fifth approach, to move from recognizing nature to trying to master it, permeates the work of Bacon and (again) of Descartes. Machiavelli (1469–1527), though no scientist or metaphysician, was the significant predecessor of them all, approaching politics (and hence ethics) not through any understanding of natural law but through our human capacity to construct our own political universe.

The second approach, foreshadowed by Scotus, appears again in Grotius' simple neglect of sin in general, while we find an outright denial of original sin in the deist Lord Herbert of Cherbury, then in Hobbes, the Cambridge Platonist Cudworth, Locke and even the 'counter-revolutionary' Leibniz. The effects of such denial were immense; it opened the way to optimistic accounts of human moral capacity both in intellectualists like Descartes and Kant and such moral-sense theorists as Hutcheson, Hume and Smith: indeed providing both necessary background for virtually every subsequent account of the person and his morality and one of the clearest indicators of the coming eclipse of European Christianity. It still persists, despite the gruesome history of the twentieth century, as one of the principal bulwarks of contemporary anti-Christian liberalism.

*

In the opening lines of the preface to his *Discourses on Livy*, Machiavelli claims (not entirely accurately) that his approach to historical material is original to him. What he seems to mean is that he is unconcerned with morality but writes about how and by what means power can be obtained and retained by great men and great commonwealths. In that respect his approach reminds us of the seemingly 'value-free' sections of Aristotle's *Politics*, but of course, for Aristotle that is far from the whole story. In the case of Machiavelli, his originality consists in the fact that, contrary to earlier Christian writers, his approach is entirely consequentialist; he determines good policy not in terms of the virtues of good men, but by whether the policies adopted (moral or not) have succeeded. Apart from his daily observation of the realities of the power-struggles in the Italy of his day, we may wonder why he might have adopted such an untrad-itional, indeed radical approach to the moral universe, hence to us who inhabit it.

One factor is that he was deeply influenced by the newly recovered Epicureanism of Lucretius: not of course that it propelled him towards a political career; ancient Epicureans consistently urge us to stay clear of politics as far too dangerous and a threat to our peace of mind. Rather Machiavelli found in Epicurean physics a radical rejection of traditional accounts of the ordered world. For whereas Aristotelians saw the world as governed by natural law, Lucretius taught indeterminacy in nature and a consequent unpredictability in human affairs. For the 'Epicurean' Machiavelli, not natural law but 'Lady Fortune' – ever unpredictable and needing to be manhandled – governs our lives. Given that situation, we must construct our own moral universe, forcing the 'world' to do as we will and, if necessary and if we are 'virtuous' enough,[1] imposing our will and its consequences on others by force and by fraud. For Machiavelli the prime model of such virtue is Cesare Borgia (*Prince* 7), except that he blotted his virtuous escutcheon by failing to factor in that he might fall ill at the time of his papal father's death; which he did, being thus rendered incapable of preventing the election of Giuliano della Rovere as the Pope's successor. That, as Machiavelli intones, led to his ruin.

Power for Machiavelli is understood as the ability to control the minds of others for our own advantage. For the serious politician all means to that end are acceptable: lying, defaming, cruelty and killing. Virtue, as traditionally conceived, can and should be flaunted if convenient but, where necessary, supposedly vicious and obviously non-Christian means are to be adopted. As Machiavelli puts it in the *Discourses*, 'Our religion has shown us truth and the true path' [in some 'ideal-world' sense of 'true'] but 'treats humility, abjection and contempt of worldly things as the greatest good'. In this *de facto* rejection of Pope Innocent III's influential *De Contemptu Mundi*, Machiavelli maintains that Christian teachings cause us to neglect the practical demands of honour and that greatness of soul essential in public life, leaving us open 'to be plundered by wicked men' (*Discourses* 2.2). The 'wicked men' are, it seems, Machiavellians who use Machiavellian virtues for purposes of which Machiavelli himself disapproves!

In his account of human nature Machiavelli is ultra-Augustinian: 'Anyone who assumes human beings to be good is likely to be ruined' (*Prince* 15). Men, he believes, prefer vengeance to gratitude (*Discourses* 1.9) and are easily bored with goodness (*Discourses* 1.37); hence we must assume that all are evil either openly or in secret (*Discourses* 1.3). At the same time, he turns the basic Augustinian vice of 'lust for power' (*libido dominandi*) into sagacious 'virtue' in the politician.[2] Like Scotus, he looks back to medieval times; but he proceeds far more boldly towards the modernity of Hobbes, his successor in notoriety. Following his death Machiavelli became for a time a by-word in Europe for the cynical politician – and some politicians duly took note: as (in newly-Protestant England) Thomas Cromwell and Lord Burghley.

---

[1] 'Virtue' now reclaims its Latin root (*virtus*) and is roughly equated with 'virility', so seen as shorn of moral content. Greek *arete* could have a similar sense.

[2] For more on Machiavelli, not least on his version of Epicureanism, see Rist (2014: 166–172).

Prophet Machiavelli apart, it is fair to note that before Descartes the Mainline understanding of persons was in process of formation within an unambiguously theistic context. After Descartes, and especially after Locke, it was assumed that persons exist and that they are human, but that as human beings their identity as persons, their personhood, is to be determined by their possession or otherwise of certain mental characteristics, normally consciousness, self-consciousness or memory. Psychology is beginning to replace 'anthropology'. Those 'humans' who lack the assumed mental capacity can be designated sub-humans, or indeed not or no longer humans at all: certainly not to be classed with those who are legal persons (some of whom are to be regarded as possessing rights).

Scotus – despite himself – had raised the possibility of God's non-existence; a similar view was attributed – again as mere hypothesis – by Francesco Suarez (*De Legibus* II.6.3) to the earlier Augustinian Gregory of Rimini. Suarez himself rejected Gregory's version of the claim that even if God did not exist, moral rules would (and should) be binding on a still supposedly fallen humanity.[3] Nevertheless, admission of the possibility of a godless universe – even as the basis for thought-experiments – throws the nature of morality into doubt. And the existence of God will become problematic if the effects of his presence can be otherwise attributed, let alone if he seem altogether unnecessary. He certainly seems irrelevant and unnecessary, even undesirable, in the political theorizing of Machiavelli – even though 'Old Nick' sought and received absolution on his death-bed!

*

Many extra-philosophical and extra-theological features of the early modern world are recognized as affecting its intellectual life. One of the more obvious is the invention of printing; a second, immediately relevant to attitudes to human individuals, is the discovery of the Americas, and especially the colonization of what is now referred to as Latin America. The Spanish *conquistadores* enter into our story because their brutality towards the native populations evoked a strong response from a number of members of the Catholic clergy. One of earliest to protest was Francesco de Vitoria (1483–1546), the 'founder' of the neo-Thomist Dominican school at Salamanca and a pioneer in the developing science of international law, who in academic pamphlets argued that the Indians

---

[3] For further comment see Rist (2014: 195–197).

were human beings like the Spaniards themselves, similarly formed in God's image and likeness and therefore deserving of much better than the savageries meted out to them. A later Dominican, Bartholomé de las Casas (1484–1566) saw the atrocities at first hand and his developing attitude to the subjection of the Indians points clearly to the recycling of older ideas about human dignity to form the groundwork for later theories of human rights, especially the right to freedom of religion. Las Casas saw his championing of the Indians as a mere matter of that justice with which rights-theory, generally, concerns itself rather than with love or even goodness. His position is that if Indians are created in the image and likeness of God, then their dignity must be respected; indeed they have the right to be respected. God-given dignity entails that those who receive it have the right to be treated justly insofar as is possible in any given society.[4]

Las Casas was at first himself a landowner and none too scrupulous, early in his career arguing the morally incoherent case that it is wrong because unnecessary to enslave the Indians when more black slaves could be brought in from Africa. He later – now a Dominican and soon to become bishop of Chiapas – urged the rejection of all slavery and mounted vigorous campaigns against it, in 1550 engaging in a famous debate at the Spanish court with Juan de Sepúlveda in which he denied that any humans were slaves by nature.

At the theoretical level the whole dispute turned in part on the traditional over-interpretation of texts about natural slaves from the first book of Aristotle's *Politics*, probably intended originally to identify (and fatefully also to name as slaves) a number of human beings as incapable of self-motivation.[5] Those unfortunates, according to Aristotle, are only capable of understanding and obeying orders. In my youth some such were quite common and were often referred to as 'village idiots'; they are probably to be understood largely as resulting from excessive inbreeding in close communities, as well as from the sporadic phenomenon known

---

[4] For a detailed and generous treatment of Las Casas' activities see Lantigua (2016) and more generally Clayton (2012). Las Casas' concern was especially that the Indians should be allowed freedom of religion, though in supposing that they would give up human sacrifices without such continuing military action as would amount to conquest strikes one as rather naïve. For earlier (patristic) Christian rights-talk see the Appendix.

[5] I suggested that Aristotle had been misinterpreted long ago (Rist 1989: 249–252), but the book may have been published in the wrong place. To my knowledge my reading has not been refuted. In more recent discussions (e.g. MacIntyre 2016: 85–86) Sepúlveda's interpretation has been assumed.

now as 'Down's Syndrome'. Traditionally, Aristotle was read as teaching that such individuals – undefined but easily to be defined racially – should, in their own best interests, be reduced to chattel slavery. That is now seen to be obviously problematic, not least when *race* is thought not only to indicate incapacities but also sub-human (therefore appropriately slavish) status. What Vitoria and Las Casas protested against was the claim that such arguments justified the enslavement, on racial grounds, specifically of the Indians.

In the debate with Sepúlveda both sides claimed victory, but Las Casas' position – though largely ineffective in changing the situation on the ground – is historically of great significance since it amounted to arguing that it makes no sense to urge that some human beings are not persons and therefore need not be treated as such. Although Las Casas could hardly have realized it, the thrust of his stance was to deny what was later to become explicit in the writings of Locke and his successors: namely that for some reason – it need not be race, though in notorious cases it has been – there exist merely apparent persons.

*

Las Casas was a Catholic, and in effect used the Christian Gospel as a basis for arguing that no human is a non-person. Hugo Grotius (1583–1645) also paid attention to rights in his rewriting of traditional accounts of natural law, but from the point of view of the continued application of the tenets of the Mainline Tradition, his work represents a challenge – as that of Las Casas does not – in its insertion of ideas about the possession of rights into a world 'necessarily' to be freed, for commercial purposes, from earlier ideas of God and his role in nature. Grotius, a Protestant and certainly no atheist, tried to build the non-relevance of the *Christian* story about God into a new version of natural law which would be still coherent within a less specifically theistic and providentialist world-picture. Such a reconstructed version, he supposed, was now a necessary prerequisite for settling commercial disputes in the wider world currently opened up by the explorers in both East and West. According to Grotius, the principles of a rational and apparently binding version of natural law could be reconstructed not on traditional understandings of human dignity but as something like the Roman *ius gentium* (though without the at least tacit backing of Roman religion), perhaps buttressed by the now fashionably revised Stoicism of such as Justus Lipsius (1547–1606).

Earlier natural lawyers based their claims about man's duties, responsibilities and worth on the concept of human dignity – in pagan society dependent on social and civic standing, in Christian terms (officially) on equality in the eyes of a God who is no respecter of persons but who values his creation, especially the human race, and thus bestows dignity on it. Grotius approached natural law very differently, believing that the 'problem' which resort to natural law must solve is that human beings are aggressive and self-seeking yet at the same time sociable. Our Janus-like character will necessarily lead to disputes, and natural law is required as a mechanism for dispute resolution; subjective-rights, as Grotius sees them, are to be determined by litigation – rights-theorists, as we have already noticed, are bound always to be litigious – as being concerned with justice and fairness.[6] Nevertheless, although much Christian theology seems outside Grotius' concerns – no attention is specifically paid to sin of any kind or to redemption – he assumes a beneficent God and that our present confused and divided condition is the result of God's will and goodness.

But he has a novel and contorted way of explaining how that goodness transpires in the human condition. Instead of claiming that as children of God we have a natural dignity, he supposes that for our own *protection* we have been endowed by God with subjective rights, and not only active but passive rights against being treated unjustly. Since therefore we are both social and aggressive – and possessed of these subjective rights (whatever metaphysical status such rights are supposed to have) – unjust aggression is to be condemned as an attack upon them (*On the Law of War and Peace* 1.2.1).[7]

For Grotius, perfect rights accord with divinely-given laws of justice and the intrinsic justice of certain behaviours; hence the rights of others are not to be infringed. Yet although his argument about rights depends on the existence of God, his project of reconciling human sociability with human aggressiveness appears to be independent of theology. And although he allows rights a divine origin, others might claim them as

[6] For a good discussion of the association of rights-theory with control of the body-politic by judges, see Pera (2015: 69–71); see also below.

[7] This is not the place to consider the 'origins' of rights-talk, or of whether rights could be shown to be compatible with political ideas of Aristotle or Aquinas or any other medieval thinker. Two things, however, are clear: that there is no specific talk of *subjective* rights in Aristotle or the medieval Aristotelians; secondly that rights talk in the Middle Ages concerned the rights not of individuals but of groups, such as popes, kings, bishops, lords, guilds, etc. against one another. For an introduction to the continuing debate see Tierney (1989 and 1997); also Lamont (2011).

merely legal protection to be recognized pragmatically – even if God does not exist. Indeed, Grotius himself wants to argue that rights are the endowment of all human beings, apparently independently of the notion of a divinely bestowed dignity, and indeed designed to serve quite other – wholly secular and pragmatic – ends. In omitting to raise the question of the necessity or non-necessity of a divine sanction for rights as the ultimate sources of obligation, he produces a confusion that has lasted until the present day: we can still hear atheist rights-theorists talking (as Grotius might well have done) of rights as 'sacred'; a habit that goes back at least to the deist Jefferson's first draft of the American Declaration of Independence.

Nevertheless, although the effect of the introduction of rights as some-how basic – indeed perhaps *the* basic building block of moral theories, secular or religious – cannot be overestimated, we should remember that Grotius thinks not of *universal* human rights, but of the rights of individuals engaged in particular activities. Indeed, the same is true of most of the discussion of rights which, particularly in the English revolutionary period, further developed Grotius' ideas. In England, with one or two remarkable exceptions, rights were claims for a particular group: that is, for property-owning adult English males – neither for slaves nor for women and certainly not for human beings in general. To put it bluntly, the implications of the 'rights-theories' of Vitoria and Las Casas – both deployed within the Mainline Tradition – were more radical, if less productive in the short run, than those of Grotius.

Richard Tuck has pointed out an exception to the rule that rights are, in this period, rather limited (as Grotius, though not Las Casas, would have seen it). A near contemporary of Grotius, the English Leveller Richard Overton, primarily concerned with the rights of 'the Natives of this Land', yet clearly thought more boldly of rights as universal and certainly as inalienable.[8]

Whether Overton's claim included the rights of women is unlikely. Lynn Hunt has argued that the first reference to the phrase 'rights of man' (meaning 'mankind as a whole') – as distinct from the 'natural right' of Grotius and others – is as late as Rousseau's *Social* Contract (1762).[9] Even treating of the later eighteenth century, indeed, we need to be careful: the American Declaration of Independence, in bestowing universal and inalienable rights, still excluded women and slaves from the

[8] Tuck (1979: 149–150).   [9] Hunt (2000: 9).

beneficiaries.[10] John Adams, seemingly worried as to an absurd proliferation of human rights-claims, mocked the idea of female suffrage in an
ideal society. Only in the French tradition of Condorcet, Olympe de
Gouges and others – as then of Tom Paine and Mary Wollstonecraft –
were women's rights acknowledged at the immediately political level. As
for the French revolutionaries, they eventually fixed on regarding
women's citizenship as 'passive'. (A more outspoken contemporary version might be recognized in the comment of Malcolm X that 'the only
position for women in the revolution is horizontal'.)

The 'mature' Grotius rejects any kind of Aristotelian virtue-theory root
and branch. God-given rights – their relationship to a fundamental
human dignity remaining unclear – can explain virtue, for the man who
respects the rights of others is virtuous; whatever his motivation, he is
acting justly. Virtues – legalistically – reflect the observance of rights, not
vice-versa. Nothing in this pragmatically-developed theory, of course,
enables us to recognize which rights are properly claimed and which are
not. Grotius lists life, body, freedom and honour, apparently unaware as
to how the scope of rights was to prove peculiarly hard to determine; his
position, as summed up by Schneewind, is that 'the virtuous are simply
those who obey the law where it is specific [thus respecting perfect
rights],[11] and stay within the bounds of the permissible where it leaves
room for discretion'. That seems reasonable if the lawgiver is God, far less
so if we are dealing with human lawyers in a godless world.

Although Grotius treats less of rights-claims that I make on my own
behalf against my neighbour than about the offence to objective justice if
I act aggressively, his position entails that it is just that I claim my rights
for myself. Hence it is scarcely surprising that such claims, rather than the
pursuit of virtue, came to represent a revised version of the first principles
of morality. Thus, however unwittingly, Grotius' position is in this respect
revolutionary. For however easy it may be to include rights-claims in
scholastic ethics, none of the medievals would have wanted anything to
do with the proposition that rights provide the *first principles* of moral
thinking: rights, that is, claimed against other human beings, let alone
against God.

How does this affect the story of the person? Despite Grotius' apparent
'realism', his claims about rights are not empirical; they depend on his

---

[10] On differences between the English Declaration of 1689 and the American Declaration
see Zuckert (2000).
[11] Schneewind (1998: 78).

restricted application of voluntarist theism. If God, then subjective rights; if no God, then subjective rights need some other justification: this problem remains to haunt rights-theorists down to our present time. But we can now identify a second problem, clearly recognizable in the work of Vitoria and Las Casas: is there a distinction between persons and human beings? If some humans are not persons, then, *pace* Grotius, they might not be accepted as possessors of rights. This difficulty is not raised by Grotius, but it underlies his thesis and will surface in Hobbes and in Locke's writings on personal identity.

Put differently, Grotius has bequeathed to his successors the task of re-examining the question of what constitutes a person – and in the new context of rights, legal or otherwise and their related responsibilities, rather than of the achieving of virtue or the development of excellences, moral or other. It might have seemed, and still seems to many, that problems about persons – recast as about personal identity and related specifically to questions of rights and responsibilities – begin with the early modern age. We have seen, however, that their roots go back to ancient debates: not, of course specifically about rights and their origins, but about the relationship between man and the cause (in some wider sense theistic) of the cosmos; what marks the modern period – inaugurated in this respect more or less by Grotius in the footsteps of Scotus' voluntarism and potential agnosticism – is a set of new and potentially corrosive approaches to older more basic certainties.

For the 'demythologizing' of rights (implicit or explicit) and their potential separation from serious considerations of human dignity and its origin, is paralleled by the replacement (as found in Bacon) of 'natural' theories of the cosmos, as well as of human political structures, by inferences that the state is not natural but constructed (as in Machiavelli) and that all we can know of the cosmos is summed up by the mechanistic laws which we ourselves infer to describe it.

*

Grotius' project might seem eminently sensible, given the conditions of his day. Confronted with a new world far wider than the more or less homogeneous society of medieval Europe in which we must now trade not only with monotheists in the world of Islam but also with the culturally more remote Chinese and the native inhabitants of the Americas, we need a new code of natural law – not specifically Christian – if only to regulate our now wider commercial dealings. But with the new programme seeming incomplete and in some respects dangerous, Samuel

Pufendorf (1632–1694) tried to 'correct' and complete it. Normally, and more conventionally, he starts with duties and obligations, imposed, as any voluntarist would agree, by a superior. But rights, now perhaps correlative with duties,[12] are soon in sight again (and sometimes as coming first); nor are they any longer, as with Grotius, part of the structure of the justice of the universe but are to be considered qualities ('entities') imposed by God on human beings. Each human being (or person) is endowed with inalienable rights and subject to divinely imposed obligations as a quasi-forensically identified individual.

As for how to interpret and deploy his new natural law of rights and duties, Pufendorf specifically – and intelligibly in view of the litigious world he evokes – rules out any role for theologians; duties and rights are henceforth to be determined by philosophers and lawyers. The implication, whether or not clear to Pufendorf himself, is that the rights of individuals (persons) are nothing to do with a wider theology or with traditional accounts of virtue, but strictly matters of law, whether made by God or – better – by man.

What then would happen if God were removed, as had already been envisaged? The dignity of humans as bearers of divinely endowed rights disappears, while the only sort of rights (and duties) which remain must be man-made codes – even though it might be considered useful (and more 'user-friendly') to endow them with some kind of murkily 'sacred' nature. Perhaps persons too could be man-made. In a highly significant move in light of the Christian emphasis on the good of existence over against the pagan view that what matters in humans is their excellent qualities, Pufendorf, in contrast to all his more theologically-minded predecessors, dismisses the notion that goodness subsists in a universe (*De Jure Naturae* 1.4.4) traditionally – but no longer – supposed to be good insofar as it exists – holding that *moral* goodness depends solely on God's will. Thus, in the footsteps of Grotius, he leaves the door yet more widely open for the view that morality is to be established not on the investigation of the nature of human virtue as divinely revealed, but on the proclamation of rights – and (as he hopes) their corresponding

---

[12] Correlativity is attributed to Pufendorf by Tuck but disputed by Mautner (1989). Mautner sees the roots of correlativity in Hutcheson and a clear early example in Thomas Reid's *Essay on the Active Powers of the Human Mind*, Essay 5, chapter 3 (1785, reprinted by MIT Press, 1969). In the case of Pufendorf, Schneewind (1998: 134, note 26) hedges his bets, but he notes the emphasis on rights as moral first principles already in Gassendi (268).

responsibilities – for some, but again presumably not for all members of the human race. That will depend on who is now to be accepted as fully human, and who, and on what grounds, is to be disqualified as, yes, a human being but a non-person.[13]

---

[13] It was not only the Nazis, as we shall see, who developed such disqualifications, distinguishing in their case racially between humans (primarily Aryans), sub-humans (Slavs) and non-humans (Jews). Analogous divisions of humanity are now common in the philosophical (especially the bioethical) literature: the disqualifying factor being normally a non-developed or damaged mental capacity such as memory. Grotius is not usually mentioned in this connection, but the influence of Descartes, especially of Locke, and even more of Kant, is often recognized as lying behind disqualifying proposals A good example is to be found in H. Tristram Engelhart Jr (1986: 107–109) who writes of 'human non-persons' (i.e. the unborn, infants, the senile, etc.). I shall return to the theme in later chapters. Contemporary writers often find the views of the 'Founding Fathers' of contemporary philosophy a bit embarrassing, but Hill Jr (1992: 202) is frank enough to admit that in Kant's account of persons 'the status of infants and the mentally incompetent remains problematic'. (I owe the quotation from Hill to De Koninck (1999): an invigorating and refreshing essay.)

9

Descartes on Soul, Self, Mind, Nature

Although ancient and medieval thinkers regularly discuss self-awareness and Augustine emphasizes the importance of the 'I' and the 'first-person' stance, we have seen that pre-modern accounts of persons involve far more than identifying the personal with consciousness or self-awareness; indeed, they pay specific attention to the nature and activity of the complex subject-substance which is self-aware. Hence a basic concern – not only among dualist Platonists of various sorts – was the relationship between the 'I' and the world, including the body; and in the first instance between the 'I' and a soul which is not merely a mind yet in some way controls and is responsible for the body. The problem, as we have seen, goes back to the pseudo-Platonic *Alcibiades*; it disturbed Augustine who came to abandon the identification of the person with the soul but could not explain the nature of the 'person' – that strange 'mix' of soul and body – and it was temporarily resolved when the 'mix' was accepted in the Middle Ages as explicable in Aristotelian terms as the soul's being the form of the body: I as person am not a soul, but exist as my soul and body, and I can be understood as what I am via that inclusive combination.

These pre-modern debates were about the 'soul', not the 'self'; hence Augustine's account of '*cogito*'-style arguments is very different from that of Descartes who sees the soul as conceived by the Scholastics as able to do little useful philosophical work.[1] Hence, and abandoning the medieval view that it acts as the principle of living things, he identified it with

[1] For interesting comment see Spaemann (2012: 150).

consciousness of self, by extension virtually deploying the term 'soul' to represent what later came to be referred to as 'the self'. But before Descartes the soul had functioned as more than a life-principle having – and especially but not only among Christians – an essentially religious function, not least by way of its possible immortality and what Christians, especially following Paul, referred to as the 'spirit', the relationship of which to the soul, however, remained somewhat obscure.

This association of the soul with religion may be read more widely: not only with reference to worship, but also to it as the organ of aesthetic, moral and other such activities as we may broadly term 'spiritual'. Christian writers often distinguish our body from both our soul and our spirit. Thus, soul may have a broader or narrower sense in that it may be treated as spirit as well as the driver of more 'naturalistic' activities. But as soul became self, there emerged a risk that such spiritual capacities lacked adequate explanation; that we might come merely to suppose we have them. In any case, most pre-Cartesian thinkers hold that the soul – whatever its precise relationship – is not to be *identified* with the mind, let alone with the brain. Once identified with the mind – especially if the mind is represented as performing more purely rational functions – it is likely that claims about a wider human, indeed personal, richness will be increasingly reduced to third-person 'scientific' comment.

A good pre-Christian example of how possible ambiguities can rise about the relationship between soul, mind and what later came to be called spirit occurs when in Plato's *Republic* we find mind viewed as an aspect or kind (*eidos*) of soul but viewed too as the possessor of 'spiritual' functions. Our problem then is how to describe 'soul' if the word conveys more than 'mind'. Furthermore, the relationship between soul and mind will vary with differing accounts of mind. Plato's account of the mind is different from Descartes'; hence when the latter's operations of the mind seem to be explicable entirely naturalistically, we notice a marked tendency to *reduce* soul to mind, until eventually 'soul' may become otiose, or at best be left to theologians: a group, as we have already noted in Pufendorf, to be accorded less and less intellectual respectability

A major aim of Descartes' overall project was to rid philosophy of what he thought of as the decadent Aristotelianism of the Schools; to show Aristotelianism as incompatible with the 'new science', then look for foundational principles for that science untainted by tenets derived from interpretations of unreliable information acquired from the senses. As with Bacon earlier, final as well as formal causes will have to disappear in physical investigations. But the study of persons is importantly part of the study of nature as a whole; are final causes to disappear there too? And here traditional Christian answers to the question, 'Why are we here?' – dependent as they are on beliefs about what we are – risk disappearing too.

It is understandable that Descartes found it necessary to claim that his work had nothing to do with theology. Where Pufendorf was to hand over moral and 'anthropological' questions to philosophers and lawyers, Descartes simply disclaimed responsibility for the implications of his views. The Inquisition was understandably unimpressed: not least perhaps because such disclaimers served only to encourage the belief that much of the inherited capital of the Middle Ages, not least the version of the Mainline Tradition promoted by Aquinas, could simply be ignored. Revolutionary changes in society, the opening up of new worlds of various kinds, as we have seen in Grotius, enabled early modern thinkers too easily to dismiss the achievements of the more recent past; it was fashionable to say something different; that may account in part for why they got away so easily with philosophically dubious proposals.

Hence, barring something radical enough to verge on atheism (as implicit in Hobbes), Descartes, as a professing Catholic, had few possible avenues to follow. Medieval Aristotelianism, however, had always been somewhat uneasily allied with that Augustinian theology whereby, as Augustine himself would regularly say, he could learn about God and the soul. Hence Descartes seems to have supposed Augustinian ideas a possible recourse for the non-Aristotelian foundations of science that he sought.[2]

Descartes thinks that we can acquire belief in the existence of God and the soul – often viewed by him as in effect the mind – without reference to the senses. That sounds somewhat Augustinian, but the use to which he wants to put his knowledge of God and this 'soul' is quite other. For Descartes, but decidedly not for Augustine, all else but God and the soul – including the human body – is brute matter, to be mastered in various ways. But while Augustine in ascetic mode can charge us to beware of sensual temptations, he specifically rejects the ultra-Neoplatonic maxim of Porphyry that we should 'flee the corporeal'. While Augustine came to hold that we are not just our souls, but rather souls somehow linked 'matrimonially' with their particular bodies, Descartes wants to revert to something like the view Augustine eventually rejected: that since we are

---

[2] See the helpful discussion in Menn (1998: especially 18–72).

necessarily incorporeal, we are to be *identified* with our souls now viewed more or less as our minds. From this position of mind–soul–self we can plot the contours of the mechanical physical world, thus ridding ourselves of any Aristotelian (indeed even *de facto* of any Augustinian) account of either body or cosmos.

Descartes' primary concern was to establish a basis of certainty for truths not only about himself but about everything else; yet while, like Augustine, he argues from the general foundation 'I think' to the claim that I exist, Augustine proceeds differently, his examples being such as 'I am mistaken, therefore I exist' and his understanding of the 'I' is very different; he wants to emphasize not only 'thinking' as such but the concrete act of thinking in which he may make a mistake. It will not be his soul or mind which makes the mistake but he, Augustine: his whole person: soul, mind, body, however understood. Augustine has learned, whether or not Descartes realized it, that we are *not* our souls – nor our minds either. As for Descartes himself, in a letter of 14 November 1640 he thanks Colvius for drawing his attention to Augustine's *cogito* but continues:

He [Augustine] goes on to show that there is a certain likeness of the Trinity in us, in that we exist, we know that we exist, and we love the existence and the knowledge we have. I, on the other hand, use the argument to show that the I which is thinking is an immaterial substance with no bodily element. These are two very different things.

And again, writing to Mersenne, he comments that

[He] was grateful to find Augustine on his side against the Sceptics, even though his own purpose, as distinct from Augustine's, was to establish the thinking self as an immaterial substance.

When we looked at the developing Christian claim that human beings, *qua* persons, possess dignity, we noted the growth from its fore-shadowings in Stoic providentialism and in Plato's belief that we should become like god precisely in our moral and spiritual perfection, to the standard Christian doctrine in antiquity – of which I take Augustine to be the most eloquent advocate – that our worth depends on our being recognized as dependent and created in the image and likeness of God.

Obviously such conclusions would recede, as we have noticed, if any or all their premises are removed: for example, if it were determined there is no God, or that his proposed existence does no philosophical work, as Epicurus believed. But it now has become clear that with Descartes there also arises a further fundamental question on which we have only touched thus far: not about God, but as to whether we have some substantial *soul* – over and above the mind – which plays some basic role in our activities even if it is not to be identified with our whole being. According to the Stoics, arguing against the Sceptics, as we have seen, if we had no soul, we would be resolved into a set of sequential selves – or a mere heap of qualities.

In *The Discourse on Method* part five and in the opening dedication of the *Meditations* to the deans and doctors of the Paris Faculty of Sacred Theology, Descartes tells us that he wants to know about, or demonstrate the existence of God and the soul. As we have noted, that is apparently Augustinian talk despite its author's view of the relation of his scheme to Augustine's. However, as we have also observed, despite the continual appearance of the word 'soul' in his writings, Descartes is primarily concerned with the self-conscious mind which is the real and immaterial 'we'. Hence one of the challenges he faces is that *we* are minds using bodies to which we are somehow accidentally connected. For although *we* are to be identified with our minds ('souls'), yet our self-concern – that is some state of our 'self' – is obvious when we experience pleasurable and painful sensations through our bodies. Yet how is this even possible if *we* are to be identified with our minds–souls–self? It is not difficult to see why Descartes' attempt to explain that we are related to our bodies via the pineal gland is whistling in the wind – and that, if I have mind and no essentially different soul, the by then Mainline concept of the person will be hard to justify. And if we cannot justify it, why not something to replace it?

On inspection, though Descartes' concept of mind has often been thought very close to that of the Platonists, it is very different and far more bizarre. Plato's soul is erotic and affective and no mere thinker, whether about itself or about the external world. No Platonist, whether Christian (like Augustine) or pagan, has to explain the relationship between the 'self' and the emotions. Descartes, however, has reduced the human being to something like an 'immaterial' computer able to reflect on itself. Were that correct, then not only the traditional soul but virtually every other 'component' of the 'person' hitherto recognized – other than the fortuitous connection to our bodies – has disappeared. Indeed, and though Descartes wrote a treatise on *The Passions of the Soul*, we may wonder what has become of the 'passions' (emotions). In that work he devotes most of his time to describing individual 'passions'; though now and then treating of how the soul is aware of them and is able to reflect on them, he merely confirms how limited an account of the human being he is offering. The conscious thinking self is able to reflect and experience the passions, but this is by way of a distraction from its ordinary and proper function of self-awareness. Thus, strictly speaking, we experience the passions but are not intrinsically bound to them.

Indeed, even the 'I' of the *cogito* is diminished. Unlike Locke, Descartes makes no attempt to write empirically about the soul or mind but argues *a priori* from an apparently certain starting point. He supposes that he is thinking of himself, but all he has shown is that thinking – and therefore (we should allow him) the existence of a thinker – is a reality. This is certainly a revolutionary start, but more sober revolutionaries were readily aware, in view of their more thoroughgoing empiricism, that – final causes gone – he has left himself unable to treat holistically of human beings possessed of minds and 'passions', let alone about persons as traditionally conceived. He might be treating of some diminished version of an angel, except that his treatment of the 'passions' hardly assorts with the angelic!

*

Although Descartes' work is replete with references to the Deity, and he claims to be writing as a Catholic, his thought reveals a number of religious novelties which his successors, not least Locke, would find satisfying. As we have noted, he explicitly disclaims theologizing; this enables him to omit several traditional Christian themes; in this respect, at least, he was right to claim not to be directly influenced by Augustine. For apart from the tendency to reduce soul to a rational mind shorn of 'spiritual' features, there are various equally significant theological lacunae: above all the total absence (as in Grotius) of original sin. Descartes certainly acknowledges his own imperfections, but these are regarded as resulting from the human tendency to make mistakes or to rush to inaccurate conclusions: not to commit sins as traditionally conceived – and far less even crimes.

In *Meditation* 4.8 Descartes tells us we have the power of free choice. This he identifies as the act of the 'will' which chiefly enables him to discern that he bears a certain image and likeness of God; and as being perhaps even exempt from *subjection* to God.[3] He further explains the will as a power to do or not do something. That points to a future (and more consciously secular) Kantian autonomy. And in the absence of

[3] Cf. the letter to Christina (Adam and Tannery 5.85).

original sin, Descartes is also free to abandon many traditional ideas about the dependence of man on God: in that respect his account of persons is more 'Promethean', as in Renaissance and later traditions which we shall duly inspect.

Nevertheless, Descartes views the 'liberty of indifference' as the lowest grade of liberty and indicating lack of knowledge. If he had always clear knowledge of what is true and good, he continues, he would never have any difficulty in determining the judgment he ought to arrive at and what choice he ought to make; he would be entirely free, never 'indifferent'. In his present state, however, he fails to restrain his will, which being in itself indifferent to understanding easily falls into error and sin, choosing the false instead of the true and evil instead of good. Sin, that is, is a strictly intellectual failing – as is appropriate if 'we' are just our minds.

We have already hinted at an even more basic change from the mentality of the medievals. Just as Descartes abandons final causes in physics, so he in effect abandons them in psychology, since we can have no idea of God's ultimate purposes (*Meditations* 1.248). That squares with his view that the good of the soul is not activity, as Aristotle and his followers – and even in another mode the Platonists – held, but contentment:[4] an appropriate goal for a mind-self held to be an inert substance underlying our actions, thoughts and desires. Understanding, he tells us, is a passivity of the mind (3.82).

*

Heidegger attacked Descartes as the fount of subsequent subjectivism and his reasoning is not difficult to understand, though it is easy to see that he is seriously misguided.[5] Descartes is basically an epistemologist, interested not in how the world we know must be created by man – since our knowledge is limited to the sense-data present to our mind and consciousness – but how he, Descartes, can justify straightforward claims about its mechanistic composition. He further wants to show that since all beyond the mind is merely mechanical, it is the vocation and almost the duty of man to dominate and control it. Hence in chapter 6 of *The Discourse on Method* he says that we can employ the material world as is appropriate to the nature of its individual parts and thus make ourselves 'masters and

---

[4] *Letter to Elizabeth*, 20 November 1647.
[5] For rejections of Heidegger's historical recklessness from very different points of view see Seigel (2005: 41–42) and De Libera (2007, 2008: *passim*).

possessors of nature'. And since even the human body is non-mental, that too at least in theory is mere matter to be manipulated; Locke's claim that we own our bodies, as we own our material possessions, is not far away, and Descartes' position will thus necessarily affect all subsequent ethical theorizing.

Descartes has little to say of persons as such, but his tendency to reduce the soul to the mind entails a rejection not only of the notion that persons are ultimately composed of two substances (soul and body) but *a fortiori* of any wider exposition of the nature of the person so composed. Nevertheless, to say that we are to be recognized in the first instance as self-reflective beings trying to understand the world in which we live – however diminished an account of the person that may imply – is far from a claim that the world is not to be discovered but 'invented' by the knowing subject. The world, divided according to Descartes into material and immaterial realities, is no construct of the mind but a hard-won, existent target of mental cognition.

Nevertheless, Descartes' dismissal of an adequate two-substance theory of the person – whether in some Augustinian Christian form or more Aristotelian – when combined with his opening moves in a process to banish the soul from the philosophical stage, might seem – if ironically and despite himself – to open up the possibility that matter provides the sole explanation of mankind in general and of persons in particular. Which leaves the problem, which many have tried and try to resolve, of how matter (perhaps understood neo-Stoically) might explain those realities of human existence which traditionally were thought of as activities of the soul.

Thomas Hobbes would be among the first to test the possibility of moving along this road. And as we shall see, Locke – and despite himself in this not unlike Hobbes – pushes us further in the same direction: not by the 'way of ideas' but again empirically. For if we are a combination not of soul and body, but of mind and body – and if it turns out that mind can be explained entirely naturalistically – then materialism, *pace* Locke himself, may be key to the universe. Unless, that is, the self, the 'person', though still no soul, can be helpfully separated from the body in which it appears to subsist. Certainly, as we shall see, Locke tries to separate it to some degree, yet in doing so he risks explaining it as a mere epiphenomenon of ever-changing matter: something like that 'harmony' of bodily parts which both Plato and Aristotle had rejected long before.

10

Personal Identity from Hobbes to Locke

I am a mystery to myself.

Augustine

Descartes defended the existence of a barely knowable God, and his account of the soul, as we have seen, is diminished and naturalized. As we read him, we find a self-conscious 'self' performing a limited number of the functions of the older 'soul'; being more or less identified with mind alone, it has lost its intrinsic connection with the physical body.[1] When we turn to John Locke, often hailed as the primary constructor of the modern 'self' and stage-setter of debates on its nature – with those thought-experiments about multiple personalities with which we are now familiar – we find that while the voluntarist God is still there, the account of the 'person' is radically changed.

In medieval times, a principal function of the term 'person' was to indicate that membership of the human species – being a 'person' – is radically different from belonging to any other species. All human beings are 'persons' and are recognized by that term as belonging to a unique species created in the image and likeness of God. We have already indicated, however, that Grotius' account of rights seems to suggest a criterion for distinguishing between a human being and a person in that *real* human beings, i.e. persons, as a means of self-protection, have been granted subjective rights. Grotius himself, however, proposed no distinction between human beings and persons: a move first implied by Hobbes

---

[1] For the 'naturalizing' of the soul see further Martin and Barresi (2000, 2001).

who – relying on his claim that linguistic usage establishes what we know of the external world and that the Sovereign determines what has to be taken as morality within a state, while denying anything like Aristotelian potentiality – writes in 1647 (the date his *De Cive* appeared in print) at 17.12:

Suppose a woman gives birth to a deformed figure, and the law forbids killing a human being, the question arises whether the new-born is a human being. The question then is, what is a human being? No one doubts that the commonwealth will decide – and without taking account of the Aristotelian definition, that a Man is a rational animal.

And again, in the *De Corpore* 11.7 (1655):

But we must consider by what name anything is called when we inquire into it. For it is one thing to ask concerning Socrates whether he be the same man, and another to ask whether he be the same body; for his body, when he is old, cannot be the same it was when he was infant, by reason of difference of magnitude; for one body has always one and the same magnitude; yet nevertheless he may be the same man.

And in *Leviathan* (1.16):

A PERSON is he, whose words or actions are considered either as his own, or as representing the words or actions of another man, or of any other thing to whom they are attributed, whether Truly or by Fiction.

The radical shift in such passages is perhaps revealed with the most clarity at *Leviathan* 1.16, where, leaving behind any traditional suggestion that man's dignity depends on his being created in the image and likeness of God, Hobbes tells us that,

The Value or WORTH of a man, as of all other things, is his Price: that is to say so much as would be given for the use of his Power: and therefore is not absolute; but a thing dependent on the need and judgment of another.

'Person' is thus reduced to no more than a word which denotes human beings insofar as they are capable of speech and action for which they can be held responsible. It becomes apparent that if human individuals are not so capable (as with the deformed in the *De Cive* passage), they are not human beings, let alone persons in any traditional sense. And the power to decide who is a person is not God (or God's law or nature) but the ruler of the 'commonwealth'. Whatever Hobbes' real religious views were – and they certainly cannot be recognized as any form of Christianity (for him Christian precepts are merely adopted by Christian states as a means to the maintenance of law and order) – they exclude – along with original sin – any kind of Mainline account of man's dignity, and therefore his possible rights. For Hobbes, not unreasonably within his own world, regards rights as mere 'liberties' which are limitless in the original natural state of man and only curbed in the interest of self-preservation for which commonwealths are established.

In passages such as these Hobbes sounds very modern and very secular: and his 'wicked' doctrines seem to have been too far ahead of his time to be influential rather than just notorious. Yet they are prophetic: in the distinction between human beings and persons (though the word 'person' does not appear); in the claim that it is for the 'commonwealth' to decide who is a person and thus possesses rights that are purely legal. To which we can add that Hobbes also notes that there is a debate about the principle of individuation: it is argued that an old man may not be the same man as he was when he was young (*De Corpore* 11.7). But to Hobbes that seems not to signify; if he is recognized as responsible, he is responsible.[2]

*

Locke's altogether more modest version of all this, presented with no immediate reference to rights or dignity, specifically distinguishes the implications of our status as humans (that is members of an animal species) from our social situation and capabilities if we have them as *persons*.[3] Unsurprisingly for his times – if strange to philosophers in our own day, and hardly Hobbesian inasmuch as it stands as a clear indication of Locke's strong religious allegiance – one of his major concerns was to make sense of the General Resurrection. How can God (and equally we ourselves) be sure that those rewarded and punished for their acts in the present life – given that their atomic composition is constantly in flux – are the same as those who performed them? Thus, and as in Hobbes, the ancient problem of the diachronic unity of the self (or soul) recurs, but in a very different physical and metaphysical context – and is taken much more seriously. Near the opening of the first edition *of An Essay*

---

[2] See further Zarka (1993).

[3] Martin and Barresi (2000: 14) put the matter somewhat inaccurately, if informatively, about the notoriety of Locke's version of the problem: 'Locke burst forth with the genuinely radical and progressive thesis that persons are distinct from humans and do not depend for their existence on retaining either the same soul or the same material body, but on having the same consciousness'. For the connection between Locke's views and those of Hobbes (cited above) see Zarka (1993).

Concerning Human Understanding – that is, before he added to the second edition the famous section (II.27) on personal identity – Locke wrote as follows (I.iv.5):

He, that shall, with a little Attention, reflect on the Resurrection, and consider, that Divine Justice shall bring to Judgment, at the last Day, the very same persons, to be happy or miserable in the other, who did well in this Life, will find it, perhaps, not easy to resolve with himself, what makes the same Man, or wherein *Identity* consists: And will not be forward to think he, and everyone, even children themselves, have naturally a clear *Idea* of it.

The problem of diachronic identity, first raised, as we noted, in the comedy of Epicharmus, then advanced by the ancient Sceptics to rebut Stoic claims about the knowledge of the wise man, has now become a pressing problem in the Christian (especially the Protestant) world. In Locke's own words, 'person' must be treated as a 'forensic' term (*An Essay Concerning Human Nature*, II.27.26): we are all human beings, compounded of soul and body, but constituted as persons only insofar as we are both able to praise and blame and liable to it, whether by man or – most importantly – by God at the Last Judgment. Although despite our ever-changing material composition each of us is identifiable as one 'man', our identity as persons depends on our consciousness, one aspect of which is our capacity to remember who we were. It might seem as though what we fail to remember (even when we are sleeping) could only be acts of another 'person'.[4] Hence because of the human weakness of earthly judges we might be 'justly' punished for what we did when we were another person, but at the Last Judgment we shall only be judged for our very own conscious acts.

Locke's forensic account of persons – broadly describable as a shift from ontology, that is from concern with persons as substances, to consideration of the implications of human psychology – needs to be seen in the wider context of the gradual eclipse of metaphysics more generally in the early modern period. What we would term psychology is beginning

---

[4] The question of whether one can be immoral in a dream has aroused considerable discussion in the wake of a fascinating paper of Matthews (1981); also Mann (1983, 1999: 165) and Haji (1999). We forget most of our dreams – which affects the problem of whether we are somehow 'responsible' for them. And for what (as in Locke) we are in fact responsible. In the *Confessions* Augustine dismisses the possibility that in our dreams we are another person and holds himself responsible. Although 'immoral' dreams are not directly intended, Augustine believes them to be an effect of original sin, and thus we are responsible for them as 'one in Adam'. See further Rist (2014: 38, 56–58).

to emerge as a new variant on physical science and a new way of doing philosophy. In treating of human beings, Locke urges that we distinguish between 'person', 'man' and 'substance' (II.27.7). He proceeds to define a 'person' as follows (II.27.9):

[a person is] a thinking intelligent being that has reason and reflection and can consider itself as itself, the same thinking thing in different times and places; which it does only by that consciousness which is inseparable from thinking and, it seems to me, essential to it: it being impossible for anyone to perceive without perceiving that he does perceive ... Thus, it is always as to our present sensations and perceptions, and by this everyone is to himself that which he calls *self*: ... For since consciousness always accompanies thinking, and it is that that makes everyone to be what he calls *self*, and thereby distinguishes himself from all other thinking things: in this alone consists *personal identity*, i.e. the sameness of a rational being. And as far as this consciousness can be extended backwards to any past action or thought, so far reaches the identity of that *person*: it is the same *self* now it was then, and it is by the same *self* with this present one that now reflects on it, that that action was done.

In this passage, we note several important claims or implications: that the self and our personal identity have no intrinsic connection with the body, though we (and others) recognize ourselves as human beings through our bodily senses and perceptions. As persons, however, we are to be defined as conscious subjects, consciousness being viewed as a necessary accompaniment of thought and especially in terms of our memory and ability to reflect on events in our past lives. That leaves it unclear whether animals have individual identity since they can neither reflect nor *a fortiori* have that reflective *concern* for themselves which in humans arises precisely through our ability to reflect on our experience of past pleasures and pains.

More immediately important, however, is the claim that Locke has made in the previous chapter that while the idea of a *man* is dependent on the linkage between thinking and the thinker's body, the idea of a *person* is not so dependent. And in section three of the same chapter there is an even more remarkable notion: if a mass is formed of atoms and the number of atoms is changed, then 'it is no longer the same mass': thus in the case of living beings, including humans, the body is no longer the same from one moment to the next – unless, that is, it is somehow held together; it still needs something like an Aristotelian (or Stoic) soul.

It is not clear how Locke intended to understand the continual dissolution and reconstruction of the human individual over time, though his detractors claimed that very serious consequences were implied by what he wrote. Thus, Bishop Butler in *A Dissertation on Personal Identity*[5] charged that the implication is 'that personality is not a permanent, but a transient thing; that it lives and dies, begins and ends continually; that no one can any more remain one and the same person two moments together, than two successive moments can be one and the same moment'. Such a charge is based, rightly, on Locke's assumption that time is a succession of instants.

Locke, of course, allows that we have souls, and that souls appear to be substances. His problem – deriving from his wider metaphysical theories – is that we do not know what they are. Nor do we know what bodies are, nor the relationship between the two, nor the precise relationship between souls and persons. He has abandoned the claim of the scholastic philosophers to be able to think about the 'real essence' of the soul; we can only deal with what he calls the 'nominal' essence: namely what the soul *appears* to us, empirically, to be. Hence although souls are substances of some sort, yet personal identity cannot be defined in terms of a 'substance' which we do not understand; rather it is to be thought of as an empirically recognizable *relationship* between our stages of consciousness. As far as the physical identity of each man is concerned, I am 'nothing but a participation of the same continued life, by constantly fleeting particles of matter, in succession vitally united to the same organized body' (II.27.5). And personal identity will depend less on continuity of substance than on the relationship between those moments of consciousness that the energy of our particles generates. As Locke himself puts it (II.27.10), 'For, it being the same consciousness that makes man be himself to himself, *personal identity* depends on that only, whether it be annexed to only one individual substance, or can be continued in a succession of several substances'.

What is the overall effect of Locke's rather chaotic theorizing? First, that we must distinguish a 'man' from a 'person', but in a way quite different from anything earlier thinkers would have accepted.[6] For a person is not now a member of the human *species* (what the medievals, as we have seen, called a 'supposit') but a member of that group of human

[5] In *The Works of the Right Reverend Father in God Joseph Butler* (2 volumes, Oxford, 1859) I, 307.
[6] It should go without saying that 'man' ('*homo*') refers to the species and not only to the male members of it!

beings who can be held responsible for their concrete acts[7] since possessed of self-reflective consciousness and recognizable to themselves and as themselves through memories. Locke still thinks that human beings have worth, since they have immortal souls, and that some of them at least will be duly rewarded by God even if their merits are unrecognizable by the morally and epistemically limited perceptive capacities of their fellow men, but – perhaps surprisingly – he resembles Descartes inasmuch as he has bisected the human being. For Descartes, we are reflective souls linked as it were accidentally to particular bodies; for Locke, although we all are members of the human species (and thus recognizable through our bodies by others in the world in which we live), those of us who are not also persons, or who through loss of consciousness – broadly defined – cease to be persons, are almost as alien to those that are as is the Cartesian body to the Cartesian soul.

For Locke, human consciousness is always embodied;[8] hence as an empiricist he is far more aware than is Descartes of the role society plays in our self-construction. Not that he would go so far as his defender Edmund Law who, in *A Defense of Mr. Locke's Opinion Concerning Personal Identity* (1769),[9] seems to have attributed to Locke the view that our 'forensic' identity is simply the product of external forces, of the way others see us and consequently of how we learn to see ourselves; that we are built up, so to speak, by our experiences. For Locke, such claims (in accordance with what would become known as associationist psychology) would seriously compromise the responsibility that as 'forensic' persons we have for our actions. Nevertheless, while Descartes can allow all human beings (or rather all human minds) to have worth, Locke is only committed – probably despite himself – to the immediate worth of those who are capable of being responsible 'persons'.

That that is a theme with a substantial future we see in our own day. It points to a further and potentially sinister aspect of Locke's position. Although he accepts that as human beings we are souls with bodies – not, that is, just souls – yet the relationship between the soul and the body is neither the Augustinian 'marriage' nor the Aristotelian hylomorphism

---

[7] Seigel (2005: 108): 'Locke was (as far as I know) the first writer to develop the idea of personal identity in terms that put individuals' responsibilities for who they are at the center of it'.

[8] Cf. Yolton (1970: 150–151).

[9] For more on Law – he became bishop of Carlisle – and on how by his time Locke's concerns about the theological implications of his work had largely ceased to disturb the intellectuals (even among churchmen), see Martin and Barresi (2000: 103–109).

adopted by Aquinas and other scholastics. Nor again is it clear that souls and bodies are *substantially* dissimilar: differing, that is, as immaterial substances from mere matter (*res extensa*). Rather we, as human beings, *own* our bodies, though with a very strange kind of 'ownership'. Given that I own a house and destroy it, I myself, as owner, survive, whereas if I destroy my body, I do not!

Locke's theory of our ownership of our own bodies already points towards the idea that we (including our 'souls') are entirely material: that is, he appears, like Hobbes – at times at least – to be committed to the idea that in the case of humans, matter can *think*. However, as a believer feeling it necessary to avoid the straightforwardness of Hobbes, he writes as follows (*Essay* IV.3.6):

We have the *ideas* of *matter* and *thinking*, but possibly shall never be able to know whether any mere material being thinks or no: it being impossible for us, by the contemplation of our own *ideas*, without revelation, to discover whether Omnipotency has not given to some systems of matter, fitly disposed, a power to perceive and think, or else joined and fixed to matter, so disposed, a thinking immaterial substance: it being, in respect of our notions, not much more remote from our comprehension to conceive that GOD can, if he pleases, superadd to matter a faculty of thinking, than that he should superadd to it another substance with a faculty of thinking, since we know not wherein thinking consists, nor to what sort of substances the almighty has been pleased to give that power ...

Thus, while avoiding the stigma of straightforward atheism, Locke has reduced the soul to mind – that is to a thinking subject – and gone on to ask whether to account for thinking we need more than matter. He thus suggests that an explanation of thought, far from demanding the existence of an immaterial substance, need only recognize thinking as an epiphenomenon of matter. Although that would imply a very different account of matter than the *res extensa* then proposed, Locke's view must surely remind us (again) of the account of the soul as epiphenomenon of matter – as a harmony of material parts – rejected by Plato in the *Phaedo* and by Aristotle in the *De Anima*. It further suggests – in despite of himself and many before as after him since antiquity – that it may be reductionist, or just plain false, to *identify* the *soul* simply as a supposedly immaterial *mind*. But if not mind, what then is the soul?

It is not enough to note that Locke may be making a basic mistake about the relationship between mind and soul. We also need to understand how 'soul' – if merely the name for an epiphenomenon of the body – can form moral and aesthetic judgments. For if as *persons* we are to be specifically responsible, our responsibility must depend on at least some degree of free will. Locke himself believes that on our ability to stand apart from our instincts and desires and to reflect on what we *should* do, the belief that we, as persons, are responsible, must depend. That ability is further conceived as our capacity to organize what we receive from the senses (for at birth mind is *tabula rasa*) into some sort of rational whole which will display, especially, the moral world as willed by God – and that despite the fact that, following in the footsteps of Hobbes, Locke denies that we have any special instinct for the good or for virtue.

Christianity, Locke thinks, is a 'reasonable' religion, and our minds can understand as much of that reasonableness as is necessary. That, however, does not entail following Charles Taylor and so speaking of Locke's 'punctual self':[10] a self, that is, which merely plays the role of the impersonal spectator; on the contrary Locke wants us to recognize God's role in the world on no basis of mere authority but on the God-given power of our reason. Although he hesitates at times as to whether our mental capabilities are up to the task of living virtuously, he normally offers an optimistic diagnosis. Certainly, original sin is to be rejected utterly; it is responsible neither for our failings nor for our inability adequately to understand our nature.[11] Yet Locke as yet is neither Hume nor Adam Smith, even though parts of his work point towards both. Above all, with God soon to be removed and the 'soul' unknowable and possibly even non-existent, while the 'self' remains inadequately accounted for, we may find ourselves left as fleeting particles of matter somehow bundled together, yet able to make what we label moral and aesthetic judgments with and about what we do not understand! It is hardly surprising that Locke himself thinks that divine sanctions are necessary if we are to be kept up to the mark – not least since his account of free will enables him only to say that we can by reflection on the effects of our acts 'suspend the execution and satisfaction of any of its [the mind's] desires' (*Essay* II.21.47).

[10] Taylor (1989: 159–176).
[11] At the opening of *The Reasonableness of Christianity* Locke rejects the idea that Adam's sin could be passed on to his descendants, none of whom had accepted that he was acting on their behalf. This legalistic view is of course at odds with what we might term the 'genetic' view of the doctrine as originally conceived.

11

After Locke

In the course of the eighteenth century Locke's work on personal identity was followed up in divergent ways: some pursued his thoughts in the same direction, emphasizing especially the 'science-fiction' accounts he gave of the possibility of brain-fission, and generating further problems not only about the diachronic continuity of the person but eventually, as in the case of William Hazlitt (whose work in this area was almost entirely neglected at the time), as to whether it is rational to worry about our future selves, immortal or not.[1] Other post-Lockeans, like Stillingfleet, Butler and Reid saw grave moral and spiritual danger in Locke's claims, above all in that he seemed to suggest that persons are to be viewed not in terms of continuing substances but in terms of relations between material parts of the human being.

Others repudiated Locke's explanation for the relationship between personal identity and responsibility – as also the sanctions of a voluntarist God – as inadequate to explain moral obligation. Hence Hutcheson and others in the wake of Locke's former pupil the third Earl of Shaftesbury developed an optimistic account of the renewed possibility of virtue by introducing a 'moral sense': an evaluating feeling or 'sixth sense' to replace the more intellectualist accounts of moral conduct prevalent hitherto. This introduction of the moral sense found both echo and stimulus in an evolution in the attitude of eighteenth-century writers and readers to the moral role of certain forms of literature, especially the 'sentimental' novels of Samuel Richardson – much praised also in

---

[1] For the advanced thinking of Hazlitt (whose *An Essay on the Principles of Human Action* appeared in 1805) see especially Martin and Barresi (2000: 139–148).

France and a pointer to the relevantly similar 'sentimental' novels of Rousseau. This development had potentially significant implications for more philosophical accounts of the human person, hence for understanding how individual humans could and should behave.

The decisive culmination of all this – or rather the reaction to it – was the attempt by Immanuel Kant and his successors to construct a radically new account of reason which could replace the moral sense – or any other form of non-cognitivism – as the fundamental desideratum both for an adequate theory of the person and then for a more 'humanizing' (and certainly less Hobbesian) account of ethical reality. This development would be a watershed, being in many respects the last hope for moral obligation in a soul-less and god-less age. For the repudiation by Shaftesbury and others of Locke's voluntarist God – preserved as a law-making antidote to hedonism in virtue of his power to reward and punish – had left a gap not only in theology but also in 'anthropology': if God is not essential as rule-maker, then – without returning to a less rule-based account of ethics, with very different implications for 'persons' – who (or rather how will we) make the rules? We would need some special capacity to do so, whether by a moral sense or – with Kant's repudiation of that – by his construction of a 'holy' and rational will.

Before proceeding to more detail, we should reiterate that (such 'reactionaries' as Butler and Reid apart) all post-Lockean developments assumed or presented a world in which the 'self' has almost replaced the soul and from which God has disappeared or at least been reduced to a comparative irrelevance: thus in Kant God's role is little more than to provide a happy ending for those who act well in the moral struggles of our earthly life. And that, as we shall see, will soon come to look like little more than wishful thinking.

*

Returning to the earlier post-Lockeans, we will merely glance first at those who followed Locke insofar as he raised the possibility of sequential selves and those who wanted to reaffirm what they took to be more traditional accounts of personal identity as substantial rather than relational, rejecting the potential materialism conjured up by relational versions. Nor is there need to do more than mention that in less 'enlightened' (or Enlightenment) circles in Europe the older Aristotelian, Thomist and Scotist accounts of the person continued to be taught, without their advocates becoming much engaged with the challenges emanating from post-Lockean or other 'atheists'. Such unwillingness to take on the opposition, letting them go by default, had (and still continues to have) serious implications for the near-eclipse of more 'traditional' views.

As we have noted, what both Butler and Reid feared as a conclusion in Locke had already been proposed by Hobbes, who thought that the identity of a material substance is governed solely by the structure of the matter of which the individual beings, including humans, are formed. As also noted, that kind of epiphenomenalism had long ago been repudiated by Plato, Aristotle and their followers of various stripes. Yet in the context of seventeenth-century mechanism it seemed far more plausible, even though the principal difficulty it raises is to understand how any *organized* structure comes to be established. As yet and before Darwin, that might still seem to be left for God, or perhaps for Descartes' 'ghost in the machine': the immaterial and reflective mind. But the ghost comes to look so ghostly that it must soon be exorcized, leaving as only alternative some form of the thesis that matter can think, as Locke had suggested (though still in a theistic context): unless, that is, human activities are merely the product of their social environment. In either case, if matter can think, the soul, at least as then presented philosophically, becomes otiose.

Hobbes' radical solution to the 'problem', however, remained a step too far and older features of the soul, especially immortality, had to be whittled way before it could come into its own. That was the issue in the debate between the 'Newtonian' Samuel Clarke and a radical Lockean, Anthony Collins, which broke out in 1706 and continued over the next three years. Collins, who substituted the notion of a connected consciousness for Locke's supposedly identical consciousness over time as the explanation of personal identity, found no difficulty in attributing this continuation to successive streams of atoms forming the human mind. To Clarke's objection that since matter is divisible it cannot by itself account for consciousness, Collins retorted that this is mere guesswork: we do not understand the nature of thinking, hence to introduce an *immaterial* mind is to present us with an unnecessary hypothesis. All we know is that thinking is connected somehow with the material brain. If the soul, unless explicable solely in material terms, is not needed for thinking, it has no other claim to exist, and so – though Collins did not draw this conclusion – cannot be immortal.[2] If that is even largely correct, then almost all

---

[2] For more detail on the fascinating debate between Clarke and Collins, see Martin and Barresi (2000: 51–60). The immediate future, as they point out, lay with Collins, since the

pre-modern accounts of the person (let alone of its worth) are radically flawed.

*

Butler and Reid (following Locke's earlier antagonist, Bishop Stillingfleet), approached Locke's challenge somewhat differently from Clarke, though their basic concerns were similar. Emphasizing less the relationship of a material mind to consciousness than the possibility that 'persons' might be mere relationships rather than substances, they sought to reinstate the older concept of the soul as the *bearer* of consciousness and memory. In the case of Butler, his major concern seems to have been that without a substantial soul the notion of conscience – which he freely handles with insufficient emphasis on its formation – would disappear. But conscience is not easily investigated empirically, and we can assume that with Butler's death in 1752 defence of a substantive soul more or less disappeared from the cutting-edge debate in Britain for some fifty years, being replaced by empirical investigation into a possibly material mind. Even anti-Lockeans like Reid followed the new path; only with Coleridge do we eventually find an attempt in mainstream thought about persons or selves to recover the religious dimension. Coleridge's success was very limited, and despite Kierkegaard – who was largely ignored – and later Newman, religious thought about the self or soul, at least in Britain, was virtually abandoned until the end of the nineteenth century. In Continental Europe efforts to revive it, especially by Leibniz, were more successful for a while – until Kant, under the influence of Hume, largely deprived it of any residually Christian metaphysic, thus making anything like the Mainline Tradition about the person as 'dignified mixture' impossible. The next step was a revival of something of the pantheism of Spinoza in post-Kantian form by Hegel, pointing as we shall see, towards the progressive depersonalization of the 'person' and the as yet unacknowledged loss of his inherent dignity

*

But it is time to retrace our steps to Locke's one-time pupil and later fierce critic, the third Earl of Shaftesbury. Though agreeing with Locke that we have no innate concern for any supreme good, only for the human race,

---

study of consciousness could, it was increasingly assumed, be carried on within a naturalistic psychology which need allow no room for an immaterial, hence immortal soul. Indeed, if 'soul' is no more than a name for the mind or one of its functions (as had often been assumed and remained largely unchallenged), the 'future' was bright for atheism.

Shaftesbury castigated as unworthy Locke's insistence on the necessity of divine sanctions on bad behaviour if hedonism is to be avoided, emphasizing, like the Cambridge Platonists before him, self-determinism rather than mere obedience as the core of morality. Hence he (and others) saw Locke's claim that we have no natural instinct for virtue as implausible and grossly threatening to morality, letting Hobbes in by the back door.[3] And since we cannot be reduced to the immaterial, impersonal, purely ratiocinative minds proposed by Descartes, it follows that we must possess in our very makeup some kind of sense of right and wrong, some '*moral* sense': and that sense might be the distinguishing (perhaps the only) mark of our humanity, hence of our value. Though Shaftesbury seems not have been the first to use the phrase 'moral sense', he was certainly the first to be recognized as powerful wielder of the concept. But what could a moral sense be? How could it be relied on? Indeed, how could it be recognized? And why should it, in and of itself, bestow more value than any other human capacity?

In offering a solution to such questions, Shaftesbury – though, like Leibniz, his interest was in old-fashioned virtue rather than rights – could hardly have been unaware of Grotius' thesis that human beings combine sociability and aggressiveness, and he was determined to reject a 'correction' of Hobbes that views us as ultimately concerned only with survival in a world in which sociability, and the virtue of benevolence associated with it, is irrelevant or but a convenient veneer. The moral sense, Shaftesbury thinks – by now almost anachronistically – enables us to feel ourselves part of an objective and harmonious cosmic order and able to reflect on our passions and desires, approving some, disapproving others, and so possessing 'cosmic' worth. It is activated by reflection on our primary feelings and emotions, such that we experience 'another kind of affection towards those very affections themselves, which have been already felt, and are now become the subject of a new liking or dislike'.[4] As with our aesthetic sense, the moral sense has to be

---

[3] Voitle (1874: 119) [cited by Schneewind (1998: 296, n.20)] cites a letter (of 1709) of Shaftesbury to Michael Ainsworth as follows: 'Twas Mr Locke that struck the home Blow (for Mr Hobb's character and base slavish principles in Government took off the poison of his Philosophy). Twas Mr Locke that struck at all Fundamentals, threw all Order and Virtue out of the world, and made the very ideas of these … *unnatural* and without foundation in our minds.'

[4] *Inquiry into Merit*, in *Characteristics of Men, Manners, Opinions, Times, etc.* ed. J. M. Robertson (London, 1900) I 251.

nourished, being by no means fully available to humans as such. As Shaftesbury views it: 'Tis undeniable, however, that the perfection of grace and comeliness in action and behaviour can be found only among people of liberal education'.[5] Thus he leaves us to wonder whether other persons possess much in the way of human dignity.

Nor is it entirely clear how Shaftesbury thinks that the feelings of approval and disapproval which the moral sense provokes relate to *reflection* on primary experiences. The moral sense enables us to cultivate the appropriate approvals and disapprovals and hence we 'recognize' that morality is rational and 'harmonious'. Yet this is by no mere cultivation of a 'taste' for the harmonious, since Shaftesbury (in contrast to many later moral-sense theorists) is convinced that the feelings of benevolence which the moral sense engenders reflect an *objective* state of the universe and point toward a wider context for virtue.

For Shaftesbury's moral-sense successors, however, feeling alone seemed more and more to be what matters, what motivates, and could show us more of our nature as individuals and as human persons. As Shaftesbury's continued sense of cosmic harmony (with its Cambridge Platonist ancestry) began to fade, and as Locke's account of the original blank sheet of our inert minds came in its place, our feelings, rather than our cognitive powers, were held to mark our individuality, our personal 'identity' and – however illogically – our dignity. Such a backlash against the Cartesian attempt to reduce humanity to arid rationality could not ultimately be (or should not have been) ignored. In Shaftesbury's time, however, there burst upon Europe no disastrous emotivism and 'life-assertion' such as would follow Kant's attempt to construct his own arid cognitivism – though the warning signs are generally recognizable in retrospect. The reflection which for Shaftesbury's successors stimulates the moral sense still seemed able to generate moral commands, implying that to be guided by the moral sense is at least to learn self-control, hence to be valued members of society if nothing more.

Self-control, the old Stoic virtue, certainly underlies Shaftesbury's thinking, eliminating the need for divine rules and sanctions, and in later moral-sense theorists (especially Adam Smith) it will be promoted to the front rank. For as Shaftesbury already says (*Inquiry* II 103), it is the mind (in his vision of it) which 'superintends and manages its own imaginations, appearances, fancies ... modelling these as it finds good': that is,

---

[5] *Inquiry* I 125.

harmonizing them. However, with or without cosmic harmonies, and given the widening vision on offer of a blend of feeling and self-control, we can recognize that the concept of a 'person' (but hardly of the soul) is potentially both enriched by an enhanced attention to affect and at the same time diminished by the underlying reliance on mere rationality: diminished certainly in its 'religious' aspects.

Nevertheless, a dogged supporter of the Mainline Tradition in the eighteenth century needed to allow that that tradition – despite the influence of Augustine – had paid too little careful attention to our feelings and emotions, whether or not properly disciplined. For perhaps even the pre-Cartesian account of the mind – in contrast to that of Plato himself and of Platonists like Augustine (who believes that one of the tools by which God draws us to himself is a proper feeling of pleasure) – had become too arid, too rationalistic, so that the *attraction* of objects of value or worth had been significantly neglected in favour of their mere existence.

*

According to Shaftesbury, the mind is active and still traditionally virtue-seeking. For Francis Hutcheson (1694–1746),[6] it is inert, capable only of responding to emotional experiences rather than effectively discriminating among them; hence *only* feelings and emotions, provoked by what we meet in the external world, are capable of stimulating action. That implies that if we are to enact the benevolence which Hutcheson regards as the chief characterization of the moral life, we must be endowed with a *feeling* for goodness such that when we meet the world, we 'feel' accordingly. Such feeling is not, apparently, a Platonic capacity to recognize the good in the universe or in a transcendent world, as Shaftesbury and earlier the Cambridge Platonists had taught, but it enables us to react benevolently to natural external stimuli: to *feel* how to act well. If we ask why any such feeling will inform us correctly, Hutcheson can only answer that that is how we are, that God must so have created us. Yet it is clear that without God, there would be no reason to believe Hutcheson rather than Hobbes – or Bernard Mandeville, whose apparently amoral *Enquiry into the Origin of Moral Virtue* (1723), a revised version of his earlier *Fable of the Bees*, became for Hutcheson – as also for Bishop Berkeley – an immediate target. Berkeley, however, was mistaken in supposing when

---

[6] Quotations from Hutcheson's *An Inquiry into the Original Ideas of Beauty and Virtue* are from the fourth edition (1738).

he wrote the *Alciphron* that Shaftesbury's increasingly old-fashioned deism was the more serious threat to Christian thinking about persons and morals, even though he realized that for Mandeville deism was merely a last-ditch attempt to prop up a Christianity far more seriously threatened in Europe than he dared allow.

An exile from Holland who had learned to hate Catholic and more generally religious persecution, Mandeville saw the world through essentially secularist eyes. Though purporting to advocate traditional virtues, as he felt obliged to insist in his reply to Berkeley (1732), and evincing no more respect for rights than did Hobbes, he claimed to be being merely honest in his depiction of the real world where – in this language recalling Machiavelli's – virtue impedes national well-being. 'Vices' such as drunkenness, prostitution and especially greed are the engines which encourage money to circulate, commerce and the exchequer to prosper: that is, private vices promote the public good. But in Mandeville's wider picture of society, which leaves religion aside and sees virtue as damaging 'worldly greatness' and commercial success, what role does virtue actually play? And beyond that do individuals, whether virtuous or vicious, have more than economic and social worth?

Mandeville's answer is ambiguous: though virtue must lack its religious grounding, it is helpful in that it encourages people to be concerned with social prestige and strive to be of good repute. Its downside is that being virtually unrealizable as well as financially detrimental to the state, it can only – albeit this too has its benefits – encourage hypocrisy, a recognized vice of his age which nevertheless helps bind society together. Beneath this amoral, quasi-Thrasymachean approach, lie Mandeville's reflections on the arguments of Grotius that in society we must learn to harmonize human aggressiveness and sociability. With Shaftesbury's ideas about basic human goodness dismissed out of hand, in the world of Mandeville 'Moral virtues are the Political Offspring which Flattery begot upon Pride' (1.51)): a world, that is, full of virtue-signaling hypocrites, driven in part by the desire for respect and fame while promoting policies which create public wealth from private vice, plus useful social inequalities: as maintaining a poor educational system which allows for the perpetuation of an under-class necessary for labor-intensive agricultural work (and in the future will provide a needed industrial proletariat).

Berkeley and Hutcheson naturally repudiated all this, recognizing its radically post-Christian character. Hume and Adam Smith, while professing to disown him, found Mandeville a valuable source of insights about economic development. Mandeville indeed acquired for a century or so the notoriety of Machiavelli and Hobbes as subverters, affecting Continental and especially French thinkers as well as British. His mockery of morals and religion attracted Voltaire while Rousseau was impressed by his apparent 'honesty' while hardly recognizing his basic amoralism in exposing polite (and other) society as the hypocritical charade it really is.

Compared with Mandeville, Hutcheson's latter-day Christianity and account of human worth can only look naïve. In his view as an unorthodox Presbyterian, justice, duties and rights are all to be explained not as profitable hypocrisy, but as acts of love, or, rather, in his language, of calm and disinterested benevolence. When our feelings are (somehow) favorably evaluated by the moral sense, they will generate happiness, for the greatest human pleasure, he claims, lies in making other people happy (*Inquiry* II, VI): a remarkably non-empirical claim for an empiricist. If we ask why (or how) we are capable of so acting, Hutcheson, as we have seen, falls back on God: we are happy if benevolent because we know we are following God's providential ordinances, hence acknowledging God's own benevolence. What then can Hutcheson say about those who apparently enjoy torturing people? Nothing, except that the existence of a benevolent God shows that torturers would be happier if they gave up their trade. The argument is beginning to look circular.

Indeed, we must ask – analogously to our question to Grotius – what happens to such optimism if God should disappear? Would we not have to revert either to Hobbes' war of all against all, or at best to the conflict between aggression and sociability that we find underlying Grotius' proposals? Perhaps the moral sense may be compared with Butler's conscience, but we have already noted Butler's unresolved problems about the formation of conscience, and without the cognitive aspects of conscience claimed by him, it is hard to see how Hutcheson's benevolently presented moral sense would be any more morally effective. It is one thing to claim that we are aware of morality, that we live in moral space, quite another to assume that we know how to navigate that moral space with any consistency. Indeed, lacking Butler's greater emphasis on autonomy, Hutcheson's restricted account of free will would seem to make his difficulties the greater, until it seems that only dependence on God and a knowledge of God's Revelation can save the day. Is there no other path for the 'sentimentalist' to preserve his undeniably benevolent intentions unscathed?

12

Sympathy or Empathy: Richardson, Hume, Smith

Help came from an unexpected quarter. Soon after Hutcheson's work was published there appeared a series of novels of sentiment ('sentimental') from the pen of Samuel Richardson. They differed substantially from the earlier and more 'libertine' tales of Aphra Behn and Daniel Defoe and earned the contempt of Henry Fielding who offered alternatives in his own picaresque novels and parodied Richardson's seemingly hypocritical Pamela in the person of his own blatantly hypocritical and immoral Shamela. Nevertheless, Richardson was directing the novel into new and very popular territory. In *Pamela* (1740) and *Clarissa* (1747–8) he highlights the moral and psychological dilemmas of very ordinary people, especially females. But his heroines are no longer the free-thinkers, libertines or whores – whether or not eventually penitent – of Behn and Defoe, but sweet – at times almost sugary – 'nice' people, hence to be read as moral exemplars by ordinary folk.

For these moral heroines and their fellows are no longer to be found in the aristocratic or élitist world of Renaissance humanism, nor even in the whiggish and self-consciously high-minded circles frequented by Shaftesbury. Richardson's novels encourage us to take account of a peculiarly obvious feature of humanity, commonly ignored by philosophers – including those in the Mainline Tradition – but helpful to moral sense theorists: the ability to empathize or put ourselves in one another's place.

Nor is this to be understood as Aristotelian 'pity and terror' as evoked by Greek and classicizing playwrights dramatizing the dread consequences of a *hero's* fall – though Aristotle in the *Rhetoric* also considers ordinary feelings and emotions and how to arouse them – which might look more Richardsonian. Still less should Richardson's novels be thought of as some sort of quasi-philosophical attempt to solve the post-Cartesian problem of 'other minds', but as an appeal to our ability to 'get inside' characters as though we were they; to be able, that is, to feel a *sympathy* (what would later be called *empathy*) with them: not as great women or men but as ordinary folk like his readers. Even if pointing to such feelings may be of little help in determining how we *ought* or might have an obligation to behave, it reveals features of our perceptive capacity which (with few exceptions, such as Augustine's *Confessions*) had been scarce examined by earlier writers, indeed hardly at all by philosophers since antiquity.

It has often been observed that the intellectual world in which Richardson's novels were composed was much influenced by the Puritan habit of diary-keeping, viewed as a way of tracking that moral care for the self that the godly sought to develop. Such awareness of oneself and one's own feelings can be seen as a precursor of the novelist's attempts to 'get inside' the minds and consciousness of others and as a by-product further to understand ourselves. Later, and with similar tools, Rousseau would aim more directly at exerting his influence and would be even more successful. That being so, it is worth further examining what Richardson helped to draw to our attention about human nature and about ourselves as individual persons: namely that capacity – among other animals unique to humans – to *identify* with others, or at least to attempt to do so in a way that may satisfy us that we have done so: the caveat is important, since it is impossible to be certain that one has identified with an individual *qua* individual, rather than with an individual *qua* member of the human race: *nihil humani alienum*, as the Roman comedian Terence has it. Nearer to our own time, such considerations were to form an important subject-matter of 'debate' on empathy between Martin Heidegger and Edith Stein.

An effect of the sentimental novel will be for readers to ask themselves: what would I think (or how would I feel) if I were in that situation? The novelist induces them to attend, vicariously, to the emotional situation of another particular person; this Denis Diderot recognized when in his *Eloge de Richardson* (1761) he wrote that *on se met à sa place ou à ses cotés: on se passionne.*[1] For Diderot such empathy is an essential requirement for virtue, providing some check on the unbridled egoism, which would appear to deny even the possibility of altruism, with which he toys

---

[1] Helpful contemporary discussions include Watt (1957), Taylor (1989: 286–287) and Seigel (2005: 160–161). For a broader prospective see Starobinski (1978).

in *Le Neveu de Rameau*.[2] And Richardson also gives his or her readers the opportunity to compare their favourite character with those 'others' that other people identify with – recognizing the common features and thus colluding to praise or blame, or be moved to reward as behaviour is judged to require it.

But then the problem of what to do in moral space arises in another form; the technical skill that produces these effects on readers can have its more negative side: a 'sinister' aspect relating to failure to recognize that feelings (moral or not) must be rational or irrational. It is hard to know, that is, how moral sensitivity can be separated from powers of rational discernment. The appeal of novelists is emotional – to moral sensitivity, to moral feelings – but although Richardson is normally scrupulous in 'rewarding' and encouraging virtue and castigating vice, his later (and especially his modern) successors have often done the opposite, following the patterns of traditional demagogues in using emotional appeal as vicious propaganda to whip up the vicarious passions of a lusting, dehumanized and uncritical mob until they experience what Max Scheler has called 'emotional contagion'. (Thus, contemporary demagogues may appeal to an unthinking 'moral sense' in those hostile to 'racism' to castigate behaviour which has nothing to do with race.)

Already in Plato's *Republic* we learn in detail how emotionalism can be morally dangerous; for novelists of the eighteenth century, it is nevertheless a basic feature – some might say a 'fallen' feature – of ordinary human nature, recognizable in different forms in different individuals. Yet empathy, as we can readily understand, is open to abuse not only if we are induced to identify with 'evil' or misguided characters, but also if we are led to confuse literary or sub-literary characters 'existing' only in the simplified milieu in which the writer has placed them with individuals we meet in real life. Our own world of virtual humans, virtual life, virtual emotions might seem in the eighteenth century to be already around the corner. To that we shall return, pausing now only to note that if God has disappeared and reason found inadequate to motivate, and if the moral 'sense' seems ambiguous (however informative about human nature and revealing of our capacity to sympathize), we must conclude that, yes, humans live – somehow – in 'moral space', yet have no easy means of

[2] The 'nephew' is famously treated by MacIntyre (1981: 47–48); he returns to him in MacIntyre (2016: 137–138). Already by Diderot's time – indeed at least since Hobbes – altruism had become problematic.

identifying *how* to move within it: even in general, let alone in the particular circumstances of their lives.

*

In both classical antiquity and in 'Christian times', one of the most basic – if not the most basic – human weaknesses (or sins) was identified as an ambition to challenge the gods: we find a version of it in stories of the Titans and others as early as Hesiod's *Theogony* – not to speak of Adam and Eve. By the mid eighteenth-century, atheism was becoming respectable; David Hume had small inhibition about identifying himself as an atheist, and he believes he can retain his atheism and at the same time reject the claims both of the Hobbesians that our basic passion is the desire for survival, and of those like Hutcheson who can defend their respect for benevolence only by referring it to the goodness of God. In the spirit of the Enlightenment, he believes he can do better than God.

Hume goes well beyond Hutcheson in spelling out what he sees as the implications of the 'moral sense', concluding that, although our behaviour is normally determined by our instinctive feelings (439)[3], these cannot be identified as true or false: facts are to be sharply distinguished from values (469–470), so that our feelings are subject to approval and disapproval only. When we witness a murder – and the 'we' is important since Hume appeals to what he assumes to be 'normal' human reactions, not merely to our individual and perhaps quirky feelings – we feel the killer deserves blame (468–469). Yet we may reasonably ask Hume, as Hutcheson, how our moral sense has 'decided' on feelings to approve, and how such approval is justified? That is where sympathy, now openly evoked as a capacity to share in the feelings of others, enters in as a major guide to 'virtue' and as the hoped-for corrective to unashamed Hobbesian self-seeking.

In the *Treatise* Hume tries to explain how this sympathy works (317); we observe what we infer as the bodies and behaviour of other people, hence their affective state. Consequentially, we form an impression of 'such a degree of force and vivacity, as to become the very passion itself, and produce an equal emotion as any original affection'. Martin and Barresi compare this experience to [Scheler's] 'emotional contagion';[4]

---

[3] References to Hume's *Treatise of Human Nature* are to L. A. Selby-Bigge's second edition (revised by P. H. Nidditch, Oxford, 1978).

[4] Martin and Barresi (2000: 90–92).

thus a baby starts to cry when in the company of other crying babies. (They also point out that Hume's account is not entirely consistent.)

Adapting Grotius' distinction between imperfect and perfect duties, Hume proposes a distinction between natural and artificial virtues – virtue not being limited, as with Hutcheson, to benevolence. Sympathy is natural; when we realize that it is also in our interest (at least up to a point), we are *en route* to developing some sort of understanding of the artificial virtue that is justice (439): a virtue – and a form of social glue – necessary if the security of any societal unit larger than the family is to be retained (491, 497). Hobbes might reply that self-interest is still basic; that though sympathy is a natural response, it would (and should) always yield to a more basic self-concern when the chips are down. Of course, while Hobbes' purpose is to determine what it is sensible for us to do, Hume thinks that ethics is only concerned with showing why we are motivated in particular ways. It follows from his premises that he is not concerned with our obligations, let alone our rights, but only with how our motives are formed, hence how we determine what are virtues.

Though sympathy is the root of justice, yet Hume believes – and somewhat as Sceptics had believed in antiquity – that the most effective outcome of self-concern will be the following of the customs of an equitable country. His list and analysis of the virtues supposed to lead to well-being (though his account of well-being seems notably banal) is unsurprisingly in tune with the conventions of his time and place. Sympathy – hence the moral sense which it primarily though not exclusively supports – thus turns out to be inadequate; morality in effect is basically conventional, albeit, like the novelists, Hume is right to attach importance to sympathy, however arising, as significant indicator of a person's humanity. That different persons will be 'prone' to it to different degrees, however, might again seem largely the product of convention and social pressure. Hume's own apparently conventional catalogue of virtues is very much the product of his age; he takes the ideals of that age as the ideals of humanity a whole: a clearly mistaken view, though many have followed him in taking it.[5]

As observed, Hume's position is not entirely coherent: thus, in the *Treatise* (19) he views moral ideas as arising from a 'noble' source, without explaining why the source, even if correctly identified, is particularly 'noble'; it seems 'we' just feel that it is. Yet it might (again) be merely

---

[5] For recent comment on Hume's variety of conventionalism, following not the customs of 'the country' but of the élite classes of his own country see MacIntyre (2016: 83–85).

conventional. Hume thinks to offer a possible route out of the dilemma. Reason is inert, merely suited to distinguishing truth from falsehood, but though a spectator or observer (477), it is an *impartial* spectator of the activity which impinges on our consciousness. Yet granted that for Hume reason is an observer of motives (for actions are merely indications of motives), it is not clear how it observes them *impartially* (77). The phrase 'impartial spectator' itself first appears not in Hume's own writings but in those of his friend Adam Smith, but the concept is visible enough.

There is a further difficulty: if we possess some sort of inner observer of our own conduct, how can Hume explain that in terms of his accounts of human nature, since especially in the *Treatise* he seems to accept all the radical implications of Locke's disintegration of the self (or soul or even mind) into nothing but a bundle of ever-changing qualities? Consider the following famous section from the *Treatise* (1.6.3, 261):

I cannot compare the soul more properly to anything than to a republic or commonwealth, in which several members are united by the reciprocal ties of government and subordination, and give rise to other persons who propagate the same republic in the incessant change of its parts. And as the same individual republic may not only change its members, but also its laws and constitutions; in like manner the same person may vary his character and disposition, as well as his impressions and ideas, without losing his identity. Whatever changes he endures, his several parts are still connected by the relation of causation.

This is a curious passage, beginning with Hume's referring to the 'soul' when clearly he means the individual. Then he seems to claim that we have some sort of continuing identity, hence a continuing impartial spectator (presumably to be supposed adequate for our being held responsible for our actions) without giving any more adequate explanation than does Hobbes of how it can assign such *personal* responsibility justly. For in a republic, who *individually* is the bearer of the continuing existence of the republic itself? Hume's apparent incoherence is partly obscured by his choice of the word 'soul', which must suggest a much more individualized continuing self than the model of a republic would normally imply. For we may not unreasonably ask why our inner moral observer is able to maintain stability within a broader 'theatre of the mind' which – unlike actual theatres – has no apparent location (This might be an argument for its immateriality!). The reference to theatres too is incomplete; Hume regards the 'theatre' as the body (or some part of it) and holds that we shall cease to exist – and so to have any identity – when the body collapses.

Hume, however, wishes to explain the apparent stability of our inner moral observer in accordance with his basic account of perception, telling us near the start of the *Treatise* that what we experience is nothing but a series of impressions; that on these our ideas depend, and that these are the result of our imaginative reading of the impressions – the imagination being presumably dependent on what we have learned since childhood. He continues (1.4.2, 193):

For philosophy informs us that everything which appears to the mind is nothing but a perception, and is interrupted, and dependent on the mind; whereas the vulgar confound perceptions and objects and attribute a continu'd existence to the very things they feel or see.

This account of what we experience – intended to show that philosophy must be uninformative – proved massively impressive to Kant, provoking him to 'solve' Hume's pseudo-problem by invoking *a priori* conditions of thinking and a 'noumenal' self free from the bonds of mechanistic physics. It is none the better for that; Hume had to invoke the imagination solely because he fails to recognize what is actually given in perceptual experience. For we do *not* recognize an endless flow of impressions but rather disparate objects which since childhood we have learned to identify as examples of 'things': houses, elephants, colours, etc. Given such an error about perception, the invocation of the imagination as a *deus ex machina* becomes a necessity if Hume is not to be convicted of conjuring up a world unrecognizable to anybody, even himself. For 'our reason neither does, nor is it possible it ever should, upon any supposition, give us an assurance of the continued and distinct existence of body' (193). Nor, then, is the stability of the impartial spectator any the more firmly based.

Furthermore, Hume's account of the moral importance of sympathy would seem to contradict his claim about impressions, for on his own showing how can we know that the sympathy we feel relates to more than what we *imagine* to be the feelings of others rather than their actual feelings? And the difficulties run deeper: a further aspect of his philosophical background should not be forgotten: his acceptance (and development) of much of Locke's radical account of the self as a kind of fictitious entity useful for social and especially forensic purposes. This was formulated less immediately in the context of moral philosophy, where we have seen it being applied – nor even in that of perceptual experience; rather it is part of Hume's ongoing empirical onslaught on Descartes' concept of the self. Some philosophers, he tells us, believe we have an idea of our continuing selves and that we are certain of our 'perfect identity and simplicity' (1.4.6, 251). The striking passage from the *Treatise* (1.6.3) is well known:

For my part, when I enter most intimately into what I call *myself*, I always stumble upon some particular perception or other, of heat or cold, light or shade, love or hatred, pain or pleasure. I never catch *myself* at any time without a perception, and never observe anything but the perception. When my perceptions are removed for any time, as by sound sleep, so long am I insensible of *myself*, and may truly be said not to exist. And were all my perceptions remov'd by death ... after the dissolution of my body, I should be entirely annihilated.

Leaving aside that if someone should stab me in my sleep it would not be murder, this is a powerful attack on the inert but always self-conscious mind of Descartes. What it fails to address is the earlier Augustinian-Thomistic account of the person as always in act; by Hume's time, in progressive quarters, that was forgotten, misinterpreted or simply written off as one of the old monkish beliefs. However, Hume does not go so far as to say that in sound sleep he does not exist, but that I 'may truly be said not to exist'. Despite the word 'truly' an ambiguity remains, and it is only at death that Hume unambiguously asserts that he will be entirely annihilated: reasonable enough because only then does the series of sequential selves come to an end. In any case, the questions, 'What is a person?' and 'What is personal identity?' are distinct and it would be a serious mistake to suppose that the problems of the first are resolved by the raising of the second.

Whatever the philosophical origins of the differing versions of Hume's account of the self, they surely reveal considerable incoherence, and the extreme version I have outlined is seen to sit uneasily not only with the apparent stability of our impartial observer but with Hume's call for a continuing self as the only explanation for the human ability to communicate. Like Locke, he wants to be able to hold people responsible for their actions, as is clearly implied in the following section of the *Treatise* (262).

Who can tell me, for instance, what were his thoughts and actions on the 1st of January 1715, the 11h of March 1719 and the 3rd of August 1733? Or will he affirm, because he has entirely forgot the incidents of these days, that the present self is not the same person with the self at that time; and by that measure overturn all the most established notions of personal identity.

Yet, as we have seen, Hume also offers a Lockean account of the self which would make responsibility an unjust imposition and render such questions empty. Nor is the problem diminished by the fact that his account of the relationship between memory and personal identity differs somewhat from Locke's: to indicate a far more conventional, indeed pragmatic, approach. For while Locke thinks that memory alone secures *identity* of consciousness, Hume maintains that each self needs only a resemblance to previous selves, and that that can be provided by a succession of conscious states. Thus:

> As memory alone acquaints us with the continuance and extent of this succession of perceptions, it is to be considered, upon that account chiefly, as the source of personal identity. [Should he not have said 'of the illusion of personal identity?'] ... Having once acquired this notion of causation from the memory, we can extend the same chain of causes, and consequently the identity of our persons beyond our memory ...

Whether or not Hume could have reconciled his more metaphysical and more pragmatic accounts of the self, it was the more sceptical version that had the most effect on succeeding thinkers and is therefore our present primary concern in this account of the history of the 'person'.

   There are other and more basic differences between the stance of Locke and that of Hume, if not on personal identity, then certainly on the *importance* of personal identity *sub specie aeternitatis*. Unlike Locke, Hume's disbelief in God and reliance on conventional morality to an extent lets him off the hook: perhaps as ever-changing bundles of qualities we – but who are 'we'? – are *not* really responsible for our actions and it is merely socially convenient and therefore desirable that, by convention, we can be called to account for them. Hume has no need to fear – as Locke should – this making God a party to injustice; in effect he may have returned at this point from Locke to Hobbes. In any case it is clear that – at least at times – he has carried Locke's demolition of the substantial person a stage further.

   With God taken out of the equation, Hume – a more consistent empiricist than Locke – has no reason to posit souls, mortal or otherwise, rather than minds. No bishop, no king: no God, no soul (though we have noticed that Hume will retain the word 'soul' in a context where another less 'archaic' term might suit him less). And with both God and soul absent, the older concept of the person, painstakingly built up over centuries, has more or less disappeared. Theologians, of course, keep on using the word 'soul' – and hymns are written in which souls apparently play their traditional role – but they increasingly are seen merely to echo past 'errors' by the more advanced *cognoscenti* who now speak only of mind, selves (whatever they may be) and matter.

Nevertheless, the problem of accounting for moral judgments and especially moral obligations persisted. If sympathy – however human – is found inadequate to provide what is conceptually needed, are there other possibilities – or, like the clear-headed Hume, have we to admit that so-called obligations are simply feelings which merely *seem* to oblige us to act 'justly' (498)? And if such may be claimed to constitute some kind of obligation – how convenient that we are naturally non-Hobbesians! – yet whatever we may 'feel', they, being rationally indefensible, are hardly worthy to deserve the title '*moral* obligations' rather than seeming tendencies towards morality. Hence persons, even if recognized as normally sympathetic, will be under no substantive moral obligation. Some would say this is in effect to dehumanize them; certainly it is to subtract something important from Mainline accounts of what it is to be a person.

*

As consideration of Richardson has shown, if sympathy is to provide us with obligations, it needs to be reinforced. But in Hume's godless world no reinforcement is available, reason – an obviously possible candidate – being dismissed as only (and in Hume's view properly) a slave of the passions (415); convention thus remains all-important. Hume's friend Adam Smith, successor of Hutcheson at the University of Glasgow and the last of the 'sentimentalists' to make much mark for more than a century, seems to have recognized the problem. Unlike Hutcheson, he prefers to speak not of a moral sense (which might seem to invite a comparison with the five physical senses), but of moral sentiments, especially (again) the feeling of benevolence. Looking for an explanation of why we are naturally benevolent and why our feelings are surely liable to point us, regularly enough at least, in the right 'moral' direction, he observes that someone who judges cruelty and treachery acceptable is morally depraved (whatever the person judging may 'feel' about it) (323):[6] pointing to the 'fact' that God, whom he calls the 'great Superintendent of the universe' (87, 277) has ensured that the morality that goes with happiness is within our grasp by placing an 'impartial spectator', his own vice-gerent, within all of us (130). This act of divine foresight might solve Hume's problem about why the spectator should be impartial, but again at the cost of an optimistic account of human motivation which

---

[6] References to Smith's *The Theory of Moral Sentiments* (1759) are to the edition of D. D. Raphael and A. L. Mackie (Oxford, 1976).

Smith and Hume can no more dispense with than could Hutcheson, but which for Hume matters less, since the judgments of his impartial spectator depend not on theological claims about the inner nature of human beings but on following the customs of the country.

For Smith, that pragmatic recourse is unnecessary, but there is a price to be paid in the high estimate of our actual moral capabilities which such as Hobbes and Mandeville could dismiss as naïve. Indeed, such naïveté is an essential part of Smith's broader outlook, appearing again notoriously in *The Wealth of Nations* where in a well-run economic system the 'hidden hand' is expected ultimately to work things for the adequate good of all: though we should also note that even this good is the mere sum of individual goods. Smith lacks any sense of the common good such as the Mainline Tradition would require.[7]

Thus in retaining God as the guarantor of an adequately 'moral' content for the moral space in which we operate, Smith has reverted from Hume to the earlier sentimentalism of Hutcheson, but his account of sympathy and the sympathetic imagination – he allows what Hume sees, that it may be a matter of mere emotional contagion but insists that this is far from the whole story – enriches the versions not only of Hutcheson but of Hume himself. Here there is no need to go into detail,[8] except to note that like Hutcheson Smith again puts much emphasis on the fact that we are by nature such as to be made *happier* by mutual sympathy, which helps to alleviate our own obvious weakness and is but recognition (*pace* Hobbes and Mandeville) of the simple fact: that we benefit from the kindness of others. A related feature of Smith's more sophisticated account of sympathy that also deserves skeptical attention is his optimism specifically about self-mastery enabling us to direct our sympathy appropriately.[9]

More remarkable, however, than his view of self-mastery is his account of the related subject of conscience. According to Smith (113):

When I endeavor to examine my own conduct, when I endeavor to pass sentence on it, and either to approve or condemn it, it is evident that, in all such cases, I divide myself, as it were, into two persons; and that I, the examiner and judge,

---

[7] Cf. MacIntyre (2016: 92).

[8] For details see especially Seigel (2005: 142–145); Martin and Barresi (2000: 94–102).

[9] While it is true that Smith's account of sympathy is more psychologically scientific than the proposals of Hutcheson and Hume, it is misleading to say [with Martin and Barresi (2000: 94)] that his investigation required no statement of his epistemological and metaphysical views. As we have seen, his religious beliefs are very germane to his conclusions.

represent a different character from that other I, the person whose conduct is being examined and judged of.

Later (135), Smith asserts that we know there are two persons because there are two roles:

The first is the judge; the second the person judged of. But that the judge should, in every respect, be the same with the person judged of, is as impossible, as that the cause should, in every respect, be the same with the effect.

In these passages Smith appears to have ignored not only traditional accounts of persons, but – despite the splitting up of an individual – also the reflections of Locke on personal identity and to have reverted to the ancient Roman account (developed by Panaetius and recounted by Cicero, who may have been Smith's source) of a person (or *persona*) as a kind of mask which enables an actor to perform different roles in a play. That, however, is to cut the knot cut otherwise by earlier sentimentalists, for Smith assumes that our internal spectator or conscience can by persistent self-control and self-mastery be developed such as to become genuinely impartial and recognizable as such. That is getting very close to Stoicism, but the Stoics were obliged to admit that the sage may need many years of reflection and self-analysis before he can be sure, by inspecting the consistency of his extended behaviour, that his *motives* are pure.

To sum up: in Smith's treatment of persons (or *personae*) there is hardly a thought not only for the Mainline Tradition as developed down to the time of Aquinas, and even a curiously cavalier attitude to the revival of ancient doubt about personal identity introduced by Locke. It seems Smith was wise to shift his attention from moral philosophy and 'anthropology' to economics.

*

By the end of the eighteenth century all that remained in Britain of traditional Mainstream thought was an assumption that we can control what we are and thus improve our character, especially in becoming benevolent, plus claims about rights, usually proposed with no foundation other than an assertion that we want them and therefore ought to have them. Such an etiolated philosophical condition raises new problems. With God abolished and man left to his rights and sentiments, is it possible to find some account of human nature which could justify a claim that we are competent constructors of anything seriously to be thought of as moral rules? For a spectre lurks behind the eighteenth-century Enlightenment: we want rights and moral principles but may have to fall back on convention (perhaps for Hume intended to represent pre-philosophical experience) or on unvarnished self-seeking – including usefully helping others if convenient – with Hobbes. Or perhaps the cake may be iced (à la Mandeville) with moral rules acceptable only to hypocritical dupes gulled by political manipulators who have induced them to believe that there exists 'out there' some objective morality.

It looks like a dead-end, or at least that any further advance would have to be radically different – perhaps originating from outside the United Kingdom. And so it turned out; two radical options (not unrelated despite their huge differences) were to be set on the table. The first, that of Rousseau, was that sentiment and the moral sense, coupled with a benevolence springing from supposed pity, must be supplemented by alignment with a 'General Will', so toughened up into something more rawly emotional, full-blooded, revolutionary, egalitarian – and certainly less godly. The second option (apparently) would be to accept Hume's dissolution of the *empirical* self in his mechanistic universe and argue that this argues the need to return to a less flabby version of the Cartesian mind; not this time inert but to be seen as a 'holy' will to obey what it holds to be rational for all to obey. This is the proposal of Kant, thus blending the democratic instincts of Rousseau with Hume's sceptical account of perception and contempt for any theory which might be taken to derive moral 'ought' from naturalist 'is'. Both options threatened further to subvert the Mainline Tradition.

13

Ambiguous Rousseau's Soul and 'Moi'

[By 1720] it was no longer considered well-bred to believe in the Gospels.
Cardinal de Bernis, Mémoires (cited by P. Gay in
The Enlightenment: An Interpretation)

Hutcheson, Hume and Adam Smith, in their different ways, thought that sympathy/empathy was the key which would free us not only from what they saw as the morally impotent rationalism of many of their predecessors but also from imprisonment in the obsessive self-serving on which Hobbes was convinced the honest man must rely to escape, by force or fraud, from the war of all against all in which he is otherwise trapped. Smith went so far as to claim that sympathy with others could be an engine by which to develop those powers of self-control which he judged the foundation-stone of the moral outlook

It is now time to cross the Channel. Hutcheson and Hume, as well as Locke, were influential well beyond the British Isles, especially on Rousseau; for a time, indeed, Hume was on close terms with him – until Rousseau's increasing paranoia ended the friendship. We have already seen that the 'moral sense' of these philosophers finds a parallel in the sentimental novels of Richardson, whose deliberately 'ordinary' characters – Pamela especially – were widely and enthusiastically welcomed by a growing reading public in France as well as in England as emblematic of an everyday but attractive world where readers could feel at home – or, in Diderot's phrase, 'find their place'. Pamela and Clarissa are ordinary females capable of arousing our sympathy: far from aristocratic and like ourselves, so it was supposed, driven by their feelings, whether 'moral' or otherwise, but arguably too polite, too bloodless, too merely bourgeois.

Rousseau and Diderot were not the first French intellectuals to relish the British philosophical scene: attention to Locke and his radical views of the self can be discerned earlier. Thus replying to Pascal on the question of the self's (or soul's) diachronic unity, the Abbé de Condillac observed that it is true, as Pascal had argued, that the self cannot be reduced to a bundle of qualities, and that '*le moi*' must be understood as founded on some sort of bearer-substance. Otherwise, if I loved someone I might be supposed (reverting to the old 'pagan' view) not to love them for themselves but for some quality of theirs which might, like beauty, be ephemeral. Nevertheless none of that implies that the self (or soul) must be immortal: nor, we might add, immaterial! We are immortal, concludes the Abbé, not by nature but by grace, in effect offering a back way of reaching what had been a Christian theme since Justin Martyr in the second century.

Pascal's original remarks might be read as an attempt to restore a more genuinely Aristotelian account of qualities in refutation of a Cartesian misreading which compared them to packages on the back of a (very substantial) camel. But while supporting the correction of mistaken readings of Aristotle, Condillac reiterated an authentic if neglected Aristotelian belief that nothing about the immortality of the soul should be inferred from the relation between its substance and its essential qualities. Unlike Pascal, and closer to most of the British post-Lockeans, he is not interested 'philosophically' in the immortal soul, but in the empirically observable and explainable self: in psychology, not in metaphysics. Souls and their possibly intrinsic worth-bearing qualities can be left (as in Descartes) for the theologians. However, although Condillac is unwilling to follow Locke very far in his doubts upon the diachronic continuity of the human person, he agrees that such continuity (also defended by Pascal) depends (as in Locke) on continuing consciousness and correspondingly on memory,[1] but draws no ethical conclusions: in that, as we shall see, differing radically from Rousseau.

For while Rousseau agrees that memory explains the self's diachronic unity, he is less concerned with its ontological significance than with how

---

[1] For Condillac on memory see his *Essai sur l'origine des connaissances humaines* in *Complete Works* (Paris, 1798) 1, 1: 53, cited by Seigel (2005: 181).

we acquire it: a theme approached rarely in earlier treatments of persons. Writing of young children, he observes (*Emile* 157):[2]

> With their strength there develops the knowledge that allows them to direct it. It is at this point that the life of the individual really begins; it is then that he acquires self-awareness. Memory extends the feeling of identity over all the moments of the individual's existence; he becomes one, the same, and consequently already capable of happiness or unhappiness.

This seems to suggest that before conscious memory the individual (*qua* person) does not 'really' exist. When the child can remember (and presumably for so long as it continues able to remember), it is what *we* would call a person; otherwise it is only a human unit: not, then, a person with unrealized potential but a potential person. Perhaps that is not exactly what Rousseau intended, but what he says is open to that (very modern and radically non-Aristotelian) account of what it is to be an immature human being. The potential person has, in more recent times, played an important role in the construction of bad arguments in bioethics.

It seems that Rousseau, intentionally or not, has used the debate about diachronic unity – as did Locke – to determine who should be deemed a person and who should not. His treatment of sympathy, however, represents an advance on that of his British moral-sense predecessors. Sympathy for Rousseau – whatever its theological or philosophical causation – is a two-edged sword: its merits or demerits depend on the kind of people with whom one is drawn to sympathize. To understand this, we need to delve deeper into his account of the soul – or in his more usual term, influenced by Locke and by Hume, of *le moi*.

Broadly expressed, Rousseau thought that in our primitive natural state we assume ourselves to be – or rather simply act as – solitary individuals. Though he is unclear whether any humans were actually in that condition, he considers it as our original state. In that state, we exhibit *amour de soi*, a naturally self-regarding attitude which, when we enter into society and concern ourselves with our standing with others, is corrupted into *amour-propre*. Furthermore, in our natural state, apart from our harmless self-love, we had feelings of pity for the sufferings of other sentient beings, though whether such a claim is plausible, rather than merely guaranteeing for Rousseau an assurance of a basic benevolence, is far from clear.

---

[2] References to *Emile, ou de l'éducation* are to the edition of C. Wirz (Paris, 1969) and those to *Julie, ou la Nouvelle Héloise* to that of M. Launay (Paris, 1967).

The distinction between something like self-respect and a selfish indul-
gence is well worth making; it adds up to a claim not only that we
consisted, but that we still consist, as it were, of two selves in tension, a
natural and a social self. Rousseau remains ambiguous about the latter,
for the social self is not simply the effect of corruption but on the positive
side also the guarantee of a certain stability imposed by our intercourse
with those others among whom we are obliged to present ourselves over
time; such coherent stability makes up for the rather Humean view of the
self as the product of an ever-changing series of impressions provoked by
the senses: our individualistic lot in the 'natural' state.

Despite Rousseau's sense of its necessity, this stability brings with it a
desire to keep up appearances which appears problematic as being unnatural. For the drive towards social commitment hampers the activity of the
free and autonomous self which – albeit in an unreflective form – the
natural state allows us to indulge. This natural and pure self (at least
occasionally, and perhaps with a bow to Rousseau's continuing theism,
even at times near-Christianity) is isolated, feeling no bourgeois sense of
obligation to others. Which does not imply that Rousseau thinks we
should not be concerned with others; only that such concern should be
'natural', free from the social pressures which deform it. It depends on our
'conscience' which Rousseau denotes in *Emile* (286, 290) a 'divine
instinct, an immortal and celestial voice ... an infallible judge of good
and bad which makes man like unto God': a conscience being presumably
identifiable as an authentically 'developed' voice of that pity which in our
primitive state enabled us to feel for the sufferings of others. Certainly, in
Emile it is associated with sentiment (235).

Rousseau's notion that we should conform ourselves (or be induced to
conform) to the General Will is apparently an attempt to explain how, at
its best, our conscience can point us to an authentic social life, thus
dissolving the effects of our also socially-derived ill-will.[3] Such autonomous conformity gives us uniformity of purpose free from the alienation
supposed to result from a mere dependency on others. In such concern
that our moral actions be authentic as well as autonomous, we see one of
the many areas in which Rousseau exercised a deep influence on Kant,
and so beyond Kant on ourselves: indeed, an influence perhaps deeper

---

[3] The idea of the General Will goes back to Malebranche, though there it is associated with
the activity of God. It is to be found in contexts more like that of Rousseau in Diderot: see
Schneewind (1998: 467, 474). For a fuller discussion see Riley (1986).

than Kant – however explicitly grateful to Rousseau for democratizing his approach to his fellow human beings – was prepared to admit.

We cannot recover even a revised version of our hypothesized natural condition (not even in the less nostalgic form which is all we can hope to manage) without being subjected to manipulative educational processes. A tireless writer himself, Rousseau claimed that he hated books (*Emile* 290) because they distract us from any revised version of the natural state. Hence the young must be kept free of most of them – together with any other corrupting social instruments – while they are educated in self-sufficiency, and not only because books might teach them to dilate on what they do not understand, but more basically because children might 'learn' sympathy with people who should not be so viewed and into whose shoes we should not put ourselves. Here then we see a more thoughtful – and more sinister – development of the naive attitude to sympathy which readers of the novels of Richardson or the philosophical writings of Hutcheson and other 'sentimentalists' might seem to advocate. To be sympathetic to 'bad' or 'corrupt' people would only make us corrupt; indeed, even to feel sympathy with those of a higher social status induces envy and frustration (*Emile* 341–342). But who is to determine what it is to be 'corrupt'?

As is often observed, the only novel which Rousseau seems to find free of such possibilities for corruption (apart, presumably, from those he wrote himself) is Defoe's *Robinson Crusoe* (*Emile* 290–292): a tale of an isolated castaway who learns to be self-sufficient, remaining free of all taint of the corruptions induced by luxury. The darker side of this liberation, however, is the plausible growth of unconcern for other people. Perhaps more than any other thinker, Rousseau is at the root of a contemporary inability to commit to the long-term projects implied by marriage. He indeed proved incapable of caring for his own children, preferring to leave them to the tender mercies of an orphanage; the social demands of looking after them would have impinged undesirably on his own 'authentic' naturalness and isolated if shifting selfhood.

Nor can we allow the darker side of Rousseau's educational project to pass without further scrutiny, even granted that the intended aim was to put an end to the ambiguities of our social existence. This he himself found impossible to resolve in his personal life, requiring him to resort not only to the irresponsibility that results from a lack of commitment, but to that self-pity and hypocritical self-justification (at the expense of others) which his life reveals as the accompaniment of moral inadequacy.

In *La Nouvelle Héloise* Rousseau shows himself not only the self-indulgent self-justifier of the *Confessions* but also, in his struggle to avoid the ambiguities of the tension between our natural and social selves, the manipulative educator whose technique, as Starobinski put it, is to make sure that while the child thinks he is developing his sense of autonomy, he is being induced to wish only what his instructor wishes him to wish.[4] Indeed, Rousseau reveals himself through his characters as himself double and ambiguous – even reminding us of the analogous if more straightforward self-bisections of Descartes, Locke and later Kant. In *La Nouvelle Héloise*, where we find Julie's lover Saint-Preux sheltered from society and re-educated by the atheist De Wolmar,[5] Saint-Preux stands for the innocent self of the natural Rousseau being groomed for the 'real' world, while De Wolmar (apart from his atheism, except that he suggests that as a desideratum of Rousseau himself) represents the real Rousseau: an omniscient educator who points the way for Saint-Preux (that is, for the primitive Rousseau) to become that self-determining human male – the 'male' is important – presented as model of a developing *amour de soi* kept clear of the temptations of *amour-propre*.

Yet the characters in *Julie* do more than indicate our natures as double and ultimately irreducible, given the impossibility of extracting oneself, Robinson Crusoe-like, from society. In Rousseau's account of the divided self we find a rather sophisticated attempt to resolve (or present as unresolvable) a major dilemma of Western thought we have found occurring at least since Descartes. For already in Descartes and in Grotius we identified an uncertainty as to how two conflicting features of the human person can be induced to live in harmony: in Grotius' version it is our social and aggressive selves. Beyond which discord lies the deeper problem of whether – however well concealed 'underneath' – we are basically good by nature (to become the basic conviction among moral-sense theorists as theism declined), or whether we are basically corrupt, as Calvinists and other continuing Protestants supposed: a view which could only lead ultimately to a radical pessimism once the religious explanation of Original Sin had been finally jettisoned – as indeed it already had been, and not only by Hobbes and Locke. According to Rousseau, in our original (but now unattainable) natural self we are basically good; in our normal social self, however, we are corrupted and even at best cannot

---

[4] See the perceptive comments of Starobinski (1988: 198–199).
[5] See further Shklar (2001).

avoid hypocrisy.[6] In the approaching restored naturalness to be acquired by a Rousseauistic 'education' we are on the way to a kind of redemption which Rousseau himself, especially in the *Confessions*, complacently admits that he has not be able to achieve.

How to sum up? Rousseau sensed the uneasy relationship between theories of the nature of the person as earlier developed and problems of personal identity re-introduced by Locke. Again, we see attempts to develop a naturalistic psychology, with God and the soul omitted, and a corresponding tendency to limit any claim to personhood for those lacking self-conscious memory. Yet those who remain somehow more human than these others – which is all even apparent human beings – are treated as both possessed of rights and at the same time in need of a social relationship aligning them with something 'more' (or less) than personal: in Rousseau's case the General Will. Hence and despite his concern to understand how human beings develop, Rousseau must be recognized as not only pointing to a further 'depersonalization' of the human individual but to an egalitarian concept of rights for those who though possessed of them are unable to exercise them until their nature be radically re-written. In older times Christians had looked to the New Man, the Christ-likened unique person generated by baptism and religious observance. With Rousseau we envisage a very different New Man, produced by educational manipulation, devoted to 'sincerity' and the unexamined pursuit of authenticity and self-fulfillment, possessed of rights which seem more and more contradictory and justified only by appeal to arbitrary feelings and random desires.

But the General Will, to which we must somehow be assimilated, might be made more concrete, indeed actualized as that Progress of History (however understood) into which our personality, indeed our unique personhood, can be duly submerged. For Rousseau is a well-spring not only of the bourgeois democratic morality of Kant but of the General Will, with all its revolutionary violence, hypocrisy and claims to enforce universal rights, of the 'people's democracy' of Paris 1789.

---

[6] For a brief introduction to inevitable hypocrisy in Rousseau's own career see Rist (2014: 270–272).

14

Kant's Rational Autonomy

> Dilemma: A Polish soldier stands on guard. He sees an armed German approaching on the right, an armed Russian on the left. Which does he shoot first?
>
> Solution: The German, because one must always put duty before pleasure.
>
> Anonymous, from Warsaw

As we have seen, Boethius and Duns Scotus are hinge-figures; Kant is another, for two reasons: first because he marks a significant point in the gradual shift from talk of human dignity, which is Christian language, to rights-talk, which at least was to become post-Christian; and second, and relatedly, because Kant seems to many to offer the best chance of preserving human dignity and human rights without recourse to religious premises.[1] I believe this hope delusory.

In *Groundwork* (4.434 *AK*) Kant distinguishes two types of evaluation: humans may have a price (as Hobbes had put it) or they may have dignity, as he himself believes, and that dignity is of inestimable value; possession of it is the mark of all human beings as members of the kingdom of ends. But unlike traditional accounts of such worth, which, as we have seen, derive from man's creation in God's image and likeness, Kant's version depends on his claim that in virtue of our autonomy we, alone among creatures, are able to prescribe the moral law for ourselves. There is no need to bring in God, at least in this part of the story. We must

---

[1] For a clear understanding of the difference between 'Catholic' and Kantian dignity see Rosen (2012).

therefore look at the background for such a claim, which, as will appear, is radically opposed to the beliefs of traditional Christianity, though still purporting to allow for the universal and inalienable dignity of all human beings.

As he himself says, Kant was woken from his dogmatic slumbers by Hume who persuaded him that the attempt of Leibniz and his follower Christian Wolff to revive much traditional metaphysics – and with it older accounts of human psychology – was a failure. Hence, he mistakenly accepted Hume's account of perception. But if he was to defend the new knowledge of the physical universe established by Newton, Hume's resort to imagination seemed quite inadequate. Since Newtonian physics could not be dismissed as near-fiction, what was to be done? Kant's answer was to propose what he considered *a priori* conditions of thought. We have the mental capacity not to *imagine* what underlies our Humean perceptions, but to infer from them the mechanistic laws of physical nature. And we have a further mental capacity which operates 'freely' and points us toward a radically new – albeit not entirely unprecedented – moral theory.

There are at least four basic principles of Kant's mature ethical stance: human beings are autonomous and possessed of free will, this free will being viewed as independent of our sense-driven desires and other effects of the Newtonian and mechanistic world-structure;[2] all human beings should be treated as ends and never only as mere means to an end,[3] for man is an end in himself; we must respect the moral law viewed as a categorical imperative; and the ability to formulate such a law binding on all is the 'form' of morality and constitutes our claim to be moral – indeed human – beings.

We shall inspect these interrelated principles in order to see how Kant came to conceive the human person, recognizing how, though no atheist, he in a particularly significant respect places Man on the same level as God, thus leaving God morally otiose. It is true that Kant only rarely seems to suggest that the human will, as well as God's will, can be described as holy (*Groundwork* 4.414; 4.439), but such passages must be taken seriously, for as moral law-giver Man is like God in so far as he

---

[2] Taylor (1989: 363) is helpful.

[3] The 'only' is important, since there are occasions when I can quite reasonably use others as means: Rosen nicely (2012: 82) cites the case of a man sheltering behind others in a bus queue to keep out of the wind and rain. That shows that Kant must mean that we should not 'make use' of others when it does them harm, physically or emotionally: 'make use' does not entail 'use' (in the sense of manipulate).

can correctly prescribe the dictates of his rational will. And it is by virtue of his noumenal self (that is, as we shall see, his real self) that he is indeed able so to prescribe, being unpolluted in that real self by desires and inclinations – and to have that capacity (which is shared by all humans) is to be holy and moral.

As for Kant's God, he does not will morality, as most of the early modern natural lawyers – not excluding Locke – held, but proposes it rationally out of respect for the moral law. As do we, and we propose and accept it because, like God, we are rational beings: 'We have no need of God to make moral judgments' (*Lectures on Ethics* 27.277 AK). In that sentence is summed up the difference between the Mainline tradition and Kant, as followed almost universally (though often in distorted form) by those of our contemporaries – including atheists – who accept intrinsic human rights.

Nevertheless, since Kant believes we have been *created* by God, he must assume (though often seems to forget) that had we not been so created with the capacities we have we should not be able adequately to respect the moral law as he believes we do. Strictly speaking, therefore, Kant's position still depends on God's activity – therefore should not be available to atheists. Where he does differ from the Mainline Tradition is that he believes that God has given us the capacity to be moral, while leaving us to determine moral content – as does He.[4] In that thesis, Scotus' univocity is back centre stage, not exactly ontologically, but in matter of rationality. And all this radical theorizing is built on denial of *theoretical* reason and the abolition of metaphysics, because 'I had to do away with knowledge to make room for faith' (*Critique of Practical Reason* B XXX). Here we see the beginnings of the ethics of wishful thinking and deception: of 'as if' accounts of morality and of man's nature and responsibilities in the world.

Let us examine autonomy. Kant tells us he had learned from Rousseau that every human being is able to grasp, without the assistance of professional or learned expertise, his basic dignity, hence his capacity as a moral law-giver, hence that in human affairs our possession of rights is of paramount importance:[5]

---

[4] *Religion within the Limits of Reason alone* (AK 6.50).
[5] *Observations on the Feeling of the Beautiful and Sublime* (1764), cited by Beiser (1992: 43).

I am myself by inclination a seeker after truth. I feel a consuming thirst for knowledge and a restless desire to advance in it, as well as a satisfaction on every step I take. There was time when I thought that this alone could constitute the honour of mankind, and I despised the common man who knows nothing. Rousseau set me right. His pretended superiority vanished and I learned to respect humanity: I should consider myself far more useless than the common labourer if I did not believe that one consideration alone gives worth to all others, namely to establish the rights of man.

Inevitably, with God already largely disappeared among intellectuals outside Prussia, the next stage in our story will reveal human beings as the *only* source of prescription in an otherwise value-free universe. Engagement in such moral construction reveals us as possessors of that self-imposed, self-asserted, yet intrinsic dignity now, as then, acclaimed as the basis of our rights. Man has properly appointed himself the *de facto* god. We have dignity as members of the kingdom of ends and that dignity is revealed by our holy will.

Although Kant rejects Rousseau's 'sentimental' account of conscience,[6] he believes that we all have the capacity to recognize the force of the rational will. But immediately problems arise, not all relevant to our present project. What does Kant mean by 'rational'? What does he mean by 'will'? Is Kant's concept of the freedom of the purely rational will intelligible? What sort of freedom is in question? How could such a will *guarantee* human rights? Above all what specifically does the rational will tell us, and how does it speak to us? That last question is especially important since Kant shows little concern for the development of character; seeming to assume that we just have a capable rational will and if we do not exercise it – here is a curious echo of Hume and Smith – that is out of an unnecessary lack of self-control.

Kant understands his emotionless rationality in a roughly Cartesian manner. When we are motivated by the rational will, we identify moral truth without any pandering to our desires or inclinations. The rational will is – or appears to be – devoid of any emotional or erotic features such as (for Kant) disfigure its Platonic predecessor; it 'exists as an end in itself,'[7] that end being outside the natural and mechanistic world. For Plato and the Christian tradition which follows Augustine it is impossible to know the Good without loving the Good, the mind being loving, even

[6] Cf. Schneewind (1998: 314).
[7] *Groundwork of the Metaphysics of Morals* 4.429. He also rejects a somewhat similar account proposed by Schiller.

passionate, rather than aridly calculating. For Descartes, and now for Kant, the holy and rational will possesses a *purely* cognitive capacity. That presents the problem, identified by Hume, that on Descartes' account of ourselves as rational beings – and on any relevantly similar account – we lose the capacity to act; for we act not because we know something about something, but because we *want* to act upon it. In a Platonic version that occurs because we *love* to bring something about. If we are Cartesian selves, however, we are in effect inert; yet as Hume points out, whenever he looks into himself, he finds no inert mind or self but an engagement in thinking, judging, wishing, etc.

Kant's holy and rational will, however, is far from inert, at least as it is capable of respecting the moral law, but to protect it he has to construct a dual-natured human being. As with Descartes and Locke, though in a very different mode, his account of the real 'I' – now autonomously centre stage – effectively involves partition of the person. But whereas for Descartes we are souls (minds) and not bodies, and whereas for Locke human beings are divided between those possessing personal identity – and who therefore are persons – and those who are not, Kant's defence of human freedom (and therefore of responsible moral action) depends on our being bisected into our 'phenomenal' and 'noumenal' selves. The former is governed by the harshly determining laws of Newtonian mechanics – hence providing no grounds for responsibility and obligation; the latter constitutes a 'kingdom of ends' where the real 'I' lives in a rational world in which we prescribe moral laws for ourselves: these being laws which everyone, including ourselves, should rationally respect and in accordance with which we should act.

Moral action is dutiful, and our sense of duty indicates our respect for moral law. As Kant himself puts it (in one formulation): 'Act only according to that maxim through which you can at the same time will that it should become a universal law' (*Groundwork* 4.421). And in the rational autonomy by which we so respectfully act we recognize the dignity of man,[8] which in turn guarantees 'intrinsic' human rights. The concept of dignity, of course, is traditionally Christian, and Christians, as we noted, were the earliest developers of rights-theory. But since ancient times they had recognized their dignity as a gift from God, ontologically dependent on our creation in God's image. For the Mainline Tradition our capacity to be moral and rational, in so far as it exists, has not

[8] So Taylor (1989: 83, 365).

reached us by chance; it depends on God's determination as creator and our continuing dependence on his grace to be able to recognize what is right and good, to act in accordance with virtue and to recognize that the moral law we respect is none other than the nature of God himself. Yet although our rational will, for Kant, is still created by God, its traditional dependence is far from meeting the conditions for Kantian autonomy; that indicates that the foundations of Kant's account of human rights diverge substantially from the Mainline Tradition. His substitution of human moral capacity for a traditionally 'humble' recognition of human moral and intellectual weakness is an essential feature of his account of autonomy – and that account might look like wishful thinking.

And why assume that the real 'I' is my 'noumenal' self? Apparently because unless it is, Kant can find no freedom in the will, and if there is no freedom of will, there is no moral responsibility. He splits the human being because we must both have freedom of the will and be responsible for our actions. But why must we? The claim looks like mere assertion or a desperate recourse justified by little more than a desire (however well-grounded in itself) to escape a mechanistic universe. It is based perhaps in part on the assumed axiom that 'ought implies can', but is splitting the person the only recourse available for defenders of responsibility? And *does* 'ought' always imply 'can'? Are we prepared to mangle human nature and turn ourselves into something like non-corporeal angels? There are many occasions when we know that we ought to do something or other but find ourselves unable to do it. It is to avoid the possibility of accepting such an undignified feature of human persons that Kant tells us in the preface to *Groundwork* to seek for the moral law not in the nature of man – that is, as empirically experienced in a mechanistic world – but in pure reason.

Kant's human beings are able to propose laws which must be applied universally, but they are unable to obey them. So why does Kant claim that the capacity to formulate and act on such laws is an essential characteristic of human beings? Not least because only by living in the under-determined 'kingdom of ends', and in virtue of our real and noumenal selves, can we recognize that we possess some kind of equal, indeed infinite worth. For worth being tied to moral responsibility, it is hard to see how in a strictly deterministic universe anything could be of worth; hence we must (hopefully) somehow live and have our real being outside it. And if we are to be autonomous, our worth (whatever its origin) must depend not on God but on our 'noumenal' selves and their constructive powers.

Yet whether or not being somehow morally responsible, why do we know we have any non-conventional value in the first place? Kant's most famous moral claim is that we must always treat one another as ends, never only as mere means; in human interaction we must never lose sight of our priceless nature. Here, however, he is again puzzling. Why is our nature so priceless? We can hardly reply, 'Because we live in the kingdom of ends', because it is not clear, even in Kantian terms, how far we so live, or even whether such a kingdom exists. Has it not rather been proposed merely to enable Kant to get round the question of the origin of our dignity and moral responsibility? Kant supposes that the ability to formulate a categorical imperative somehow shows that individual human beings – or perhaps persons – have intrinsic worth – but it is hard to see how it enables any such thing; rather it implies only that we would like to have such worth, or think we deserve it.

Kant claims that we should show respect for every human being, but what he appears to have done is to accept from his Christian roots that we are valuable (that is, have dignity in God's eyes as His creation), then try to demonstrate that such a desirable evaluation can be achieved '*etsi Deus non daretur*' (as Scotus, Gregory of Rimini or Grotius might have put it). But for all the attractiveness of the principle that we should always treat human beings as ends – and the impressive build-up of Kant's formulation of it – we seem only to be able to establish it by assuming Christian (or at the least theistic) premises:[9] premises which imply that we are dependent on God but in obeying which we commit the extreme Kantian sin of being not autonomous but heteronomous. We are left, then, with a choice: either we are autonomous and of no necessary value or we are of value but necessarily heteronomous since dependent on God. Nevertheless, it is unsurprising that many of our contemporaries have taken refuge in Kant as a hoped-for, even if incoherent, advocate of two incompatible desiderata: autonomy and rights.

Associated with the problem of value are difficulties about the will. According to Kant there is nothing strictly moral about *loving* something, for his account of willing demands liberation from any such eudaemonistic, let alone hedonistic, impulsions. But it is hard to understand how anything can be 'willed' – let alone voluntarily acted upon – if it is merely *known* to be moral. Thus, I may know that I should, say, pay my taxes in

[9] As Schopenhauer – cited by Crosby (1996: 208) – already noticed.

full, and this is because of the needs of a society of which I am a member: rational enough, except that I may be in love with a certain motor-launch I can afford if a make an 'adjusted' declaration. If I do not *want* to subscribe to a principle, how can I voluntarily subscribe to it even if it looks rational?

Indeed, as already noted – and even granted that we both ought to subscribe to such a principle and want to do so – if we have no capacity to do so, then, whatever our autonomy, the categorical imperative is of no use to us and may even distract us from reality. In Christian thinking up to and before Kant's time, this sort of problem was solved insofar as it was believed that God could – if we accepted his grace – give us the strength at least to try to love the way of goodness, even though we are unable to do so completely and regularly in our present life. Kant's autonomy is a claim to a capacity to do for ourselves what previously only God could enable us in part to accomplish. Yet it might seem obvious that Augustine and those who followed him in the Mainline Tradition were right: it is highly counter-intuitive to suppose that we have the capacity to be autonomous in the sense required by Kant. And unless respect itself provokes desire (and this Kant rules out as self-serving), it alone will not be enough.

Even if that obedience to the moral law we prescribe for ourselves avoids the charge of heteronomy, it is hard to see how mere obedience, as such, can generate virtue, even if it can generate an impersonal justice. Yet even that more limited clam is suspect, for to claim to know what is just (even if we prescribe it for ourselves as well as for others) seems empty unless we know what is good (or really good). Thus the standard charge against Kantian ethics that it reveals itself as purely formal has serious purchase. It might be possible, it seems, to obey a law out of respect for its rationality without understanding what it is to be good. Kant's reply (at the opening of the *Groundwork*) is that – strictly speaking – rationality *is* the only good.[10] That again is wildly counterintuitive and would diminish rather than enrich human life in that it fails to determine which other apparent goods are good merely as rational. Thus, Kant's position collapses (at best) into the claim that ideally we should rationally pursue whatever good is rational and only in so far as it is rational.

To avoid that difficulty, we would need to do what Kant himself is unwilling to do: namely recognize that our rational will gives us the

---

[10] At *Groundwork* 4.412 the will is said to be nothing other than practical reason.

capability not only to prescribe universal moral laws but, by what might look like mere *preference*, to determine the content of those laws. Most modern Kantians, unlike Kant himself, are preference-theorists in this sense; they assume that their rational will will always decide, in specific cases, what would be recognized as right by all other 'rational wills'. All such preferences would thus meet with universal acceptance, at least among Kantians. But this not only has not happened, it could not happen.

What then has happened to that human person whom we should always treat as an end, never only as a mere means? He or she seems to have been replaced. Kant has disassembled the account of the person as proposed by the Mainline Tradition in a parallel though far from identical way to that suggested by Locke. We are free rational beings but not free persons in any traditional sense because our value is now strictly tied to our hypothetical noumenal – and in effect bodiless – self, through which we may rationally respect the moral law without knowing what it should prescribe.

Coupled with this diminution of the complexity of the person is an excessively minimal account of human excellence: a diminution analogous to the attempt by religious fundamentalists to diminish and consequently debase the concept of truth. For the religious fundamentalist only 'saving' truths matter; anything approaching a wider vision of a flourishing humanity is abandoned in favour of obedience to the moral demands of a God who seems to have decreed that all except a (narrowly understood) moral life is unimportant; that what matters is only what is 'right' (however determined), not what is good, or even – leaving aside strictly religious claims – what is true. Analogously, for Kant, our humanity is displayed not in our overall capacities (which include, of course, our moral capacities) but in our acceptance of his esoteric notion of what it is to be moral. In this way Kant has accepted the demand of Rousseau that moral action should be available to all on the same terms, at the cost of putting us all aboard the same dreary – because inhuman – boat. Anything like an Aristotelian concept of human flourishing has been replaced by a narrow (and actually unlivable) moralism; eudaimonism, however, is not so easily disposed of. Nor, for that matter, is pleasure.

Apart from the unsatisfactoriness of reducing the good life to the narrowly moral life, and the moral life to the readiness to act solely out of respect for the moral law, the Kantian structure depends, as we have seen, on the division of each human person into his 'phenomenal' and 'noumenal' aspects. Most contemporary Kantians, while assuming themselves to be Kantian 'constructivists' in practical ethics, are prepared to

abandon the bizarre psychology that Kant thought essential. But there is –
again – a price to be paid for cutting Faustian corners in that way. Kant
proposed the noumenal self because he did not see how without it he
could avoid the hard determinism of a mechanistic universe. Were he alive
today he would surely see the same problems in any purely naturalistic
account of the cosmos (of which human beings form a part). He would
fear that without a noumenal self, freedom will disappear and with it
moral responsibility. He would notice that this diminution is an ever-
growing phenomenon.

Those who think they can salvage Kantian ethics without Kantian
psychology must explain why such fears are unfounded. If they cannot,
they are left – and they normally are so left – not only with no means of
exorcizing the spectre of determinism but with little more content for their
moral space than what they happen – even deterministically – to prefer:
an option to be rejected as unkantian. Just as utilitarians now often
suggest that we should maximize the good, whatever it is, so 'Kantians'
find themselves only able to prescribe the content of moral space on a
similarly 'preferential' basis.

If the concept of the human person is to be further developed for our
times, we need to recognize that Kant – despite his prestige as a Founding
Father of contemporary assumptions about the rights of man and the link
between human freedom and responsibility – has added nothing defensible to the Mainline Tradition but subtracted much. His merit will be to
have drawn attention to important features of that Tradition, primarily
about the unique worth of individuals (however badly he has defended it);
his demerits include ignoring obvious facts about human dependency (the
price of secularizing earlier accounts of human dignity) and trying to
construct a more acceptable version of the Cartesian error in supposing
the real 'I' to be entirely non-material. Long before he wrote, we viewed
self-awareness as determinative and supposed that human beings have a
certain dignity, and therefore the possibility of possessing subjective
rights. Kant's aim – sufficiently laudable even if inadequately argued –
was to try to get that conclusion *sans* the traditional role of God. Like the
modern post-Lockeans who want Locke's conclusions as to rights without Locke's theistic premises, so Kant's latter-day followers want human
dignity with its capacity to determine the content of the moral law
without even admitting Kant's (false) premise that God has created us
with that capacity.

In as much as man is substituted for God as our source for the moral
law while God as creator of Man is left aside, 'Kantian' claims about the

worth of human beings, though ardently advocated, have little philosophical justification and look horribly like wishful thinking. Contemporary 'preference-theory' seems the ultimate but debased way of defending some principles of Kant's approach. An old-fashioned Christian 'mainliner' might comment that what *Genesis* calls the tree of the knowledge of good and evil refers to human nature's capacity to *experience* – not merely to know about – the difference between right and wrong. We now live in a world so complex that we may have immense difficulty in case after case in distinguishing the one from the other, and even if we distinguish them, we may be so ruled by a *nostalgie de la boue* as to prefer the wrong and evil, and make these, by choice, our goods. If that is the truth of the matter, then Kant, so far from preserving morality, has taken a big step in the direction of nihilism. And perhaps the underlying reason for that is less that he was mistaken about the content of morality (much of which – not least that we have duties to ourselves as well as to others – he inherited from his Christian forebears), than that with his doctrine of univocity he eliminated the philosophical foundations of the radical distinction between God and man. Where Scotus had been the forerunner of a link between the univocity of being and the irrelevance of God to the making of the moral law, Kant pointed clearly to what that link implies when taken seriously.

PART III

TOWARD DISABLING THE PERSON

15

Introducing the Five Ways

> The West has lost Christ; that is why it is dying, that is the only reason.
> Dostoievsky, *Notebooks* (1871)

With few exceptions, Kierkegaard being the most prominent – and leaving aside for now the radical critique of modernity offered in the novels of Dostoievsky – it is hardly misleading to claim that after Kant theism in any Christian form disappeared from philosophical psychology – which in its empirical version increasingly presented itself as a separate discipline – until the Thomist revival at the end of the nineteenth century. Of the early neo-Thomists many did little more than attempt to reinstate the past, or revise Aquinas to sound like Kant, becoming thus unable to do much further to develop the Mainline Tradition. More recently a number of less Thomist theologians (such as the Jesuits Rahner and Lonergan) have pursued the same inconclusive path to nowhere.

Also in the twentieth century the historico-biographical insights of Augustine were still largely left by the wayside, despite arousing interest among a few outside the guild of professional thinkers. Instead, it was a combination of an incomplete Thomistic synthesis of earlier thought about persons with the new phenomenological movement and with a certain 'personalism' having distant connections to Augustine – together with a gradual return outside Thomist circles to more ancient modes of thinking about ethics – which inaugurated a possible rehabilitation of the Mainline Tradition. By then, however, the basic intelligibility of that tradition had been first widely challenged and then increasingly disregarded for anti-metaphysical, scientistic (and therefore anti-theological) reasons. The next stage of our enquiry will be to consider the nineteenth-century swamp that a twentieth-century brand of theistic or so-called personalist philosophers needed to drain.

For all the seeming novelty of Kant's approach to human nature, there are important features of his work which had been in the air for many centuries, some of these constructive, others subversive. The idea that man's nature can be implausibly close to God's had already resurfaced in the Renaissance, the creative artist being often considered at least super-human if not virtually divine. Yet such notions were preached in a society in which belief in God was still more or less universal; even Machiavelli never *claimed* to be an atheist nor did Hobbes, who about a century later still presents himself as an implicit rather than explicit unbeliever. For advocacy of any human 'divinity' or even self-sufficiency had still to jostle with the 'real' God of traditional Christianity. Thus, in the case of Pico della Mirandola, we find a promotor of the divine man at the same time an ardent supporter of the rigorist castigator of un-Christian morality and preacher of a return to authentic Christianity, the Dominican Savonarola.

But by post-Kantian times things were very different. With atheism increasingly common – nature being often treated as a divinity-substitute among the more philosophical classes, especially but not exclusively in Northern Europe (including France) – we find a growing tendency among the Romantics in Germany and England – in some sense literary succes-sors to the sentimentalists of the previous century – either to express themselves as near-divine creators or to think of themselves as the voices of an all-encompassing Nature. Even in the more pantheist version the presentation of the person as a man or woman of (often extreme) feeling is obvious enough,[1] Kant's efforts to revive the person as rational and noumenal self seeming to have little immediate effect.

Certainly in England it took some time for Kant's work, let alone that of Fichte and Hegel, to become known. Coleridge was one of the earliest to recognize its importance; Mill notes as late as 1838 that in his youth the intellectual stars were Coleridge and Jeremy Bentham.[2] Meanwhile in Germany the subjectivism which Kant had tried to exorcize persisted among the romantically inclined, and in the person of Fichte took

---

[1] De Tocqueville (*De la Démocratie en Amérique* II.1.7) notes the spread of pantheism in his own day, but rather surprisingly thinks it especially notable among 'democratic peoples'; it appealed, he claimed, to the egalitarian mentality.

[2] Mill's essay on Coleridge can be found in volume 10 of his *Collected Works* (Toronto, 1963–1991).

centre-stage, becoming ever more associated not only with a strong hostility to metaphysics and to theism more generally, but – as in France in the previous century – an increasingly virulent hatred for Christianity in particular. All this boded ill for the Mainline Tradition, which had attained its current form in an exclusively Christian milieu, earlier pagans (such as Socrates) having often been read as proto-Christians.

For all the implications of a continuing subjectivism, there persisted both among the Romantics and (for that matter) among the followers of Mill if not of Bentham the 'liberal' belief that the person is of unique value; that, as Kant had argued, he or she should never be viewed only as a means to someone else's end but always treated as an end in his or her own right. Even Bentham and the Utilitarians who followed him tried to show that they were not mere consequentialists: that they could protect the individual – even if what Kant thought of as rights were, in Bentham's words, 'nonsense upon stilts'[3] – and that the pursuit of the greatest good of the greatest number could still – somehow – be reconciled with the search for justice for each and every human being.

Yet despite his belief that man's moral capacity was like God's, despite his *de facto* attempt where 'convenient' to put man in God's place, despite his belief that man's justification of the moral law is as valid as God's, Kant had retained God in the background, if only to set us up with a moral capacity and to ensure that in the last resort things work out well for the just. And there is little doubt that those who already thought, for Christian reasons, that people should not be manipulated, found it easier to accept his view that they should never be treated as means to another's ends – whether or not they also accepted (or even understood) his arguments to induce that conviction.

Had Kant thought – which we may hope he did not – that with God largely removed from the scene the moral landscape could remain unchanged, he would have been sadly mistaken: and not only, as the voluntarists also supposed, because post-mortem rewards and punishments need to be factored in. For it is nothing short of ridiculous (as the more able nineteenth-century anti-theists understood) to suppose that human action and character development will remain the same – in point of moral behaviour – whether or not God exists, or whether or not we believe he exists. That remains the case despite the surface objection that

---

[3] For Bentham's famous and reasonable remark in an atheist universe, see P. Schofield, C. Pease-Watkin and C. Blamires in the *Collected Works* (Oxford, 2002), p. 330.

individual non-believers may behave, whether from knowledge or true opinion, better than believers.

So as Romanticism faded into the more cynical, world-weary post-Romanticism of Stendhal and Flaubert, there arose for some a sense (rather than a conclusion in the first instance) that man cannot, after all, live happily – even contentedly – on his own, however autonomous he might wish to be. And with God's aid, however understood, for the moral life removed, there seemed to remain at least five options for some sort of 'salvation' – all of which involved rendering the 'person' either grotesquely megalomaniac, committed to deception, or irrelevant. All five options pointed variously to homogenization, debasement and ultimately nihilistic despair as the destiny of the human race.

Thus perhaps God can be substituted by some ideological claim about identification with the March of History or – simultaneously – with the Aryan (or other) race or class – or by the search for 'equality' derived from understanding liberty as egalitarianism. Or we might adopt a stronger version of the Promethean stance: live for our autonomy in contempt of God, especially the Christian God (who anyway does not exist) and of those human beings unwilling to commit themselves to our heroics. Or we might advocate such 'high-minded' ideals about humanity, however intellectually unjustifiable, as we happen to like the sound of. Or – a more recent development of that last option – while privately among fellow élitists disbelieving in, if not despising, morality and virtue, we might nevertheless seek to promote them in order to bind society together: whether as merely to protect ourselves or – more or less as a hobby – to promote the contentment of others. Or we might re-open the path taken by some of the more extreme post-Lockeans of the eighteenth century, arguing that since the person is an illusion and God does not exist, we have to put up with the fact that nothing matters, unless ephemerally.

I dub these various procedures 'Assimilation and Homogenization', 'The Way of Prometheus', 'Whistling in the Humanitarian Wind', 'Virtual Morality: Propaganda as Social Glue' and 'The Way to an Absolute Nihilism', but although such classifying can be helpful as a mode of exposition, we shall find that the different Ways often overlap or, in the last resort, collapse into one another. Indeed, some or all of them may be held by the same individuals, even in disregard of logical consistency; just so contemporary adherents of 'gender ideology' both urge it in the name of autonomy (and therefore, presumably, of the desired triumph of a radical individualism) while at the same time longing for the homogenization of the human (or post-human) race which, if realized, their proposals would encourage: with the enhanced risk (or hope) of authoritarian manipulation by the vanguardists.

I shall look at each of these Ways in turn: to see more precisely what they claim; to understand why they are presented as either attractive or inevitable; and to determine what each implies for the Mainline Tradition. I shall argue that each of them, with its distinct philosophical flavour, promotes the 'virtues' of depersonalization (as well as homogenization), of escape from the soul: hence the irrelevancy not only of metaphysics and morality but also of art and literature.

16

Assimilation and Homogenization

For Hegel, freedom is the right to obey the police.
                                        Bertrand Russell

In the eighteenth century, as we have noticed, God gradually disappears from philosophical reflection on human nature, the soul tending to be replaced by the mind or self. But these too gradually begin to be dissolved; already a number of thinkers are proposing to explain mental activity entirely in material terms, the mind being regarded as an epiphenomenon of the brain. And since for hundreds of years, ever since late antiquity, the soul had been understood not only in terms of a form of the body or as the real 'I' as well as more theologically as the bearer (whether or not naturally) of human immortality in a theistic universe, it is hardly surprising that reflection on the soul became transmuted into discussion of the self. Nevertheless, generally in the eighteenth century the self was still treated as a substance, albeit the accounts of the person proposed by Locke and his successors had introduced the reduction of both the self and the person to convenient illusions.

The most extreme propositions are those of William Hazlitt, in his youthful *Essay on the Principles of Human Action*, published in 1805, throwing doubt on the assumption of self-concern which had predominated in accounts of the self at least since Descartes. According to Hazlitt[1] – whose view of the self relied largely on his acceptance of Locke's explanation of it as dependent on memory and consciousness – although we are

---

[1] For a stimulating introduction to Hazlitt's work see, Martin and Barresi (2000: 39–48).

reasonably concerned with our own past and present, our future selves are products not of memory but of imagination; hence it is no more reasonable to be concerned about our own future (including our post-mortem future) than about that of anyone else. This line of argument, as I have noted, was for most too far ahead of its time; its future was to be revealed in the latter half of the twentieth century, making it worth recording here as a strong indicator of the way the wind would eventually blow. We shall return to it in a later part of our story.

For the moment we must inspect other assaults on the ex-soul, that is, the self, for Hume soon had continental successors, most strikingly Ludwig Feuerbach, and it will be helpful to sketch something of the larger philosophical stage on which he walked, for Feuerbach cannot be understood without reference to the general situation in German philosophy at that time, dominated as it was by Kant, and more immediately by Hegel. The extent of that dominance is particularly clear if we recognize that while in earlier times Leibniz had taken part in debates across the European philosophical spectrum, paying special attention, as did Kant, to France, England and Scotland, Kant's own achievement seemed for many years to induce Germans to regard philosophy outside the German-speaking world as but a sideshow.

As we have seen, Kant's metaphysical structure – and despite Kant himself we use the word 'metaphysical' unblushingly in his case – is open to a number of challenges, not least in that his noumenal self might seem little more than a tool for the rescue of a revised rationalism – and with it a morality – from the corrosive demon Determinism otherwise poised to swallow up the human person. But there is also a further and more basic difficulty in that Kant had rejected most of *traditional* metaphysics and theology because he held the range of the human mind to be limited by our spatiotemporal spectacles such that we judge the physical and determined world only through the appearances which the senses convey to us. Nevertheless, he also believed, behind these appearances does lie an unreachable reality of 'things in themselves'. Of that, however, and despite the traditional metaphysicians, above all the followers of Leibniz and Wolff, Kant thinks that we can know nothing.

The inevitable next step was to deny Kant's 'things-in-themselves', and this was taken by Fichte – eventually deprived of his university post as an atheist – who saw no reason to assert their existence: our world – and not merely, as with many of our contemporary Kantians, only our moral world – is what we can make out of our experiences: what matters is not what exists 'out there' but what we make of it; the self, the 'I' – whatever that is – being at the centre of the only world we can know so that, as far as we can know, what it constructs is what there is. And though with that many problems remain, I shall limit myself to two of them: first, what about all the other 'I's'? And then what if the 'I's' are themselves illusions? Hegel took up the first of these questions, Feuerbach – as accompaniment to his version of 'theism' – took up the second – demolishing in passing, as he hoped, Hegel's answer to the first.

In effect Continental – or German – thought can be seen to have caught up with Hume's, now agreeing, at least tacitly, that Kant had failed to rid himself of the difficulties conjured up by the man who had woken him from his dogmatic slumbers. Yet it also differed from Hume, often reliving the dreams of the *philosophes* of eighteenth-century France: for while Hume was an 'academic' atheist, the mood of nineteenth-century German atheism (or antitheism) was far from merely 'academic', its insistent aim being not to demolish theistic claims in the name of rational argument but to replace them in the name of some form – whether individualized or historical/social – of the supremacy of the Will. We are not merely to abandon theism and fall back, with the sceptical Hume, on convention, but to replace it, if possible, by the worship of our own intense desire for Authentic Life.

But what if that is not possible and we are not, after all, in best shape as our own masters? We may need to be assimilated into a wider unity, and of that unity there seemed in the nineteenth-century to be two versions, one authoritarian (if not totalitarian), the other the product of 'democratic' egalitarianism. The former – and more widely noticed – we shall treat of first, before passing to its less recognizable partner.

*

Hegel was, directly or indirectly, a major influence in Germany for most of the nineteenth century and beyond, but we can limit ourselves for present purposes to how he came to view his system as assimilating all that was best in Graeco-Roman, Christian and Enlightenment thinking. Like Aristotle, though with far less reason, he supposed his work to be the best possible completion of the efforts of all his philosophical predecessors. As he himself put it at the conclusion of his *History of Philosophy*:

The latest philosophy is the outcome of all those which went before it; nothing is lost, all the principles are preserved. This concrete idea is the result of the efforts of the human mind through nearly 2500 years ... of its most serious effort to objectify and recognize itself.

Unfortunately, at the time, at least in Germany, many philosophers more or less accepted that philosophy had come to an end; that some new 'form of life' would replace it. Part of philosophy's culmination – in the first instance – was held to be Fichte's 'correction' of Kant's account of the relationship of the thinking self to the apparent cosmos. Indeed from Hegel's extraordinary claims one can disinter that his over-riding aim was to eliminate Kant's separation of the noumenal from the phenomenal self: to show how the 'I' objectifies itself in the world, thus bridging the Kantian gap between Spirit and matter; hence that the individual 'I' (or rather all individual 'I's) are to be identified with the Absolute Spirit as it progresses through historical time; that progress being depicted by the history of philosophy which culminates in Hegel's own work.

The point philosophy has reached, Hegel came to believe, is that Absolute Spirit (with the absolute self) is to be identified with matter. Thus included in his new philosophical synthesis is something of Spinoza's pantheism, as well as the belief that we need neither follow Kant in separating the two worlds nor omit the lasting historical impact of Christianity now to be seen in a distorted pantheistic form as instantiating one important phase of the journey of Absolute Spirit.

Perhaps the most striking thing about this is that anyone took it seriously, though the fact of its being couched in densely abstract language presumably helped – and helps – to give the impression of profundity. Yet taken seriously it certainly was, and not least the suggestion – in line with similar suggestions of Fichte – that the most recent incarnation of the Absolute Spirit could be recognized in the Prussian state. There is much that is bizarre about that, but most strikingly that, as Hegel and other 'historicists' assumed, our ability to learn from the past entails that we can predict the future and what would be best for us in that future; yet in human history radical and largely unpredictable changes are common – if only because of early and unexpected deaths.

In sum, Hegel's system was intended to include the best (some might say the worst) of Spinoza's post-Cartesian pantheism, Kant's defence of the rational will and the nationalism of Fichte, as well as that strange version of Christianity which Hegel eventually found acceptable. As early as 1805–6, in the third part of an unpublished text – *The Third Jena System, Philosophy of Spirit* – he was arguing that we know the universal will as our own will, that we become aware of our own existence (*Dasein*) from this identification of the self with its objectified and universalizing counterpart. Similar themes persist in Hegel's later work, reminding us of the dependence which despite himself Rousseau identified in our relationship with the General Will, and now, perhaps predictably, present in less abstract form: namely in identification of the self with the German state and German society. As we shall see, this provides the clue as to how our dependence on something analogous to the General Will – or to our own objectification as Absolute Spirit – could be maintained when the notion of a fixed self had begun in Germany – as already in sceptical Britain – to be dissolved.

Yet if the self already exists only in an objectivizing process, we may wonder whether it can still be identified as what was previously considered to be a person. The dependency of the self, had, of course, had a long earlier history in the more theistic world: it depends for its existence on God and for its flourishing insofar as it respects God's laws. But in those days its relationality depended on its being a substance. If that substance is disintegrated, its being is seen as relational without being substantial – in defiance of all the rules of Aristotelian logic. And although in our contemporary world a number of theologians are indeed prepared to think that the person may be purely relational, our nihilist disintegrators know better. If the soul/self is not dependent on God (or at least something like the Hegelian Absolute Spirit), then it can be seen to be entirely dependent on its social surroundings, and to flourish best if those surroundings are ideal – as Hegel had suggested was the case (more or less) in nineteenth-century Germany. For if the soul/self is not to be dependent on God, it must be assimilated to some social construction. And, of course, the German state was not the only option, even for Germans.

*

Hegel was not the only thinker both loved and hated by Feuerbach, but we need to look at two perhaps even more influential sources of his work: the theologians Friedrich Schleiermacher and David Strauss. Of these each points to a different aspect of the intellectual collapse of German Protestant Christianity as its historical and sacramental/liturgical base became ever more effectively whittled away. Yet surprisingly the *fons et origo* of the new battering Christianity experienced derived not from philosophy itself nor from theology, nor from the often explicitly anti-Christian Romantic poets, but from the new science of classical philology, of which the techniques were soon to be applied to the scriptural sources of Christianity.

It is common to identify the beginnings of German classical scholarship with the publication in the 1770s of Friedrich Wolff's *Prolegomenon to the Study of Homer*. The effect of that work, and of those that followed it, was to show that careful scrutiny of ancient texts, especially those handed down in centuries old traditions – whether oral or in writing – can reveal that they have constantly been reworked, that the names and dates of their authors may be (to coin a phrase) fake news and that we must try to understand their original social contexts as far as possible. When such techniques were applied to the Bible – both the Old and the New Testaments – many traditional assumptions were called into question: Did Moses exist, let alone write? Who wrote the books of Isaiah? Why do the Gospel accounts of Jesus, though not old by comparison, seem so variable? Why should we accept even as much of traditional Church teaching as was acceptable to the sixteenth-century Reformers: to Luther, to Zwingli or Calvin? Since we can *know*, as was supposed, so little about the origins of Christianity and the person of Jesus, ever being reduced to what was guessed or projected by the early generations of believers, we should recognize that *feeling*, not knowledge (nor even faith), should be accepted as the essence of religion.

A major effect of all this was that what the British Sentimentalists had done for ethics, Schleiermacher and his followers could do for Christianity. Religion is, in his phrase, your feeling of dependence – on what? You don't know the faith and learn its dogmas; you feel its power, and that feeling (as again with the British Sentimentalists) impels you to act. All this, of course, ignores that one man's feeling of Christian truth is another's feeling of traditional Christian error. Again we recognize a parallel with the history of ethics. Bentham, a genuine philanthropist, was asked why he helped people – and apparently answered that he liked doing so. Analogously with the religious situation: others like more harmful activities, such as killing people.

But if Schleiermacher reduced religion to feelings – however such feelings are to be explained – David Strauss, a second acknowledged influence on Feuerbach, tended to reduce it, in the case of Christianity, to historical error or ignorance. In 1835 Strauss published his *Life of Jesus Critically Examined*, to great acclaim in Germany and beyond. By that time Feuerbach, who had started his intellectual career as a devotee of Hegel, had begun to have serious doubts, publishing an essay in 1839 entitled *Towards a Critique of Hegel's Philosophy*. That was followed in 1841 by *The Essence of Christianity* and in 1845 by *The Essence of Religion*.

Feuerbach's immediate objection to Hegel's religion was that it disregards the imagination, hence feelings and longings, that are the essential marks of religion – and certainly reminds us of the 'feelings' of Schleiermacher. Following in the footsteps of Strauss, Feuerbach goes beyond accusations of abstraction, both Christianity itself and Hegel's blend of Christianity and Absolute Spirit pantheism falling victim to his major claim: that all religious claims to objectivity can be unmasked as projection: all gods are man's desires and aspirations in corporeal form.

Feuerbach, however, declined to be dubbed an atheist; he had, he believed, simply given a better explanation of what it meant to believe in a god, and of how such beliefs had arisen at a certain stage of human development – or as the result of a human unwillingness to recognize reality. Such beliefs he thought basically demeaning; we exalt gods as ideals, while debasing ourselves to celebrate their majesty. Still visible in all this is the influence of Hegel's thesis–antithesis–synthesis. The thesis is human aspirations, the antithesis is the alienation our dependence on 'god' induces; the synthesis is the recognition that humanity as such *is* god.

Thus Hegel's thesis has been cast back in his teeth, for while Hegel claimed that he can objectify his 'self' as the Absolute Spirit in such a way as to show that he is in some sense a representation of that greater Spirit, Feuerbach argues that where Hegel sees an objectification which can be recognized as revealing an Absolute, the reality is that such objectification is merely the effect of a debasing projection. All religions are nothing but the projection of our futile longing for a god: creatures of the misguided self, nothing more. Thus exactly where Hegel has corrected Kant's account of the noumenal self, Hegel is corrected by Feuerbach. The Hegelian Absolute has gone the way of any version of the Christian God: two birds with one stone. As Feuerbach himself put it, 'The turning point of history will be the moment when man becomes aware that the only God of man is man himself'.[2] He seems to have been prescient.

But Feuerbach went further, stung by criticism that although he had erased Hegel's abstract Spirit, the self, as inherited by Hegel from Fichte, and indeed from Kant, remained to be eliminated. He set out to examine what he (or others) might mean by such phrases as 'the human essence'. Surely that sort of 'spirit' was a hangover not only from Kant and Hegel but also from earlier soul-talk and deserving of critical scrutiny. And Feuerbach pens much such scrutiny, calling – especially in his essay entitled *Spiritualism and Materialism* – for a return to nature, more or less understood in terms of a mechanical universe explained by Kant only as partial and phenomenal, and from which he had vainly attempted to escape.

In his later writings Feuerbach went the whole hog, arguing that human beings are organisms with a set of drives to a contentment which is nothing more than the satisfaction of bodily needs. There too is to be found the origin of what we call morality, since without such contentment and its opposite no distinction between right and wrong can be discerned.

---

[2] Discussed by De Lubac (1995: 10).

Thus if Feuerbach's *The Essence of Christianity* was to provoke Strauss to call it 'the book for our time', Engels to recall in 1888 that he found it liberating and Marx (not least in his *Theses on Feuerbach*) to join in the accolade, Feuerbach – and not Hegel – marked the end of Classical German philosophy (or rather he dispatched it). Feuerbach accepted such comments as a spur to completing his task: with God discarded, his image must follow suit; the self, being dependent, has nothing to depend on. For the future, he concluded, philosophy must change the world, not describe it. Unlike Marx, he declined this task for himself.

Feuerbach eventually concluded that the self, though relational as Hegel had claimed, is no fragment of the Absolute Spirit but an idealized creature of society; that would lead any would-be moral 'reformer' to suppose that a better world could only be achieved through the sort of social or political activity which could better determine our individual mentalities. Society makes us, and the more we allow the right sort of society to assimilate us, the 'better' we shall be. With God, the Absolute and the autonomous self abandoned, any traditional notion of the special and unique character, value or worth of each individual person has disappeared. Given that all that is left of traditional religion – according to Schleiermacher – is its recognition of humanity's felt need for something greater than itself on which to depend; and given Feuerbach's individual, at risk of dissolution when reliant on its own resources, some sort of secular social assimilation must seem the best option available. But which sort? The Prussian State had already been on offer, but Marx and Engels were to supply an alternative; Heidegger, in the next century, an even more brutal variant.

*

In many respects Marx remained a Hegelian, not least in his revised version of the construction of the perfected self. But Hegel had put the 'I' at the centre, and explained its objectivity with reference to the Absolute Spirit, while Feuerbach, whom Marx found 'refreshing', abolished the Spirit and abandoned the self as a construct of bodily and social experience, seeking to lay down what kind of bodily (or more broadly human) experiences are best for us and following Hegel's tenet that we need to be attuned to the progress of history – though not in Marx's case to the history of the Absolute Spirit or of the Prussian state; for Marx, the progress of history is governed by economic – that is materialist – determinism.

Further, the inevitability of progress tells us which social experiences we need at any particular point in historical time if we are to be rid of 'alienation', which is to be overcome not by seeing ourselves objectified as the Absolute Spirit but in the 'cosmic' developments of society. In our present historical phase, we suffer from an alienation that warps the character of both the oppressed and the oppressors, and we can be rid of it by freeing ourselves not only from the trappings of religion – the main concern of Feuerbach and Strauss – but also from bourgeois capitalism – under which head Marx's collaborator Friedrich Engels would most insistently include the private family.

For a key feature of Marxism, as of its neo-Marxist successors – all heirs not only of an authoritarianism derived from Hegel but also of the actual totalitarianism of the French Revolution culminating in the total mobilization of the population ordered by Napoleon – is its implicit critique of much earlier authoritarianism for allowing enemies of the 'correct' régime to retreat into private life. By contrast the Jacobin descendants of Rousseau had insisted that the family should afford no protection for enemies of their imposed society, thus paving the way for more 'advanced' thinkers, like Marx and Engels, to follow their progression from authoritarianism to totalitarianism. For the Jacobins there was to be total war, total mobilization; for the Marxists, there is to be the total state from which there is no escape – since only a fool would want to escape from paradise, and fools are to be eliminated. We are all to be 'educated' to love Orwell's Big Brother. There are no natural rights; here the atheist Marx agrees with the atheist Bentham: rights, being merely proposed protections for egoism, being thus necessarily irrelevant to the perfected 'communist' society.

As already noted, an important prerequisite of Marxist assimilation – emphasized less by Marx himself than by Engels and in more recent times given a neo-Marxist colouring, especially a feminist one by gender-ideologists – involves significant change in the role of the family within society. For it is within the family, in which we normally spend our most formative years, that the possibility of a socially non-assimilated self can be early developed. Engels saw this clearly and marked the family down for elimination from the communist paradise. Ironically, more recent attacks on the family, though historically deriving from Engels, are concerned to *liberate* the individual from *any* particular social structure rather than to transfer his or her loyalty from the family to State or Party. In fact, however, they also expose the individual to greater jeopardy of totalitarian manipulation and victimization.

It has been recognized at least since Plato's *Republic* that families, especially if extended into clans, can be a threat to wider citizen loyalties. The internecine civil strife that split the Greek *polis* – as it would the city communes of Renaissance Italy – challenged philosophers, beginning with

Plato, to attempt reform of the relationship of family and society. The alternative seemed to be civil war, or at best an endemic weakness which made the small individual cities easy prey for larger political predators; this happened in Greece where the *poleis* were swallowed up by Macedonia and in an Italy plagued by political and military weakness in face of the 'barbarian' (meaning largely French) aggression castigated by Machiavelli.

Yet the motivations of Engels and his more recent feminist epigoni are not identical. For Engels, the family is the source of a loyalty to its own and to a separateness of its individual members which may reveal itself as hostility to the totalitarian goods and goals of the homogenizing State. For his feminist (and more recently 'LGBT') descendants the problem is the family as standing in the way of what they view as the personal, primarily sexual, liberty to experiment and self-construct. Of course, in earlier times too – not least in the Athens of Plato – the responsibilities of the family promoted much more than individual fulfilment or autonomy. Family-generated women were to bear children not only for the clan but also 'for the city', while men might be called on to fight and often to die for it. Modern 'third-wave' feminist individualists look on the family as threatening in a very different way not only from Engels but also from older theorists.

The older view considered our bodies and sex as at the service of both familial and civic obligations. Both parents and the state wanted, and needed, children, the state to ward off foreign enemies, the family to ensure that property be kept secure: aims now often considered oppressive of the individuals who have to live by them. Thus while Engels wanted the family assimilated and subordinated to the state, more recent anti-family movements would impose strict limits on family size – in practice indeed ensuring something approaching childlessness – and since the traditional (as opposed, for example, to the 'gay') family may resist that, it should be abolished altogether. Now that the individual's sexual life is entirely his or her own business (except, as occasion demands, their partner's), the family has come to be seen bar to an egalitarian liberty whereby human beings are regarded not only as 'equal' but, so far as possible, identically indeterminate and equally malleable.

The essence of such assumptions is a denial of the significance of all 'natural' social instincts; in the private 'square', as in the public, all 'personal' relationships are to be by contract, entered upon with a marked hostility to commitment and assuming no liability of stability. Nature is to be reconstructed at will, and since the development of 'persons', especially of their earlier social selves, is carried out in families with at least some degree of structure, the destruction of the family will favour the generation of 'persons' in no imperative social context and thus ripe for totalitarian assimilation.

Since persons, as recognized in the Mainline Tradition – being natural members of familial and social groups – cannot survive in such displacement, they may, in the course of time, learn to substitute virtual life for family life as apprentice citizens: a trend facilitated by mass and often brutalizing entertainment purveyed on the computer and the mobile phone. At best they may develop a spurious, statistically-based 'love' of humanity, an impersonally conceived mass benevolence, believing themselves global citizens but with little understanding even of those they know, of those who should represent for them what it is to be an actual person. At worst this is Plato's project gone mad, designed to replace a possibly restricted but creative loyalty by an uncommitted membership of an extended set of scarcely identifiable, free-floating human items. But, as we should have learned from Aristotle's criticism of Plato ('Better to be a real cousin than a Platonic son'), such a project, in destroying the person, can only produce narcissistic sub-human units, predictably sexually errant since sexual instincts must be re-directed.

History was supposed to end, for Marxists, with the construction of the Communist state, but recognizing that such a state had not been realized, some of them – especially Chairman Mao – thought backsliding even among the new élites inevitable; hence perpetual purges and perpetual revolution would be features of the best *possible* society: a conclusion at least revealing of the contradiction inherent in Marx's original vision of human progress and indicating that his failure – if there was to be a failure, for science unimpeded by ethics might in time be more successful – was due to the fact that the developing self's desire in each generation for a certain autonomy, however limited, could not be gainsaid and so would have to be repressed. So far, the assimilation – at least the total assimilation – of the self looks to have failed and will continue to fail as new generations of humans struggle to be more than homogenized, colourless units until (to adapt the words of Hitler) the last man has killed the last but one. Total assimilation, that is, can only succeed by entraining the end of the human race.

*

So far, I have followed the majority of political analysts in thinking of human assimilation as some kind of political programme for the deliberate destruction of human nature by a totalitarian state or society. There are also non-totalitarian (or at least not obviously and immediately totalitarian) versions of the Way of Assimilation. These depend less on the force and fraud of their more obviously totalitarian sisters, being effected rather by immediate gratification: the desire for an inert, comfortable life rather than by a desperate hope that anything like this cosy condition might be secured by submission to a brutal and incoherent ideology. This quieter route to assimilation, as was recognized by Tocqueville, is more 'democratic'; at least it derives its original impulse from more democratic desires: above all the desire – again in the spirit of the French 'democracy' of '89, if less brazenly so – to view liberty as *égalité*.

Tocqueville (in *Démocratie en Amérique* II 1.8) connects equality with a theory of the indefinite perfectibility of human beings (in the present life goes without saying). In his analysis of the United States of his day he may well have been right; even so, the conjunction remains incoherent. There is no necessity that what Tocqueville thinks of as the dictatorship of the majority (I 2.7) should produce *both* 'democratic' egalitarianism *and* the notion of infinite human perfectibility – except that it is possible to combine the drive for the humanist perfection which formed part of the mentality of the Founding Fathers with a feeling among the general public that it is much more comfortable to conform – which conforming means at least a degree of homogenization such as Tocqueville saw in American social *mores*. In that case homogenization – driven by a taste for *la dolce vita* – may be identified as the path to an egalitarian version of democratic perfection. Nor, of course, should we forget that even when the 'dictatorship of the majority' is modified by some recognition of minority rights, both majorities and minorities within a 'democratic' structure can be manipulated by élites who control the supply of information (as of bread and circuses offered for gratification) to the general public. Democracies – increasingly – are no exception to the general rule that power ultimately resides with some oligarchic élite.

We conclude that both the totalitarian and the superficially non-totalitarian forms of assimilation derive from a similar feature of the human condition: a fearful desire to be comfortable with whatever our lords and masters (of whatever stripe) can, by force or by bread and circuses – or now by social media – choose to offer us. The Greeks regarded pleasure and pain as the twin enemies of the good life: that maxim still applies in contemporary societies. And in the longer run the offer of a mindless contentment may be more corrupting than the more obvious threat of violence: *occultior non melior*, as the Roman historian put it in another context. Yet for those who follow the Mainline Tradition a couch-potato fiddling with a mobile phone is no model of the perfected human being, however many millions are content to be such.

17

The Way of Prometheus

> The arts generally make life possible and worth living.
> Nietzsche, *The Birth of Tragedy*

The myth of Prometheus can be read diversely: as a challenge to mankind to aspire, to challenge the gods, even in effect to claim to be a god; as an example of arrogance which should not be imitated and should be punished; or as all of the above. In the early nineteenth century the first of these would be promoted, by those who hated the Christian God, denied his existence and aspired to fill the gap with super-humans. Protheans had not always been so apparently coherent in their claims about human capacities – whether moral or more normally artistic in some form; in the Renaissance Prometheus was usually invoked by those who still retained much of their Christian theism. In that earlier time, such views were in part a reaction against an extreme of self-denigration often preached in the Middle Ages – typified by Pope Innocent III's *De Contemptu Mundi* – but already they could go beyond what had previously been recognized as orthodox Christianity, a fact recognized not least by Luther. Thus, Ficino's 'Know yourself, divine race in mortal clothing'[1] comes perilously close to the Platonic view, always recognized as unchristian, that man is naturally immortal rather than made so by grace. A century later Giordano Bruno – a pre-enlightened voice anticipating the omission of historical Christianity from the Charter of the European Union – went much

---

[1] In Ficino's letter to the human race, *Epist.* 1.1.642a.

further; we should abandon the Christian centuries and return to a revised version of Graeco-Roman paganism.

Ficino and his associates managed to remain Christian, and though their account of human nature and human worth exceeds that of the ancient pagan Platonists – Plotinus could have dismissed it as Gnostic – their Christianity imposed limits on their worship of the 'superhuman' artist or literary genius. That was in part because they considered moral as well as aesthetic excellence as indicators of human perfection. And humility had ever been held the mark of the saintly – in sharp contradiction to the 'great-souledness', however understood, which marked the pagan traditions, not least that of Aristotle.[2] Only the most 'Christian' of the pagan writers, Plato, claimed that when thinking of our proper attitude to the gods we should be 'humble' (*Laws* 716a) – by which he, of course, did not mean sniveling hypocrites of the Puritan type ambiguously praised by Mandeville and regularly caricatured in English literature: as Dickens' Uriah Heap (a self-styled 'very umble man') or Trollope's Reverend Obadiah Slope.

After the Enlightenment things were very different. Hume's atheism annoyed comparatively few. But, as we have seen, while for Hume atheism was largely a matter of private belief and encouragement, with no obvious and immediate political or more generally public and social implications, that was far from true for the atheists of France: as a rule, they wanted not merely to reject but to blot out (as Voltaire put it) the infamous scandal of Christianity. And soon that vehemence found an echo in England, notoriously so the youthful Shelley whose *Necessity of Atheism* (1811) got him expelled from Oxford, while in a letter to Thomas Jefferson Hogg of the same year he observed that 'I wish I were the Antichrist, that it were mine to crush the Demon'.[3] Such vehemence could only imply a very different account of the worth – if any, and however justified – of the human person. In the case of Shelley, it is clear that man as a rational animal capable of religion should be replaced by man as a rational animal capable, in multifarious ways, of art. And while Shelley wanted to be the Antichrist, there were soon those who thought that they had achieved it.

---

[2] For interesting criticism of Aristotle, especially of his unwillingness to admit that all humans, not only the young, the old and the disabled, must in an honest reading be recognized as dependent on others see MacIntyre (1999: 127).

[3] For comment see Beckett (2006: 399–401).

In Shelley much of this might be dismissed as adolescent display and a self-admiration become typical of artists, especially since Shelley's time: these have often come to see themselves not only as guardians of memory and promoters of the fame of great men (as Horace put it, there were great men before Agamemnon but until Homer we knew nothing about them) but as creators – hopefully *ex nihilo* – in that respect replacing the Christian God, or at the least as demigods like Prometheus, whose 'creatures' Beethoven was at about the same time to serenade. And whereas Protagoras had told us long ago that man is the *measure* of all things, with Feuerbach the new atheists wanted to persuade us that man is the *creator* of all things: with Shelley of art, with Nietzsche – in some respects his more serious successor – we can and ought to be creatures of ourselves: a stance, which both the pagan Plotinus (*Ennead* 5.1.1) and the Christian Augustine had condemned as basic to primal sin. Popularly it is called 'playing God': a 'Nietzschean' game increasingly indulged in since Nietzsche's time, especially among scientistic geneticists and those who revere them.

The view of Nietzsche himself is more difficult to determine, not least because his thoughts evolved. The most important fact about him is that (apart from Dostoievsky who came to conclusions in some respects remarkably similar) he is the first major Western thinker to insist first that God is dead (and 'we have killed him' [*The Gay Science* 125]) and that although this is matter for rejoicing in that man is freed from a degrading and demeaning subservience, we are also now threatened by a moral vacuum, which may herald a terrible and terrifying situation for us all.

As we shall see, Nietzsche, like Feuerbach, accepted a revised 'theology' from David Strauss, but later, unlike Feuerbach, came to despise Strauss as facile; his attacks ranged over several years, but not untypical are the following comments from *Ecce Homo* (7):[4]

He [Strauss] proclaims with admirable frankness that he is no longer a Christian, but he does not want to disturb any comfortableness of any kind ... abashed we see that his ethics is quite unchanged.

And again:

Strauss has not even learned that ... preaching morals is as easy as giving reasons for morals is difficult; it should rather have been his task seriously to explain and

---

[4] Which I cite from the discussion of Kaufmann (1974: 136).

to derive the phenomena of human goodness, mercy, love and self-abnegation, which after all exist as a matter of fact, from his Darwinistic presuppositions.

So much not only for Strauss but for certain aspects of Darwinism, though Nietzsche was himself a Darwinian in accepting the thesis that we are merely 'higher' animals, a more skilled variety of the chimpanzee. That, he recognized, left him without Strauss's optimism about morality. In his earlier writings, however, he had seemed to think (however confusedly) that philosophers, artists, even saints, are indications of a certain *capacity* of mankind for something like Hegel's 'Spiritual' realm. By then he had not formulated his account of the Will to Power, offering – at a price – its single explanation of humanity's strengths and weaknesses, thus of why mankind must indeed be divided, for only a few choice specimens are capable of the higher life. But of that anon.

For Nietzsche art defeats nihilism (*Will to Power* 853). Nietzsche's atheism is not nihilism (though many of his more recent successors would have it be). That is to be explained in part by reference to those who most influenced him, who ranged from Plato the lover of beauty[5] (though not Plato the moralist) to the later discarded David Strauss, who liberated him from his ancestral Lutheranism. The 'great spectacle to be presented in a hundred acts', Nietzsche prophetically tells us in the *Genealogy of Morals* (3.27), is the desperately challenging end of Christian morality that will take place in Europe in the next two centuries and take the form of 'the most terrible, most questionable and perhaps also the most hopeful of all spectacles'. Though we need to enquire how it might be hopeful, Nietzsche was certainly less nostalgic about it than was Matthew Arnold who at roughly the same time, was writing poetically in *On Dover Beach* of the slowly receding tide of faith.

Perhaps Nietzsche's hesitation surfaces, because, like those he mocked, he remained marginally one for whom 'truth is the kind of error without which a certain species of life' – that is, most human beings – 'could not live' (*Will to Power* 493). If so, we need to identify the form of truth which survives his subversion. What is clear is that the end of Christian morality is an event of almost 'cosmic' importance: as Nietzsche put it in *The Gay Science* (125), like uncoupling the earth from the sun, which is now beginning to set.

---

[5] For helpful comment on this aspect of Nietzsche's ambivalent attitude to Plato see Wood (2010: 249).

Nor in reflecting on the sources of Nietzsche's rejection of Christianity should we forget the massive influence of Schopenhauer whose *The World as Will and Representation* had appeared in 1818, and who became another of Nietzsche's loves and hates: loved because he understood the chaos and absurdity of the universe in which we live, where all depends on the violent, insatiable and basically evil Will (note the post-Kantian emphasis on the first-person, but this time with no even projected second-person, as is essential in Judaeo-Christian accounts of God); also hated, however, as having adopted a cowardly stance toward realities that he had partially understood, urging a retreat into something like a Buddhist Nirvana.

For although Nietzsche always accepted Schopenhauer's vision of the world as bleak, almost absurd in its senselessness, he concluded that though he could not deny its reality, pessimism is not the proper response: some of us can follow the lead of the ancient Greeks (as he understood them) in finding, if not salvation, yet perhaps some kind of transfiguration in art.[6] According to the mature Nietzsche, a real 'overman' embraces the evil – or the pitilessly amoral – as well as jettisoning any remaining fragments of bourgeois morality or of the 'enlightened' moralism which purported to replace it. Art, though far from comforting, and inseparable from unredeemable suffering, invites us to recognize an illusion of transfiguration. In welcoming its pitiless creativity, we adopt the heroic stance; already in the *Birth of Tragedy* it offers a veil of beauty (25) to cover the 'horror or absurdity' (7) of our Schopenhauerian world.

It is essential – *pace* Schopenhauer (and Rousseau) – that pity, along with humility, be erased from the heroic self. The possibility of that self preserves Nietzsche from a despair which might otherwise collapse into absolute nihilism. For the mature Nietzsche the Promethean self is revealed in the form of a coherent and 'higher', indeed heroic, assertion of that very Will to Power[7] which in the ordinary herd of humanity merely generates the impotent resentment which Nietzsche claimed to unmask in most deluded humans: whether Christians, Kantians,

---

[6] For excellent discussion, in implication ranging far beyond the *Birth of Tragedy*, see Schacht (1984).

[7] It is important to notice that the 'Will to Power', absent in Nietzsche's earliest writings, emerges gradually, eventually giving Nietzsche (rather in the manner of Hobbes) a simple solution to the apparent puzzle of incoherent human emotions, especially identified as such since Grotius. What Nietzsche sometimes thought of as honest feelings of mercy, pity, etc. can now be dismissed as more complex derivatives of the Will to Power. By getting someone to pity us, we can exercise at least a minimal control over him.

philosophes or any other variety of the stinking set of disingenuous moralizers who followed in the steps if not of the historical Socrates, at least of the myth which had come to surround him. These are the people who, following (or perverting) Moses and Jesus as well as 'Socrates',[8] have invented a value-system deservedly to be dismissed as slave morality and rejected root and branch: a moralism which combines the man-destroying Christian God with a perverse rationalism which, along with our myth-making capacities, has also eliminated all hope of man's attaining heroic stature.

For in this polemic against what he sees as the life-threatening rule of an arid and trivial philosophy, Nietzsche was issuing an important challenge to a pettifogging (hence deadening) rationalism. In that (as he came at least partially to recognize when later in life he read some – not all – of Dostoievsky's novels), he had been anticipated by the prophetic Russian. Of course, while Nietzsche and Dostoievsky agreed in seeing Europe as having fallen prey to a godless and desiccated rationalism and love of abstraction which was gnawing at its soul, their prescriptions were radically different. Where Nietzsche thought that there is no going back, that the tragedy of a suffering and dying Europe must be welcomed as the possible seeding of a 'higher' human life, for Dostoievsky the 'killing' of God could lead only to the dissolution and destruction of God's image, Man.

In various ways Dostoievsky's would-be 'Nietzschean' or otherwise promotors of the superman – Raskolnikov, Kirillov, Stavrogin, Ivan Karamazov and his *alter ego* the Grand Inquisitor – represent the blind (even willful) destructiveness – in Kirillov's case self-destructiveness – of a revolutionary violence which after the elimination of God tries to create a New Man and World but can only destroy soul – so they hope – as well as body: in brief the whole 'person'. God absent, only some form of totalitarianism (offering 'happiness', in the form of material contentment rather than 'freedom') will prevail. Those, therefore, who seek to maintain a core of Christian morality (including even avowed atheists like Bentham and his contemporary followers) should pay heed to the realities which Nietzsche and Dostoievsky unite in identifying, since they make the long-term effects of disabling the Mainline Tradition particularly visible.

---

[8] Nietzsche always claimed to distinguish Jesus (though not Christ) from later snivelling Christians, misled as they were by Paul and others: 'There was only one Christian and he died on the Cross' (*The Antichrist* 39).

What Nietzsche wanted was to recast a dignity of man, of the human spirit, which he believed the image-of-God theory cannot sustain; hence he rejoiced in the fall of both Christian and post-Christian morality in Europe. In this respect his critique is pertinent to the twenty-first century as much as to the nineteenth, when he writes (*Twilight of the Idols* 9.5):

> They are rid of the Christian God and now believe all the more firmly that they must cling to Christian morality. That is an English consistency; we do not wish to hold it against little moralizing females à la Eliot ... When the English actually believe that they know 'intuitively' what is good and evil, when they therefore suppose they no longer require Christianity as the guarantee of morality, we merely witness the *effects* of the domination of the Christian moral judgments.

To be rid of post-Christian as well as Christian morality is not to be rid of 'morality' altogether. According to Nietzsche, however, *every possible* moral system can be explained as a defence constructed by inferior people (as Plato's Callicles had claimed earlier) against the natural strength and will of a master-class. What genealogy can demonstrate is that these constructions can be unmasked as resulting from the resentment and impotence of the weak. Time and again this has been spectacularly successful. Its cleverer practitioners (like 'Socrates' and Plato) persuade the strong that they should take heed of it as a proper restriction of their own will.

But here Nietzsche may have trouble: it seems legitimate to ask why, if every moral system – indeed presumably every value-system – is to be recognized as pathetic, he can legitimately proclaim the superiority of the master-morality to that of the slaves. Indeed, at this point the Hegelian 'Spirit' seems to have made something of a return, while in the process allowing for yet another division of those who superficially all look like similar human beings, but of whom most are mere animals and a few are capable of a higher life. We know some of those belonging to the master-group: Goethe, Socrates, Shakespeare, Beethoven. The problem is, what justification can Nietzsche have for holding, in defiance of Christian as well as bourgeois post-Christian morality, that such as these people are 'worth' more than the many slaves?

As we have already seen, their worth is connected with their (godlike) creativity, their capacity, above all, to produce art from misery, beauty from bleakness, in a creativity which, given the nature of the world, can only be the effect of overcoming our ordinary selves: in a process involving great courage and much suffering (*Will to Power* 1041). The 'herd' merely resort to ordinary procreation: an apparently easy and painless version of 'creation'. As we have seen, from the very beginnings of his philosophical career with *The Birth of Tragedy*, Nietzsche had associated creativity with a more-than-human suffering: thus 'I know no more heart-rending reading than Shakespeare: what must a man have suffered to have such a need of being a buffoon?' (*Ecce Homo* II 4). (We may wonder whether he has unwittingly penetrated the pain of Shakespeare's concealed recusancy.)

There is general agreement as to the influence on Nietzsche's thought of Plato's *Symposium*: at least of the relentless drive for perfection outlined there. For Nietzsche (as for Plato) that drive is for a creative greatness, although for Nietzsche this greatness is envisioned as a creativity of which artistic creativity is the greatest instantiation; it is called forth, however, not, as in Plato, by love of the external Form of Beauty, rather from subjective love of one's own aspirations to perfection. If there were gods, as Nietzsche put it (and as Plato could not) how could I endure not to be one? 'Will a self, and thou shalt become a self' (*Beyond Good and Evil* 36). 'Do we not ourselves have to become gods merely to become worthy of it', *The Gay Science* reiterates.

But why is this form of 'greatness' superior? Why is it 'greater' to be a Beethoven than a master-conqueror like Napoleon (or Caesar whom Nietzsche preferred to the French Emperor)? Is it merely a matter of taste? Is Nietzsche in the end some kind of preference theorist? And if he is, why are we supposed to prefer *his* variety of greatness, of the 'proper' kind of strength? And if that challenge cannot be rebutted, why should we not go down other roads to 'greatness', other more crudely obvious uses of the Will to Power such as that advocated by Hermann Goering: 'Power is my fist on your throat'? That thesis of course may be less brazenly expressed!

Nietzsche would reply that we (and Goering) have misunderstood the Will to Power; it is not merely concerned with the achievement of one's desires; on the contrary, it involves, as we have seen, the overcoming of one's instincts, the taming of those 'Dionysian' drives by an 'Apollinian' reason which through suffering sublimates them into a higher perfection. But this might look somewhat Kantian and suffer from the weaknesses of Kant's own moral theory. For reason still conveys no value of itself, however effective in overcoming our instincts and pushing us towards becoming the 'overman'. Like Kant, it might seem, Nietzsche respects reason (though understanding it differently), but he is no more entitled to claim it as value-bestowing (or even obligation-bestowing). Certainly, he resembles Kant in rejecting the 'Mainline' person (that blend of body, mind and soul seen as constituting an intrinsically valuable person in a theistic universe), but how are we to understand his alternative?

Ex hypothesi Nietzsche's answer, as we have seen, will be in terms of the Will to Power; we have not grasped how it presents itself in the overman. Though in the snivelling herd it is deployed in futile attempts to assert their resentments, the overman recognizes raw Will simply as what the old metaphysicians would have called the essence of humanity, the authentic self. We are not Mainline persons but raw wills, able to act either dishonestly to deceive ourselves by inventing some version of morality, or to remain unambiguously simple by vaunting ourselves as the new Greeks, as the truth-asserting masters of our destiny. That is what Beethoven, Shakespeare and the rest have done; they have *willed* to create, in that becoming godlike. On this reading man is indeed the measure of all things, but that is to be understood not as man deciding how to organize the givens of nature, but as creating nature by building up his own nature. Here, perhaps, is the little bit of 'Truth' which even Nietzsche cannot live without; here is where he is no nihilist, in that, being Will, he would rather will a nothingness than will nothing at all. Man, that is, in all circumstances is to be seen as his Will. That Will is the new 'person'. But that still leaves the question as to why creativity, through understanding and suffering, is the best 'exemplification' of that will. Perhaps in his account of creativity Nietzsche is not just making a partial bow to Plato's *Symposium* but also – after all – to the Christian idea that God's greatness is shown in his creativity and in the transfiguration and suffering of his Son!

And surely the heroic identification of man with his raw will is what Prometheanism had implicitly aimed at from the beginning: the Nietzschean version adding the imaginative, even religious, 'feeling' of earlier German Idealism to a de-humanized version of the more benevolent 'sentimental' dreams of the previous century. Tragically, however, even if we cannot create ourselves as persons, we can at least deform ourselves and rejoice in our self-inflicted deformity. If Nietzsche was mad at the end of his life, he arguably had lived out that conclusion to his theorizing.

Nietzsche's extreme version of the Promethean hope of escaping reduction to anything remotely resembling the discarded 'person' is admittedly not for the 'herd', not for those who almost deliberately deform their 'real' nature. That does not matter. Being human, let alone being a human person (if these two are, as already with Locke, to be distinguished), is inadequate, even insulting; heroically or futilely, we must work to accept the raw will in a blind universe that we are. Of course, though Nietzsche's theory makes no explicitly racist claim nor in any way panders to the homogenizing and herd-promoting state, it would be unacceptable to Ficino and probably even to those still naïve innocents of later Romantic persuasion. Nietzsche has pushed the concept of man the self-creator to its limits – even if those limits have to be embraced as unintelligible and to remain – propositionally at least – inexplicable.

Nor, of course, can the goal of Nietzsche's journey be rightly compared with the mystic's search for ways to approach (however inadequately) the transcendent and inexpressible God, since for him there is no God to be transcendent and to whom only humility could show the way. For while some of our contemporary thinkers – as for example David Braine – like to describe neo-Aristotelian man as the syntax-using animal, Nietzsche lamented that his anti-intelligible and inexpressible conclusion is far from realized: 'I fear that we are not yet rid of God because we still believe in grammar' (*Twilight of the Idols*, chapters 3, 4, 6).

Hence I conclude this discussion of Nietzsche by repeating the outstanding conclusion about him – and acknowledging the distinction he deserves for recognizing it. More than any other *philosopher* he has demonstrated what happens (or will happen) to morality when God is put to death; and what happens (or will happen) in that post-theistic universe to the person identified in the Mainline Tradition as image of God. Nietzsche 'knows' – as Dostoievsky would put it – why the Mainline Tradition is mistaken. It is because it is Christian.

18

Whistling in the Humanitarian Wind

After about 1660 much English-speaking Protestant Christianity trans-
formed itself, not least among the élites, into first Unitarianism (especially
in what would become the United States), then into an increasingly
godless moralism – and even among the godly morality was increasingly
identified as the essence of religion. The push towards seeing philanthropy
as the best religion-substitute began in earnest with the Utilitarianism of
Jeremy Bentham (1748–1832). However, philanthropy seemed to require
a revised philosophical foundation if it was no longer to be dependent on
religion; that is, normally on the worship of a voluntarist and demanding
God. And changes of religious belief will entail changes in attitudes to the
person.

By Bentham's time atheism had attained a degree of respectability
such that any purported obligation to philanthropy might seem to
require justification. Bentham proposed as justifying axiom that we
should all seek the greatest good of the greatest number of people.
That was to assume a number of underlying principles: first that people
were (for some reason) worth doing good to; second that some
humans are gifted with some sort of desire or reason impelling them
to do good to others. Pleasure seemed to provide the answer: by
definition people like pleasure, so we have reason to set about providing it for them; moreover, agents of pleasure can be induced to act
philanthropically – or will so act instinctively – so as to obtain pleasure
for themselves. It is to be noted, that Bentham himself, asked why he
was a philanthropist, is supposed to have said that he liked doing that
sort of thing.

Bentham's 'utilitarian' project did not arise from nowhere: it is indebted to Helvétius, to the Italian jurist and reformer Cesare Beccaria, and not least to Hume. Bentham thus blended an assortment of earlier ideas about goods-maximization into what appeared to be a coherent system. Achievement of pleasure and avoidance of pain are the parameters of human life. Bentham supposed that axiom would gain universal approval, ensuring that morality is not reduced to a matter of taste. Certainly, the formula looks simple, but the subsequent history of utilitarianism shows that working out how to achieve the requisite goal is problematic. For Bentham had set himself to explain why we should want to act – and vigorously – to promote the good of all others: a goal entailing far more than benevolence routinely indulged; and one which other more coherent hedonists declined to attempt. Thus in contrast to Bentham, Epicurus advised his followers to avoid political and philanthropic activity wherever possible; it involves – as Bentham would discover to his cost – much trouble and even danger; hence accompanying pain.

Bentham enjoyed being benevolent, but in that very fact we can see a major problem he had to overcome: for why should anyone else 'think' or 'feel' that they should be similarly impelled? Especially if 'converted' to hedonism, why should they suppose the trouble worthwhile? Perhaps the difficulty might be diminished – so later utilitarians like John Stuart Mill came to suppose – by improving on the crude accounting of pleasure Bentham offered. Since the time of Plato most philosophers had recognized that there are different sorts of pleasure; and taught that some pleasures are 'better' than others and therefore to be given more weight – beyond the factors of duration and intensity – than Bentham recognized; indeed, Bentham himself needed to claim that the pleasures of philanthropy outweigh the pains it entails.

Thus to the widely recognized problem of how we can perform what the utilitarians called the felicific calculus – that is, in comparing apples with oranges – is added the problem of whether Bentham is even right about pleasure and pain. Other consequentialists might agree that we should seek the greatest good of the greatest number of people – and I add 'of people' because Bentham himself would have extended his benevolence to animals insofar as they can feel pleasure and pain, a matter to which we must return when we look specifically at his attitude to the 'person' – but they might disagree as to the good being the maximizing of pleasure and minimizing of pain. The history of utilitarianism shows how serious this problem was to become, but for our present purpose we need only comment that most contemporary utilitarians (or other 'consequentialists') tend to operate in a more formal mode: maximize the good whatever we decide or prefer that it should be. That again points directly to a 'virtual morality'; to this we shall return later.

Utilitarians, not excluding Bentham, have always been charged with failing to account for justice, since treating some individuals 'unjustly' may maximize the happiness of a larger group – unless we assume that pleasures should be divided into moral and immoral pleasures, and this is to introduce standards of judgment hard to reconcile with the first principles of utilitarianism. Yet the problem of justice is only one of the difficulties which Bentham's felicific calculus – or moral accounting – seems to raise. Difficulties with justice arise because Bentham fails to notice the sort of distinction Kant would make in cases where the happiness of one is sacrificed for the greater happiness of many: namely that individual persons have an inestimable value, to be philosophically represented by the principle that in human affairs the end does not justify the means, or better that the nature of the means must be morally compatible with the end desired. Bentham's humans seem to be reduced to units whose quantities of pleasure and pain can be poured into a common pot so that decisions can then be made as to what should be done or not done for individuals in differing circumstances.

Utilitarian calculations of the better overall results abolish most of the moral significance of what are commonly denoted agent-relative acts, where the good or harm done to the agent, morally speaking, is more important than the achievement or non-achievement of the desired result – which in some instances might lead to the sacrifice of one's own life. The classic case is that of Socrates, ordered to join with three others to arrest a man to be murdered for his money. Socrates refused to obey the order, though knowing that his refusal would not save the intended victim since though he would not be a murderer, others would. Consideration of whether, regardless of my participation, the undesirable consequences are unavoidable is not part of the equation; as this example shows, a crime may be unavoidable, but I am not going to commit it.

Bentham was a humanitarian: that is, he appeared to love the human race. His moral ambiguity lies in whether he does not fail (at least in theory) in love for human individuals and their virtue. It is possible to 'love' humanity and have little love – or in extreme cases none at all – for its individual members; in that case such members are not being treated as persons.[1] That this is a real problem for Bentham (as later for Mill) is corroborated by another feature of his moral scheme: his excessive concern, based on feelings, for sentient animals capable like us of pleasure and pain. Here his position is logical enough, if anti-human and certainly anti-person. For human individuals – whether from Christian or Kantian reasons – are of greater significance in the scheme of things. Though that need not license us to treat animals in whatever way we choose, it does inhibit us from granting them the same moral standing as human beings. And that in its turn implies that Bentham's criterion for granting some sort of moral standing based solely on the principle that pleasure should be maximized and pain minimized, is – from the standpoint of the Mainline Tradition – hopelessly incomplete.

In the case of Bentham's moral judgments about animals – as perhaps even about human beings – we must rely on the concept of 'standing' – that is, standing in our own eyes (or dare one say with reference to our virtue?) – rather than on rights. In an echo of Hobbes, natural rights, for Bentham – appropriately to his atheistic world – are 'nonsense upon stilts'. Rights-talk must be restricted to legal, that is, man-made, rights. And if no natural rights for us, *a fortiori* none for animals.

In sum, Bentham's humanitarianism, though genuine, lacks a solid rational foundation; thus intellectually is little more than whistling in the warm humanitarian wind. Or, with some of his successors, as we shall see, simply in the wind. If Bentham is to be counted a philanthropist because philanthropy gives him pleasure and minimizes pain in the world, an organizer of the baiting of bears could claim that he is doing the same thing.

Bentham's humanitarian urges represent an awareness of a truth most people recognize (with a few exceptions like Hobbes who has to explain them away): namely that although human beings have base desires, they also have some which might be called good or even noble. The problem – central in modern times since Grotius – is how to reconcile these with a native aggressiveness. Bentham is inclined to think that philanthropy – better schools, hospitals, sewage disposal, etc. – will in and of itself eventually bring mankind to perfection; for that Nietzsche despised him. Yet while there is no reason to believe him, we have to recognize, as did

[1] Scruton (2017: 106–108) draws attention to Dickens' Mrs Jellyby in *Bleak House* as a splendid portrayal of such attitudes. By contrast he points out that the Good Samaritan does not ask himself whether he is increasing the happiness of the human race but just gets on with the job in hand.

Bentham, the humanitarian impulse. Some may claim (implausibly) that our experiencing it can be explained without reference to God or divine providence; we have just evolved that way. Even if evolutionary explanations are adequate, however, the fact of our limited benevolence cannot be ignored; indeed, that we are so prompted is why we are also prompted to claim further that we *ought* to be benevolent.

Perhaps we should invoke some 'error-theory' to rid ourselves of benevolent ideas which arise naturally but remain unjustifiable and are therefore unjustified guides to action. Few would take that route (or at least admit to taking it); more would prefer to follow Bentham himself and suppose there must be – somehow – a coherent justification for something like utilitarian benevolence. What immediately matters for our present purposes is that while, at least according to Bentham's account of human nature, we can easily be induced to benevolence, his view of it is of an impersonal sort, requiring us to love humanity rather than human beings. It would be unduly harsh to imply that all classical utilitarians are committed to this impersonality, yet one effect of their theorizing has been to encourage it: another to enable impersonalists to adapt utilitarian arguments to notably *in*humane social projects to which few classical utilitarians would have been willing to commit themselves.

Agent-neutral morality encourages a modern tendency to devalue the individual, to play down his uniqueness. Then if the utilitarian version of benevolence claims to help humanity at too high a price, a felt need for the improvement and maintenance of social *mores* – that is, for 'social glue' – may point to another a way forward which will satisfy – even justify – humanitarian impulses. To that 'Way' we now turn our attention, only to find it often implying self-delusion at best, blatant lying and deceiving more normally. It may look more 'humanitarian' but will turn out to promote an even more degraded vision of sub-humanity in failing the Socratic test that a life worthy of human beings must be critical.

*

Of course, not all whistlers in the humanitarian wind are utilitarian philosophers; in recent times such music has become the hobby of pop-stars and other celebs. But though their motivation may imply utilitarian ideas, they differ from the utilitarians in that they make no attempt to provide a theoretical account of the goodness of what they happen to feel – though by the sheer force of emotionalism they are as good at arousing the young to pay money into humanitarian coffers as at promoting fornication and drug-abuse at rock concerts. And while they too are hailed (even knighted) as lovers of humanity, they sometimes treat their partners – not least their sexual partners – with less than the humanitarian respect owed to persons.

19

Virtual Morality: Propaganda as Social Glue

My tongue has sworn, my heart remains unsworn.
From Euripides

Ever since the possibility of atheism, or at least the denial of providence, appeared on the philosophical scene in ancient Greece, the option was available that though religion (natural or revealed) is absurd or immoral or both, it may be used mendaciously as social glue; as the best – possibly in some circumstances the only – way to ensure harmony within a political community. It can be usefully employed by bad rulers as well as good. Plato's uncle Critias claimed that gods were 'invented' by a clever despot so as to act as all-seeing thought-police who would promote his own advantage. In the *Republic* (459cd) Plato himself is prepared to lie and deceive in the interests of the state, though insistent that lying in matters of religion is intolerable. And in the *Laws* (2.663d) he notes that if the wise lawgiver *cannot* demonstrate that the just life is more pleasant than the unjust, he would yet have to claim, for the public good, that it is. Of course, Plato himself was convinced that no right-thinking metaphysician would fail to prove the requisite philosophical point, so the need for social glue would only be relevant in a religiously- and metaphysically-cleansed society. Which society in its turn, were it to be a logically viable option, would depend on a very unplatonic account of human nature and capacity.

What was philosophical speculation in the 'god-filled', polytheistic society of fourth century BC Greece was plausible social reality by the nineteenth century after Christ. Atheism – more specifically the denial of monotheism – had been increasingly common for more than a hundred years, though less politically radical thinkers were content merely to welcome the as yet only partial disappearance of a divinity they regarded as immoral if not downright arbitrary and despotic. Religion, according to Comte, had been replaced by metaphysics and that in its turn would increasingly be replaced by science. Sociologists will be the new theologians, and all will be well.

Others were less sure. While Bentham had no time for metaphysics, let alone religion, and was convinced that its impending disappearance could only do good, his successor John Stuart Mill was less certain about the goods which would accrue in the shorter term. Aware that Bentham's purely quantitative measurement of pleasures is crude, he tried to introduce considerations of quality – even though it was necessary to invoke non-utilitarian standards to help in the calculation. Some of these standards derived – perhaps via Coleridge – from Plato, for whose concept of virtue Mill had considerable respect.[1] But problematically the standards a Platonist would invoke in treating of pleasure are suspect for Mill, who found himself in the position of admiring Plato's concept of virtue while rejecting the metaphysics on which it depended. Whether the incoherence left him looking confused, hypocritical or a would-be deceiver remained unclear.

'Confusion' – albeit flavoured by deception – is more likely, being borne out by his attitude to religion. In this he follows Comte, admitting that while he himself had never been religious he recognizes that religion may be useful to encourage obedience to moral precepts. Perhaps that is élitism; Mill is certainly not an egalitarian and seems to favour the 'vanguard' notion that while the élite know better, it is helpful to let the man in the street remain in limited ignorance until he can be brought up to the élite class's high standard and superior way of life. Be that as it may, it is clear that since as a utilitarian Mill had to be prepared to subordinate the means to the end, deception – in the form of encouraging virtual religion as well as virtual virtue – came naturally. We shall see how his tentative approach to deception by the enlightened few was soon to be adopted more wholeheartedly. The unenlightened might eventually be 'educated' out of their ignorance. Meanwhile it is 'perfectly conceivable that religion may be morally useful without being intellectually sustainable' (CW X: 405).[2]

---

[1] For good discussion see Irwin (1998).

[2] CW indicates volumes of Mill's collected works edited by John M. Robson (Toronto, 1963–1991). We should note that on Mill's account of religion, its merits are merely that it can be educative. That is why at some point he thought that a possible Religion of

That such assumptions lurked beneath the utilitarian surface was revealed with more brutal clarity in the contribution of Henry Sidgwick, whose approval of massive deception in hope of protecting society from unpleasant truths becomes unambiguous. Like Bentham, Sidgwick's humanitarian input is well known – not least in the advancement of women's education – but also like Bentham (and consequentialists in general) a tendency to patronize the unenlightened, if not to despise them – perhaps as not yet 'real' persons – is in him unconcealed. Individuals must be tricked in order that humanity may be safe: or at least it be judged to be safe, albeit when the deceived detect the deception, society may suffer worse damage than would have been incurred had truth been told.

Be that as it may, at the end of his mammoth *Methods of Ethics*, Sidgwick has to admit that for all his tireless labours he has failed to show that happiness and duty are reconcilable. Had he been the Socratic protagonist of a Platonic dialogue, he would have suggested at this point starting all over again to hunt down any mistake in the reasoning thus far. What he actually does is very different: being concerned less to have failed philosophically than that, if knowledge of his philosophical failure became public, it could have disastrous consequences (he deluded himself into believing), especially if it led to widespread disillusion with the utilitarian project. Ordinary people, he implies, cannot be treated as adults; presumably they are not adults and do not deserve to be treated as persons.

Bernard Williams tellingly denoted this attitude 'Government House Consequentialism'.[3] Certainly in the more distant past such systematic deception was associated with those concerned with the gaining or maintaining of political power. Thus Machiavelli argues that the would-be politician in his own Christian society would, if he had sense, realize that he must choose between his religion and his political career (perhaps relying on the insurance policy of a death-bed confession and conversion). He observes more than once that although it may often pay the prince to be virtuous, and will certainly pay him to appear so, virtue (as normally understood) will always have to give way to expediency when the times so require (*Prince* 17, *Discourses* 1.51). As for religion, though sometimes

---

Humanity (as advocated by Comte) would be able to do a better job – as he says in 'The Religion of Humanity' [published posthumously]) – because it eschews eudaimonism and encourages a greater degree of selflessness. Whether that represents his mature view seems doubtful since he came to recognize (ironically enough) that the rituals of Comte's Religion of Humanity 'could have been written by no man who had ever laughed' (CW X: 343).

[3] Williams (1973: 16).

useful as social glue, in the case of Italy it has been very damaging. Christian teachings not only leave us at the mercy of the wicked – and we assume that all men are wicked, either openly or in secret (*Discourses* 1.3) – but also stand in the way of our own political success. Deception is therefore essential if we are eager either to avoid being oppressed or – being more ambitious or 'virtuous' – aim to dominate others.

Our utilitarian hypocrites (and their various successors), though sharing Machiavelli's willingness to resort to deception and lying, will claim to do so for more elevated reasons. True Machiavelli might make a similar claim – namely that he wished to rid Italy of the 'barbarians' – but his 'moral' ambitions are limited. Our modern utilitarians, as most consequentialists, and following their earlier fellows, claim to theorize higher-mindedly for the good of humanity. Thus more recently – to jump forward in following the 'humanitarian' tradition – Saul Smilansky, despairing of the resolution of the free will problem (and of course unwilling to admit theistic proposals to relieve its difficulties), argues that those who believe in free will should be left in their ignorance; or, as he prefers to call it, illusion. And here we reach a 'virtual' morality; morality based on systematic delusion and deception. Citing what he considers the apt language of Jerome Hall,[4] Smilansky notes:

Certainly it is plain that unless human beings are morally responsible, unless they are free agents, to a significant degree, justice is only a mirage. We should, *therefore*, confine determinism to the area of scientific investigation, while in the realm of daily action, personal responsibility and its corollary, punishment, remain persuasive.

Smilansky argues that without illusion morality is impossible, hence that we cannot justly be held responsible for anything: that 'morality' in general and moral responsibility in particular depend on almost certain falsehood and unambiguous disregard for truth. Without truth philosophy is voided as well as morality, and who can tell whether the moral values Smilansky chooses to assume be not also illusions? Even if they are not, we can only follow them if kept in ignorance – this in the interest not only of social stability but of 'morality' itself. And if truth is irrelevant to the free will problem, why should it – for any reason other than a deceptive comfort – be relevant elsewhere? Although Smilansky may deny that as a philosopher he actually wants to *encourage* (rather than merely

---

[4] Smilansky (2002) and in great detail (2000). The quotation from Hall [*Law, Social, Science and Criminal Theory* (Littleton, NH, 1922)] appears on page 169.

condone) illusion, that seems to be what he should logically hold. Yet he claims that he is defending respect for the 'intrinsic value of the [deluded] person'.

This is several stages beyond Sidgwick; although in the same élitist spirit, it is even more contemptuous of the ordinary man or woman. We are not fit to know the truth, not least because we cannot live peacefully within it. For the claim is that we would be much happier if we give up the illusory Mainline Tradition about persons, since we cannot live up to it; better and safer to become zombies. Were this to be widely accepted, it would mark the end of philosophy as we know it and its replacement by organized propaganda. Though Smilansky and others like him may regard themselves as benefactors of what they assume to be (or despise as) humanity, others will view their project as abandoning mankind to a moral and aesthetic – not to say spiritual – desert. Impersonality, understood as reductively materialist survival (its pleasures and pains to be measured, after all, in terms of some kind of felicific calculus) is the best we can hope for. If, that is, 'hope' is the right word. Nietzsche foresees some of the banality of this when he urges that for the herd 'happiness' can be offered in exchange for 'freedom'.

*

Other features of contemporary 'ideological glue' which, if not necessarily encouraging active lying and deception, certainly involve what could be dubbed conscious, if unacknowledged, diminution of the Christian – let alone the Renaissance – concept of the dignity of man. Such depersonalization can take several forms.

First, the tendency among broad-brush 'humanitarians' of an antipersonalist stripe to close their eyes to brutalities, to promote what amounts to a desensitized humanity and to encourage their hearers and readers to do the same. In its modern form the practice goes back at least to the French Revolution and its subsequent admirers. It was not only wild-eyed, poetic youths like Shelley who could exalt in the great Revolution; as early as 1814 Saint-Simon was able to remark that 'the Golden age of humanity is not behind us, it lies ahead, in the perfection of the social order'.[5] Saint-Simon, a friend of Comte, largely saw future progress scientistically and convenient brutalities assisting the right direction could be set aside. In more recent times we have seen many parallels: thus Sartre

---

[5] Cited by Hill (1958: 61).

(surely in bad faith) ignored the atrocities of Stalin, Mao and other progressive heroes, not least of his admirer Pol Pot.

Even in such extreme cases the 'hard left' – as also their comrades on the far right – regularly seeks to minimize or even condone atrocities with a 'Your torturers were far worse than ours'! Typically, in the Spanish Civil War, according to the right all the barbarism was the work of the communists; according to the left it was obviously the work of the 'fascists'. In both cases ideology trumped truth as the desire for a propaganda coup took centre stage, and with it was revealed a contempt for the (unenlightened) victims of the deception. In this scenario, we see how only 'right-thinking' individuals can be allowed worthy of personhood. A person is now no longer the possessor of unique and irreplaceable qualities, merely a human being with 'the right' opinions; others are discussed as 'scum', a word applied by Stephen Hawking to the entire human race: 'just chemical scum on a moderate-sized planet'.[6] How easy to move from condoning brutalities to writing the human race off altogether.

And denigration of ourselves is propped up by Darwinism of varying stripes, from the 'social Darwinism' of a Hitler to the off-hand comment of Daniel Dennett on the BBC that 'we must give up our awe of living things'. (Robots are as much use as we are, or soon will be.) It is 'politically incorrect' to accuse Darwin himself of such views – even if they can be recognized in his eugenicist followers such as Marie Stopes and Bernard Shaw, the latter of whom echoed Bentham's tendencies to rate animals with humans;[7] that is misleading and demeaning to persons as defined by the Mainline Tradition.

Yet in one of his letters Darwin himself observed that 'Looking at the world at no very distant date ... An endless number of the *lower races* (my italics) will have been eliminated by the higher civilized races throughout the world'. Even if, though implausibly, this can be dismissed

---

[6] For this and other contemporary re-evaluations of human worth see Smith (2010: 187–207). One of the most influential is that of Ronald Dworkin (1993: 164), who argues that any claim about the intrinsic value of human life is specifically religious; hence that for those who read the quasi-biblical American Constitution as definitive, human life should not be legally protected since such protection offends against the First Amendment. Human beings have other rights, for 'rights are trumps', but not to life. Such reasoning seems both to uphold my own view about human dignity and its origins and to highlight the often radical antithesis between what is moral and what is legal.

[7] Not least in his reference to the need for possible eliminations in death-chambers of the 'mentally and physically challenged'. Cf. the striking if passing reference in Young (2013: 228). Hopefully not too many of Shaw's admirers would adopt a similar programme.

as mere description of a probably coming reality, the use of 'lower' and 'higher' signals a more sinister explanation. Whatever the value of evolution as an explanatory thesis, on this history of biology – and especially since much of our own future 'evolution' now resides in our own hands as the exponents and enactors of the evolutionary process – this now widely accepted post-Christian interpretation of the theory adapts nicely to a dismissal of human worth. To the question that arises as to who identifies the 'higher' and the 'lower' races, and who does the eliminating – and to whom, Hitler and others have made suggestions, as do those partisans of more and more abortion who want (following Hitler) to concentrate first on the defenceless unborn, then to move on to the handicapped and the senile.

If it be objected that 'We live in democratic times; no risk of a Hitler now', that perhaps is even true, yet a Hitler may be unnecessary; the activity of successive exponents of human indignity – for whom we are only worth being deceived for our own good – proceeds more slowly but more surreptitiously, hence perhaps in the long run the more effectively. We can observe the underlying contempt for 'persons' – indeed for human beings in general – as measured by some or other ideological standard, in a gradual shift in subject-matter regarded as appropriate for debate in a 'civilized' society.

I have observed elsewhere how Simon Blackburn, one of the more radical analytic writers on moral philosophy, compares the work of a contemporary ethicist to a sailor on Neurath's boat. All the planks supporting earlier (and more personal) moral systems can be removed and replaced, but not all simultaneously, for fear of an explosion among a public concerned that their past beliefs and standards are being discarded. 'Salami-tactics' are necessary, but the final result will be the same; a glance at Blackburn's work reveals a re-organization of our moral universe in the interest of a morally neutral individualism.

Blackburn denies he is an emotivist,[8] that is, a man who believes that moral judgements are emotional outbursts, yells of approval and disapproval; rather, they are to be compared with Locke's secondary qualities, arising from contact between an individual and the circumstances in which he finds himself. Thus there may appear to be a reality-aspect to moral judgments insofar as they do indeed correspond to factual

---

[8] Samples of his approach can be found in Blackburn 1994, 1998, 2004. The last of these is an attempt to read vices as virtues, or at least as good for society, in the spirit of Bernard Mandeville.

situations. When we observe an attack on an innocent passer-by in the street, we react by blaming the attackers. Yet our reaction cannot be accounted anything more than a combination of a sense of moral outrage with the experience of something we have conventionally learned to detest. Our judgments, by which we may be assumed as exponents of one or other of the traditional cardinal virtues, are in fact conventional reactions, mere signals of 'virtue'.

In other societies we will have been taught differently: in Iran if we see a woman in a mini-skirt we might join with those trying to settle the matter with a stoning. In our own society too, we can easily find examples of virtual morality (that is, pretense) in action. Suppose we are praised for behaving in a courageous manner if we attempt to stop an assault in the street; if the praise comes from an amoralist, it is merely descriptive, not the accolade it appears to be. And indeed if we had no more than conventional reasons to act as we did, we did not earn the accolade anyway, having in effect been duped into a reaction which we cannot defend when cross-examined as to why we bothered to get involved – unless of course, we try to construct some argument about its being in our own interest in the long run, only adding to our conventionalism.

But even the appeal to the 'long run' is called in question. Thanks in no small measure to the efforts of H.L.A. Hart,[9] we are encouraged to think that legally only the immediate effects of actions between human individuals need be taken into account: tested, that is, for harms (however crudely specified) and benefits. Hence, for example, however much we are aware (even with statistical backing) of the long-term harm done by, say, the purveying of pornography or cocaine, we cannot 'prove' this and so lack a compelling reason to try to put a stop to it: and so on until Neurath's boat has been completely reconstructed and we wake up drowning in a world in which we have no substantial idea of what its moral contents – nor even its legal contents – should be.

We thus find ourselves seemingly endowed with some sort of moral compass, but with little idea how to read it. Or, to put it differently, we live in what looks like moral space, but have no fixed idea of its contents, so we may just go for what we like or prefer; this, with Bentham, may include philanthropy, but based on no adequate account of why we should be philanthropic. The purveyors of virtual morality may not have won us over to their own position, but they have succeeded in leaving us

---

[9] For reasons to reject Hart's claims in their entirety see Laing (2004).

so confused as to seem morally impotent: hence unable to think seriously about our own nature, let alone personality, if any – unless perhaps a major shock to our moral systems is generated, as by a tsunami, a massive volcanic eruption, or the outbreak of a war. Perhaps that is what Heraclitus, he who observed that massive learning gives no wisdom, had in mind when he said that war is the father of all things. In any case, we can see how the advocates of virtual morality (whether or not as social glue), together with those they deceive, will to promote and may promote a degradation of the concept of the person as developed in the Mainline Tradition. But this time we are not assimilated, nor invited to fantasize, nor committed to an indefensible humanitarianism: we become victims of a propaganda designed to confirm that we are not fit to be honest.[10]

---

[10] There is an interesting parallel between belief in virtual morality (which can easily, it seems, be made acceptable), and a choice not to risk real pleasures but to be hooked up to Nozick's 'experience machine', whereby we can opt for all the pleasurable sensations possibly available in ordinary life (Nozick 1974). Nozick's point is that few would prefer to be wired up to the machine; mine, however, is that we find it attractive to be hooked on virtual morality, supposing in that case too that we are making a 'free' choice.

20

The Way to an Absolute Nihilism

I am completely normal. Even while I was carrying out the task of extermination, I led a normal family life.

Rudolf Höss, Commandant of Auschwitz

Virtual morality might be re-described – if hyperbolically – as a deceptive guise of moral nihilism: a recourse to what is deemed to be in the interest of safety or survival at the expense of truth. In its various mutations it is more widespread than the previous discussion has perhaps suggested, as an article by Richard Robinson, written some eighty years ago, confirms. In 'The emotive theory of ethics', Robinson (1948) claims that no moral judgments are true, yet he does not reject morality, being in this not unlike those Feuerbachian clergymen who deny the existence of God but claim not to be atheists. Such perversities should, of course, be distinguished from the opinions of moral-sense theorists such as Hutcheson and Hume whose claim that we possess a moral sense is intended as empirical, pointing to objective fact about human nature. That may be mistaken but does not involve deception, hence cannot be denoted a *dishonest* nihilism.

Yet if there is a dishonest nihilism, can there be an honest version? We must distinguish between a strictly *moral* nihilism and nihilist claims about the total meaninglessness of *all* human activity. A moral nihilism, however, may point towards absolute nihilism, hence we must examine it further to see what would be required to generate the absolute version.

And looking at Western accounts of the person in a wider context, we may recognize possible candidates for the role of 'honest' *moral* nihilist.

One of them is splendidly portrayed by Plato – ever ready to look reality in the face – in the character of Thrasymachus in the first book of the *Republic*. Thrasymachus argues that we live in a morality-free universe; there are self-centred preferences but no moral standards. He notes, however, that some 'bad' people show much sense and should be regarded as role models, thus depriving himself of the right to be an absolute nihilist.

For Thrasymachus what are called virtues are beliefs about behaviour that the naive have been duped by the more hard-headed into accepting. But whereas Blackburn, Smilansky and the others discussed in the previous chapter also want to dupe the public, they claim that this is not just for the purpose of exploitation; they believe that for the unenlightened virtual morality is a benefit. Thrasymachus, however, thinks that whether the deluded moral beliefs of the naive benefit them or not is irrelevant; all that matters is that they benefit the 'real rulers': a more extreme attitude. He does not even pretend that his version of virtual morality does the duped any good – beyond, that is, avoiding the savageries the stronger might impose on the naive if they come to believe that they should throw off their moral shackles and do what Plato treats of in the next book of the *Republic*: band together to enforce their will on the enlightened.

Bernard Mandeville, with one side of his mouth – for, as we have seen, he professes both the goodness and the practical disadvantages of virtue – offered his eighteenth-century readers something similarly Thrasymachean in his 'Enlightenment' *Fable of the Bees*. But Mandeville, though much read and much vilified, was ahead of his time, and made little attempt to draw metaphysical conclusions from his ideas about morality. And neither Thrasymachus nor Mandeville qualifies as an absolute nihilist; both offer a set of approved, even constructive values.

What about the Marquis de Sade? Perhaps his total denial of morality is some form of honest nihilism; it certainly cannot be identified as Prometheanism, since he seems to suggest there are no values of *any* kind – and *that* is no mere denial of morality. In effect, Sade claims that he is entitled to behave like an animal since nothing is forbidden by nature, but that is to assume not only that nature licenses us to do whatever we feel like – not least if we feel like being cruel and generally destructive – but that human nature can give us no legitimate sense of right and wrong. Yet we do have that sense in a way to which no animal can aspire. We can license ourselves to be cruel and destructive; animals have no option.

It seems that Sade's apparent nihilism depends on a mere and apparently willed mistake about consciousness and cannot be taken seriously as an intelligible claim to nihilism. It shares its cruelty and destructiveness with some possibly 'honest' version of absolute nihilism, but its reasons for doing so are quite distinct. In a later chapter, we shall identify the nearest approaches to actual nihilism – and its perpetrators would never have thought of themselves as mere 'natural' animals. Their 'nihilism' was a conscious decision to act nihilistically: not because they are animals but precisely because they can consciously understand the nature and 'joy' of cruelty and destructiveness.

Leaving Sade aside, therefore, we can move to a further possibly 'honest' tradition of nihilism: of those (often post-modern) would-be nihilists who claim Nietzsche as their guiding light, and ask, since we have denied their right to do so, how they are mistaken? And since we have argued that Nietzsche's position cannot be identified as nihilist, it is not unreasonable further to ask whether an 'honest' nihilism is possible, or whether it must remain an anti-personalist dream, extending far beyond the limits of mere morality-rejection, so looking analogously like a denial of the Law of Contradiction For Nietzsche's mode of composition makes it easy to misread his intentions, as would-be nihilists, presumably in good faith, have often done; hence to proceed with our enquiry, we must return to those features of his work which some have read nihilistically. It might indeed be argued that the logic of his position *should* have driven him to absolute nihilism, that even he managed to underestimate how difficult it is to be a full-blooded nihilist and to collapse a moral into an absolute nihilism.

I have already interpreted Nietzsche as an ultra-Promethean, and all Pantheons claim to follow an ideal higher than mere morality. Nietzsche goes further than many, supposing that if we are to be authentically human and face raw truth, we must accept more than the bleak absence of morality; there *are* no *other* truths, only beliefs: moral 'truths' are merely the most pernicious of supposed truths and genealogical enquiry can unmask their advocates for the snivelling wretches – driven by alienation and pride in their philistine morality – that they are. Yet although there is no moral truth, there remains the bitter truth about man and his nature as raw will in a bleak world. To believe that, however, is not absolute nihilism; those who accept that reality deserve respect.

Nietzsche comments on the variations of moral belief from society to society and finds that 'social morality' preceded what he meets among his contemporaries, concluding that there is no justification for any morality currently on offer. His claim does not, however, depend merely on inferences from moral relativism; he believes that there is no good *reason* to suppose that any *possible* moral system is more than a search for power, open or concealed; every one of them without exception is a device to console the slavish whose sense of inferiority leads them to manufacture apparent ideals (*Genealogy of Morals* 1.14). In observable nature, there are no moral values, and with God eliminated there is no further defence of morality available. Nevertheless, honest heroism, though non-moral, deserves praise, for we are capable of applauding the sort of heroic behaviour which elevates us painfully above 'ordinary' styles of life.

Marx thought religion the opiate of the people, Comte that it is something which Western society was at last learning to outgrow; Nietzsche goes further. In his view, Comte and Marx merely want to replace one set of idols by another. Whether the ending of morality is an entirely good thing is, as we have seen, somewhat unclear: Nietzsche merely invokes 'that great spectacle in a hundred acts which is reserved for the next two centuries in Europe, the most terrible, most questionable and perhaps also the most hopeful of spectacles' (*Genealogy of Morals* 3.27). He speaks as a prophet: it is going to happen, and we can either pretend it is not, or if we are 'masters' engage – as did the ancient Greeks – in whatever creative behaviour we will to pursue, in full knowledge that there are neither moral constraints nor moral-metaphysical progressions, Hegelian or other.

Nietzsche held that Callicles, the first 'natural lawyer', defeats Socrates in the last act of Plato's *Gorgias*,[1] yet he might logically have convicted Callicles – as he could not Thrasymachus – of inventing a new morality, a new set of false beliefs, even laws, about natural human action in a bourgeois-morality-free environment. While Callicles believes in a 'law' about the greatness of violence and the endless search for pleasure, and Schopenhauer, despite his roughly accurate view of the world and his pessimism, hailed compassion – though for humanity rather than for individual persons as such – yet both, for Nietzsche, are misguided, albeit Schopenhauer is the more slavish and pathetic (*Beyond Good and Evil* 1.86) since having approached recognition of the Will to Power, he attempts a cowardly, if typically philosophical, escape (*Beyond Good*

---

[1] See Dodds (1959: Appendix).

and Evil 1.86). For the Will to Power points to no ideal or moral law, only to a brute world where there are no 'truths' beyond itself.

Nietzsche's arguments are directed largely against those who hold that morality somehow deals in objective realities (Plato, Kant, etc.); he also despises utilitarians as banal and has small respect for the sentimentalists. Though moral-sense theorists have understood that there are no *objective* moral *judgments*, they look for a *morality* that does not require them. We may label such people as non-cognitivists; from Nietzsche's point of view they have merely rejected objective moral claims and tried to find some feebly sentimental substitute.

Nietzsche eulogizes 'the magnificent suppleness, the audacious realism and immoralism which distinguished the Hellenes' (*Twilight of the Idols* 10.3) and confesses that 'my cure from all Platonism has always been Thucydides. Thucydides and, perhaps, Machiavelli's *Principe* are most closely related to myself by the unconditional will not to gull oneself and to see reason in reality – not in "reason", still less in "morality"' (*Twilight of the Idols* 10.2). (A similar respect for the hardheadedness of Thucydides had been evinced by Hobbes.) Such Greek realism is to be contrasted with the slave mentality, fit, as we have noted, only for those for whom 'truth is the kind of error without which a certain species of life [he means 'most human beings'] could not live' (*Will to Power* 493).

Nevertheless, it is legitimate to ask whether Nietzsche's position (perhaps after all rather like that of Callicles) is that there is a better, or higher, 'morality' which he would wish to substitute for the slavish versions. Yet despite his unfortunate and misleading reference to a 'master morality' and a 'slave morality' – and it is clear that he prefers what is non-slavish – this is no *moral* assessment, merely a personal preference – a chosen mentality – based on claims about rationality, creativity and aesthetics. Some superior humans may act and feel like overmen, and they are 'better' than the slavish in that they have rejected *any* form of moral law; they are to be identified aesthetically and can best be recognized in the vigorous actions of heroes in Homer's *Iliad* or as presented in Thucydides' *History of the Peloponnesian War*. The correct reading of Nietzsche is that the greatness of the masters is cognitive and aesthetic, not moral, despite the phrase 'master morality'. Masters have recognized the universe for the morality-free place it is, and will accordingly.

Nevertheless, a trace of the moral mentality seems to persist in the attitude of the masters to the slaves who should be treated less with hatred than with contempt; they do not *deserve* to be hated (*Genealogy of Morals* 1.10). This may be recognized as an ancestor of Heidegger's claim, the details of which I shall examine later, that inferior humans cannot even die – that is, authentically; they merely perish.[2] Yet even if an attitude of contempt sounds no more than minimally moral, it shows once again that for Nietzsche something still matters; that in some sense 'better' and 'worse' are useful terms, that the word 'desert' has reference, hence that nihilism is not an ideal, whatever his 'followers' may wish.

And since Nietzsche – not to speak of most of his ideologically-minded upholders – fails to make the grade as more than a *moral* nihilist, the question remains open as to whether anything more extreme is even possibly defensible. Nietzsche might have dismissed his own evaluative claims as driven by an ultimately impotent will to power, and therefore meaningless, but he did not do that. Had he supposed himself an absolute nihilist (as he seems not to have done), where would his mistake have been located? Surely in his claim for the superiority of the 'aesthetic' life of the overman.

Nietzsche may have thought he had all but destroyed intelligibility – at least beyond the reality of the Will to Power – for that very Will indicates a certain meaning which it imposes. Perhaps, then, he had dismissed Schopenhauer too briskly; for despite Schopenhauer's pity for humanity he could find relief from the 'absurdity' and meaninglessness of the cosmos in no heroic stance, only in something like the Buddhist nirvana; perhaps our modern would-be nihilist successors are more in his debt than in Nietzsche's. Perhaps there is not even that one single truth, about the Will to Power; perhaps (as Nietzsche sometimes implies) the very concept of truth itself is *always* absurd.

To argue, as some did in the twentieth century, that the world – not simply claims about morality – is *absurd,* is to suggest that Nietzsche, who sometimes speaks in those terms, lacked the courage of his potentially nihilist convictions; he could have become an absolute nihilist but balked at the last fence. But perhaps it is actually impossible intelligibly to express an absolute absurdity. Where playwrights of the absurd – Beckett, Ionescu – have made the forlorn attempt, they can fall into contradiction in expecting their audiences to laugh: for their laughter and feeling then signify, just as does Nietzsche's 'Hellenic' heroism. Perhaps then the absolute nihilist will not chatter about the absurd but try merely to destroy – and for no intelligible reason. Callicles, though far from an absolute nihilist, takes refuge in imagined threats of violence when an

---

[2] *Sein und Zeit* 247, cf. a lecture to the Bremen Club, *GA* 79.27.

intelligible defence of his position becomes impossible. We shall return to this as a possible outcome.

*

Having completed our brief survey of Five Ways of devaluing humans in general and persons in particular – For Five Waysers the distinction is trivial – we may reiterate that the various Ways overlap. Some anti-personalists cannot be fitted exactly into any one group; that seems to be because though they are all driving toward a denial of the value of persons (or individual human beings) some are more unwilling to understand where that road leads than are others. More generally, the Five Ways indicate less a set of arguments than aspects of a common mentality and common culture.

PART IV

PERSONS RESTORED OR FINAL SOLUTION?

21

Parfit and Heidegger

Since Kant, if not before, British (and North American) and 'Continental' philosophers have usually taken different roads – and that despite the fact that Kant himself had and still has a massive influence north and west of the English Channel. In Britain, apart from Kantianism, we have seen the dominance of varying forms of utilitarianism from Bentham to Sidgwick to Moore and, in a striking contemporary version, to Parfit. On the Continent, we started with the various 'Idealisms' of Fichte and Hegel, then passed to Marx, then to post-Brentano phenomenology (in the first instance that of Husserl) and on to Heidegger, Sartre and other Existentialists and post-modernists.

When, however, we consider the nature and importance of the person, we can recognize that the two traditions have come gradually closer. We have noted the parallel between the attempts of Hume and Feuerbach to dissolve the self and to deny the reality of God. The parallel continued on in the scientistic, anti-personalist emphases of logical positivism on the one hand – and less obviously also in the varied versions of linguistic and analytic philosophy – and on the other in a Continental post-modernism found in such themes as the so-called 'death of the author': the claim that even literary figures are nothing more than mouthpieces of some particular cultural trend, mere flotsam on a post-Hegelian stream of history.

It is well beyond my present intentions or capacity to pursue such developments in the detail they may otherwise deserve. Rather I content myself with comparing two recent and representative philosophers. Both, being radically godless, are determined to write a philosophy minus God and thus, if a basic theme of this book is correct – namely that the concept of the person was constructed on the back of beliefs about God and the soul – both in their different ways will argue that as individuals – or as persons perhaps – we (or at least most of us) matter much less than we like to suppose. Our two philosophers, coming from very different traditions, will meet when they confront the nature and importance of the individuality of persons or apparent persons. And in both cases it will be impossible to treat of their account of persons without saying something about an inseparable theme: namely whether there exist objective values (including the possible value of persons) and hence the possible existence of God; or whether we live in a value-free universe in which any 'value' we attribute to persons derives from various kinds of human calculation or just from wishful thinking.

My two representative figures are Parfit for the Anglo-Americans and Heidegger for the Continentals. Perhaps my claim that they have much in common will seem especially strange in light of the fact that several prominent analytic philosophers have condemned Heidegger as having done more than anyone else to obscure and inhibit serious philosophical investigations in the twentieth century. Yet I believe my comparison can prove helpful in that the various ways of diminishing the importance of persons, which in the last section we have inspected in five largely nineteenth-century forms, will be shown to be still 'alive and kicking' in the more philosophically homogenized twentieth century. And beyond . . .

*

In 1986 Derek Parfit published *Reasons and Persons,* a very ambitious book of which the aim was to carry on where Sidgwick had left off: to construct a strictly secularist ethical theory whereby on utilitarian principles we could calculate the best course of life with a precision normal only in mathematics. But it is less Parfit's utilitarianism to which we should now attend; rather his attempt to make utilitarian calculation easier by following Locke and Hume in developing an account of the human person seen largely as illusion or convenient fiction, forensic or other.

Wittingly or not, in *Reasons and Persons* Parfit offers an elaborate update of the early nineteenth-century project of William Hazlitt, in arguing that mistakenly we are too concerned about ourselves, since we are constantly changing. But whereas Hazlitt thought it reasonable to be concerned with our past and present selves but that our future self is a mere projection of the imagination, Parfit argues that we have no permanent identity (except presumably for legal purposes, as with Locke – but why should we make any such *principled* exception?) beyond our *somehow* connected memory chains which he calls examples of Relation R. The 'somehow' is to evade difficulties provoked by Locke's appeal to immediate continuity of memory. Legal matters apart, Parfit thinks 'I' an indexical applicable to a persisting set of memory-qualities or quasi-memory qualities. The 'self' may over time be completely renewed, like a club the original members of which have been replaced though the club itself – in humans the body – persists.

Parfit argued that the consequent diminution of our concern for ourselves at *any* particular time – It would not matter much if we were cloned for, if I perish, my surviving clone will be as good or 'almost as good' as I am – will make us less egoistic, more willing to engage in utilitarian calculations of the general good, more prepared to think that others matter. Even if he were right about such 'rational' reactions, however, it is not easy to understand how we would take on board emotional corollaries of our much diminished importance. If we were diminished in Parfit mode, it is hard to see why we should love (even respect) ourselves, and without self-respect we would seem to have no reason to be concerned about anyone else. We might agree that in Parfit's world each of us has less importance than we supposed – or arguably none at all; that would imply that the rest of humanity shares our non-significance.

One might argue that with so diminished and impersonal an account of our own value and that of others as offered by Parfit, we would make of ourselves exactly what the totalitarian ruler (of whatever stripe) would want to make of us: mere cogs in an economic and political machine. All first-person features which we have noticed as an essential part of the developing concept of the person in the Mainline Tradition get dismissed at a stroke. All that would be left for humanity is a self-recognition as one more biological species, different from other species with a difference little more than a slight eccentricity.

Parfit[1] claims that although such impersonality may seem threatening, it would often be better for everyone. (At this point, like Schopenhauer, he cites Buddhist nirvana approvingly.) That conclusion might seem plausible if nothing human really mattered at all: a supposition which Parfit's more recent gargantuan book *On What Matters* sets out to deny[2] – giving the impression that Parfit wants to move from something close to moral nihilism to a revised version of my Way of Whistling in the Humanitarian Wind. Be that as it may, *On What Matters* is certainly surprising, not least in that Parfit now argues that many contemporary moral theories point directly (though unintentionally, even undesirably) toward that moral nihilism to which his own earlier views seemed also to point. This may indeed be the case, but what worries him is that he and other thinkers he

---

[1] Parfit (1986: 454).

[2] Page references below are to Parfit (2011), published in three volumes.

respects seem 'to disagree not only about what matters, but also about what it would be for things to matter – and about whether anything *could* matter' (2.427): that is, about an 'honest' and absolute nihilism.

To defeat that threat Parfit's solution is that 'some things matter in the … sense that we have reasons to care about these things'.[3] That seems appropriate since he now presents himself as a reformed Kantian: Kant reformed, that is, in a utilitarian direction; this perhaps would have been welcome also to Sidgwick. Parfit relies on the Kantian claim that reason can tell us not only what it is prudent to do but what we *ought* to 'care about' or respect. Yet, assuming that what is reasonable depends on what is good rather than the other way round, we would still need to discover (and not merely to speculate on) what is good and what it is therefore right to try to bring about.

But Parfit now argues – contrary to what we might expect from one of the more recent utilitarians who either assume they can determine what is good or fall back on the position that we should maximize the good whatever it happens to be – that goods, including moral goods, are good *objectively*. This claim, tied to that about the power of reason, is backed up by a sustained attempt to show that Kant and the utilitarians are closer than is normally assumed, while the objectivity to which Parfit appeals views moral truths as like 'the truths of logic and mathematics', thus having no 'ontological status' (2.487), but being what all seemingly rational people can agree on. Yet, though a would-be Kantian, Parfit offers no account of what is specifically moral; he treats rather of what is prudent or convenient or the object of some sort of (obvious?) choice or preference – implying that these very accounts point towards the moral nihilism which he now repudiates as the logical last stage of all moralities *other* than his own! Plainly, Parfit is concerned that readers understood a near-nihilism to be the goal of his *Reasons and Persons*. He of course – in line with what has been accepted as recent current practice – neglects to consider that theistic arguments can relieve the dilemma he has recognized.

Thus, and arguing now *against* moral nihilists, Parfit notes accurately enough that deniers of objective moral truths regularly 'use normative language to make psychological claims' (2.448) and strongly contests what he supposed Bernard Williams' neo-Nietzchean advice that we should forget about the old Socratic question as to how we should live in favour of asking 'What do I basically want' – thus without attending to

---

[3] Parfit (2011: 1.110). In his introduction to Parfit's book on page xxv, Samuel Scheffler summarizes Parfit's position when he writes that '"all such views" [naturalism, non-cognitivism, etc.] tend towards nihilism'.

the horrible things some humans seem determined to want. Parfit's substitute proposal, however, is equally defective, even similar: what we
should all want is to eliminate pain and maximize happiness; what is
'right' simply is 'maximizing happiness' (2.303). But that 'happiness'
seems, as in Epicurus, to be reducible to the elimination of pain; hence
unless we 'really' know something more plausible about the nature of
happiness and the human capacity to achieve it philanthropically, we are
again whistling in the wind. As long ago Aristotle pointed out, we can all
agree that humans want to be happy.

Parfit thinks that although in the past we have done a poor job of
securing 'happiness', the human race is young, and there is reason to
suppose that the future will be more satisfactory, adding, as in *Reasons
and Persons,* that it is likely we shall all come to agree about the moral
good. Sadly, there seems little chance of that – not least in the light of an
ever-increasing diversification of panaceas offered by contemporary moral
philosophers! And if (even with a stronger account of what a person is than
Reasons and Persons offers) that is all that is to be said, we have to
conclude that the moral nihilist, in denying Parfit's ontology-lacking non-
natural values, is in the strongest position after all: that those cited by Parfit
who thought it 'better' for human beings not be born are on the right track.
And indeed, in 'advanced' Western societies, many seem to be implicitly
following this apparently more attractive alternative, as thinking it not
worth having children and that the human race – or at least some phyla
within it – might just as well die out. In similar vein Todd May, a philosophy professor at Clemson University, has recently published an article in
the *New York Times* arguing that it 'might just be better' for the planet and
the animals that inhabit it if the human race died out.

It is a mark of Parfit's stance – specific in *Reasons and Persons* and
never formally withdrawn in *On What Matters* – as a notably modern
(i.e. post-Cartesian) philosopher, that he assumes the only alternative
account of our 'self' to that developed by Locke and Hume to be Descartes' concept of the ego. This rings a further change on a theme persistent in post-Second World War English-language philosophy: that the first
task of the philosopher is to demolish Descartes' 'ghost in the machine'
thesis about human beings, as Ryle put it. Indeed, we may say, 'So far so
good', for Descartes' account of persons is badly flawed.

But it is not the only alternative to following Locke and Hume and
something more Aristotelian has always been a possibility. Yet Parfit does
not consider it, so apparently impressed he is by the dogma that the
diminished account of the person offered by Descartes and other early
moderns is the only possible alternative starting point to his own – or that

it does not matter what the 'person' is so long as we can make him or her (better would be 'it') 'happy'.[4] It is hard not to conclude that Parfit has become aware of the dead-end into which much contemporary philosophical psychology – hence ethics and overall accounts of the person – has found itself, but that he has accepted the received inhibition as to the old-established and unfashionable alternative. Perhaps he is aware that, although Aristotle has been a major inspiration for the current revival of 'virtue ethics' – sometimes this being an attempt to exclude Aquinas – ethics without philosophical psychology and metaphysics goes nowhere but, as Plato pointed out in the *Phaedo*, will always finish up as the following of convention. In Plato's semi-serious conclusion its practitioners will be reincarnated 'next time' as social insects.

*

Turning to Heidegger, we see that – arguably wiser than Parfit – he foresaw the dead-end of Parfit's road and tried – though dangerously – to avoid it. The abiding key to his variable thought (as to Parfit's) is the godlessness – after a brief period as a seminarian; that placed him, from his earliest days, in a morality-free zone where man as an individual person outside the 'right' cultural background, has no worth. His influence survived his notoriety as Nazi and anti-Semite and is still immense. But what is perhaps most interesting about him – historically speaking – is that, recognizing that overcoming death is basic to Christianity – not to say Judaism – which he came to detest, he gave the first serious account by an atheist of the experience of dying. Of course, in the *Phaedo* (64a, 67e), Plato had claimed that the purpose of philosophy is to practice for death – that is, to learn to die in the right way, understanding what one is experiencing, while Christians had always assumed it necessary to make a 'good end', life being, as Gregory of Nyssa put it, a long race toward death.

Few of Heidegger's philosophical predecessors had offered much in the way of an analysis of dying, and Heidegger, profiting from his phenomenological training, claimed to explain the uniqueness of each person's experience of our mortality, dedicating some twenty-five pages of *Sein und Zeit* to the theme. In brief, his claim is that each *Dasein* that is a person is 'thrown into' the world as a living being in which he is

---

[4] A former student of mine, writing a mini-thesis on Parfit, asked him why he did not look at Aristotle's account of the soul–body relationship, and was startled to hear Parfit's reply that he did not know much about Aristotle. Philosophy really did begin with Descartes – and all the earlier accounts of the 'person' disappear.

confronted by the reality of – and the necessity of – a non-tranquillizing 'care' for his own coming death, albeit few of us are able to face it 'authentically', that is, with a recognition that what we are experiencing is our own extinction as the soul separates from the body (though Heidegger has rather little to say about souls and bodies, concentrating, as an ex-phenomenologist, on what is given to us in our conscious *experience* of what it is to die). He even is prepared to say – perhaps in a spirit of unwonted kindness to failing human beings – that his philosophical tools do not allow him to speculate on whether there is some continuing existence after the soul and body are torn apart (247, p. 292)[5]. Any such continuing existence would, of course, have to be proposed as having no transcendental or 'other-worldly' features, for that would take it – *per impossibile* – beyond the realm of Being, viewed, as in Scotus and Kant, univocally.

As is also the case with many recent Anglo-Americans, Heidegger's philosophical fame among those who, often surprisingly, still admire his contributions to thought, grew out of his hostility to the Neo-Kantians, who in his day still dominated the intellectual scene in many German-speaking universities. Also and more immediately it was prompted by Descartes' – and even his teacher Husserl's – seeming lack of concern for 'raw' existence. Hence *Sein und Zeit* won Heidegger the approval of a number of Anglo-American (as well as Continental) thinkers – not least Gilbert Ryle whose review of it in *Mind* was treated as iconic.

As MacIntyre noticed with reference to options far beyond mere Nazism, there is nothing in *Sein und Zeit* – written long before Heidegger joined the Nazi party – that 'could give one a standpoint from which to criticize it [Nazism] or any other irrationalism'. Later, of course, Heidegger was more explicit: there are inferior and superior races. The inferior races (like the animals of Nietzsche's herd) have no history; their members just come and go. At the end of their lives they do not die, they merely perish (cf. *Sein und Zeit* 241, p. 284; 247, p.291), because recognition of the finality of death is impossible for those who cannot look on life with the clear-eyed authenticity which only godlessness can give. Such people, as Heidegger puts it, are 'historically incapable of an active love of the essence of death'.[6]

---

[5] Page references to *Sein und Zeit* are to the translation by J. MacQuarrie and E. W. Robinson (New York, Harper and Row, 1962).

[6] In a lecture given at the Bremen Club as late as 1949, published in Heidegger's *Collected Works* (GA 79.27). The sheer insensitivity – I would prefer to say wickedness – of Heidegger's distinction between dying and perishing, whereby those who perish are in effect mere animals, is well demonstrated (by implication) in the comments of Sokolowski (2003: 35).

That love, however, can only be obtained by the surrender of the individual person to the right kind of (racist) totalitarian state. It is almost uniquely a privilege of Germans. Later, Heidegger claimed that the prerequisites were less racist than cultural, and that Germans shared this cultural advantage with the ancient Greeks. It seems plausible to suppose that it was not least the hardness of Greek culture – as portrayed especially by Sophocles and Thucydides – confronted by the amoral bleakness of a world which thus invited 'heroism' that impressed him, as it had impressed both Hobbes and Nietzsche. Be that as it may, we recognize that Heidegger, shrinking from Parfit's dead-end meaninglessness, harks back to the Way of Assimilation and Homogenization in its most brutal form. I defer further comment on the importance of his attitude to death.

Thus racial – later cultural – theorizing saves Heidegger from the problems in which Parfit seems trapped. For whereas in *Reasons and Persons* Parfit tries to persuade us to accept humanity as comparatively trivial – an attitude which in normal circumstances few of us are inclined to and which Parfit himself later seems to find unsatisfactory – Heidegger preaches that for potential supermen there is redemption if they belong to the master race: a travesty of Nietzsche's non-racist account of the over-man, though driven by a similar contempt for (most of) humanity. Here is the Way of Assimilation at its most extreme: if individuals (as in the case of members of the SS) subordinate their entire will to the will of the state and its Leader, they will eventually win through to Heidegger's curiously Rousseauistic and primitivist ideal of a rustic, pre-industrialized humanity. Industrialization, especially the mechanization of the Wehrmacht, having served its function of eliminating inferior races and the banality of contemporary cultures, can be kept as a defensive reserve. The remaining worthy humans have been redeemed by becoming part of an organic state where individuals are substitutable for one another. They have made the best choice: to risk an authentic death and be deprived of moral responsibility, becoming, in effect, ex-persons: drilled bodies following what they believe to be amoral 'nature' like animals.

The only 'good' point of Heidegger's insistence on national racism is that he avoids the pretentious and often hypocritical high-mindedness (this he well recognized) of the utilitarians who, following the Way of Whistling in the Humanitarian Wind, claim to love the human race. He 'knew' that a less abstract loyalty is required; unfortunately, by proclaiming that it cannot be discovered in a suitably amended humane society based on lives free from totalitarian manipulation, he sprang from the frying pan of banality into the consuming fire of murder.

After the Second World War, as I have noted, Heidegger decided that supermen are not recognizable racially but culturally; the ancient Greeks were culturally proto-Germans, though that might seem rather implausible. Yet his claim to have become disillusioned with the Nazis should not be dismissed as mere self-defence. As we have seen, he hoped that after the elimination of undesirables and the establishment of a primitivist society, those worthy to survive would be free to enjoy their peasant paradise. Perhaps his disappointment with the Nazis, though certainly no moral revulsion, was the fruit of a late realization that they were more 'radical' than he was in that their underlying will was seen to be not to set up an SS-run version of the Garden of Eden but simply a naked destruction in which they persisted long after realizing that their war had been lost.

At Nuremburg, Reichsmarschall Hermann Goering observed that he had not joined the Nazi Party because of 'all that racial nonsense', but because he was a revolutionary. His aim was to destroy (especially anything 'spiritual' or claiming to be 'objective'): 'I thank God I do not know what objective is; I am subjective'; and again: 'Every time I hear the word *Geist* I flick the safety catch on my revolver'. One of the most informative books on Nazism was written by the early-repentant Nazi Hermann Rauschning; it is entitled *The Revolution of Nihilism* (1939). Perhaps in the adherents of the Nazi Party – in their unintelligibly brutal if preferably cold-blooded ('ice-cold') behaviours – rather than in any possible theoretical account, we can at least and at last identify the honest nihilists. Many of those whose opportunities for slaughter and destruction had now disappeared made the ultimate nihilist move of killing themselves. Perhaps their basic motivation was to kill God, or at least to exterminate belief in him. That would help to explain the desperate fury they indulged to the last in killing 'God's people', the Jews, the Germans being, in this perspective, the ultimate Wagnerian pagans. Where Nietzsche argued that the proper use of the Will to Power is to create heroically, the Nazis were more realistic in seeing the proper use of the Will to Power as to destroy. God was the creator; man (or superman) the destroyer – especially of those to whom it had been originally said that they had been created in God's image. More specifically, it is the hope of every genocidal torturer to destroy not merely the body but also the soul, not least in its most 'personal' capacities of conscience and freedom to choose the good.

22

Strawson and Nagel

If the agents only said, 'Helen takes John as her husband', if they used only the third-person component and left out that of the first-person, no initiation, no transaction would be accomplished. The statement would be merely a strange sort of statement of fact, not a performance. 'I' have to *do* something for the act to occur. The third-person discourse alone is just a description: the first-person discourse alone is not a legal act.

Sokolowski, *Moral Action* (1985: 181)

After our brief glance at Parfit and Heidegger, who in their different ways represent the highwater mark of the destruction of the Mainline Tradition, I turn to two recent writers who, again in different ways, have adopted a more positive, but ultimately inadequate approach to persons. The first is P. F. Strawson, who in 1959 published a much-lauded book on individuals with the subtitle *An Essay in Descriptive Metaphysics.*[1] As this subtitle indicates, it is intended as a description of human beings (persons) as a subset of individuals without immediate attention to their possible dignity, though that is assumed, predictably, insofar as they are possessed of consciousness, as other animals are not. Since Strawson's book largely eschews even the possibility of the existence of God, one must assume that whatever value his persons have will derive, as in Kant, from their ability to operate in accordance with right reason. As with Strawson's Oxford successor Parfit, we have also to assume that norms,

---

[1] Strawson (1959: 87–116). Strawson's account of persons as interrelating – with detailed and influential analysis of 'reactive attitudes' – is developed in the first essay in a collection of his papers published in 1974.

including moral norms, derive from rational capacity: thus evil acts are evil insofar as they are irrational, though Strawson offers no more defence of that claim than do most other contemporary philosophers. Were it correct, we should have to assume that the only thing wrong with, say, the Holocaust was that it was irrational.

Strawson's account of a person is purely descriptive, but the description is not without interest, and might be re-cast as a semi-Aristotelianism; it is certainly neither Cartesian nor Lockean. Persons are describable in subject-predicate form, but unusually the predicates can stand for both material characteristics and non-material qualities. Thus, 'Jones is tall' (where Strawson calls 'tall' an M (material) predicate, and 'Jones is walking' (where walking is a P-predicate). P-predicates are identified as such because when enacted they attribute consciousness to the subject: thus, I am aware that I am walking when I am walking, when I am a walker.

So far so good, though it would have been helpful if P-predicates had been examined in more detail; some, for example, will be moral (or aesthetic) and these may distinguish the strange nature of human beings (persons) better than others. For although it is reasonable to say that I am just or unjust, it is more reasonable to say that my body is walking than that my body is just or unjust.

It is not clear why Strawson fails to make such a distinction; however, the omission enables him not to bother about persons as evaluators, moral and other. Certainly, one of the effects of this failure is clear. The ability to walk may appear easily explicable in material terms; the virtue of justice (or the perception of beauty) less so. Perhaps Strawson might reply that the Stoics thought that the virtues are air-currents; but the Stoics were not materialists in the modern sense, being better described as vitalists. To accommodate modern materialism, it would be more reasonable to develop a secular version of Locke's hypothesis that God could have made some sort of thinking matter. The difficulty there is to describe such matter in the language of contemporary physics.

A second difficulty with Strawson's account of persons, reasonable though it is as far as it goes, is that although he thinks of material bodies and persons as holding the 'central position' among individuals (*Descriptive Metaphysics* 246), he remains unspecific about the relationship between them, leading us again to suspect that his vote would go to some revised version of materialism, either that tentatively proposed by Locke, or to some variant on the soul-harmony theory – rejected by both Plato and Aristotle – whereby the soul is an epiphenomenon of the body. To hold that view is to claim more than that the soul cannot exist without the body (probably Aristotle's position); it is to insist that it is some kind of material disposition, as we have noticed (*ceteris paribus*) was the view of the Stoics.

The nearest Strawson comes to offering a clearer picture of the relationship between mind (soul?) and body appears in his discussion of the 'no ownership' account of our states of consciousness. The problem he considers originally arose from the anti-Cartesian comment of Lichtenberg that Descartes erred in arguing from 'I think'; that he should have started with the impersonal 'there is thinking'. But as Strawson notes (following many and not least Plotinus in the third century AD), consciousness cannot exist without a conscious subject; furthermore, any talk of ownership is misguided (including Locke's claim that we 'own' our own bodies). As noted earlier, we are able to transfer or destroy what we own: if I burn down my house, the house is gone, and I am still there. Thus too it is mistaken to think of our owning consciousness (or emotions or anything similar); we need to say that *we* are conscious, that *we* feel pain and pleasure, etc. As Hume realized (and as Aquinas and Augustine had earlier taught), we can only conceptually be separated from our activities. But though Strawson rejects 'no ownership' as normally understood, it remains unclear how he views the 'I' which is conscious in relation to a body that is a necessary condition of my continuing consciousness. It is as unreasonable to say that I *own* my emotions as to say that neither I nor anyone else owns them.

Strawson is prepared to consider that disembodied survival is at least possible, though unappealing in that it would be a solitary existence as a 'former' person, locked into the memories and experiences we have already enjoyed; for without a body, no new experiences would be possible. He wryly concludes that, such being the case, 'the orthodox [*scil*. Christians?] have wisely insisted on the resurrection of the body' (*Descriptive Metaphysics* 116). That, however, might lead us to suppose that he thinks that persons are something more than bodies and that some sort of (ex-personal) disembodied existence is logically plausible. But things are left at that.

*

Our second subject is Thomas Nagel who, in *The View from Nowhere*,[2] starts with a set of questions seemingly very different from those of

---

[2] See Nagel (1986).

Strawson. His basic concern has the merit of facing a fundamental problem directly: whether we can reduce the first-person stance, which we have identified as an essential part of the Mainline Tradition, especially as developed in Augustine but also prominent in that counter-Augustine recognizable in Descartes, to the 'scientific' 'view from nowhere': whether, that is, in descriptions of human beings, the individual experiences of each person can be re-described in scientifically impersonal terms without remainder.

Were that to be the case, persons as understood in the Mainline Tradition as developed from Socrates to Aquinas and beyond, disappear: we are human units, only interestingly discussed statistically as members of the species *homo sapiens*. After examining various modern approaches to the first-person stance (including Strawson's insofar as it seems relevant to his own), Nagel concludes that reduction is impossible. One of the reasons for this, he thinks, is a human phenomenon we noted in Strawson's distinction between M- and P-predicates. Human beings – persons – are apparent bearers of such double sets of predicates. At this point, however, Nagel reverts to the explanation implicit in Strawson's position: that we need to develop a 'dual aspect' theory of matter. He admits that this would involve a quantum leap from our present understanding of matter's nature but seems to suppose it to offer the only way of avoiding some sort of dreaded non-material reality. But to indulge in such desperation is to neglect a more genuine resolution of the problem: it can be argued that the very possibility of a third-person ('scientific') stance depends on the prior condition of a first person stance:[3] to attempt to reduce first-person explanations to third person explanations would then be recognized as precisely the wrong way to proceed. That said, like Strawson (and even Parfit) Nagel reveals – only more openly – considerable dissatisfaction with the way the problem of the person is thus dissolved or evaded – as too with corresponding reductionist solutions on offer. His later work proceeds further – and helpfully – in the same direction.

[3] This sort of specially helpful approach to reductionism is suggested by Sokolowski (2008: 223).

23

Personalism, Phenomenology, Edith Stein

Thus the serial selves in the mould of Hume and Parfit, as well as Cartesian Egos, do not live up to the claims of their proponents, while social and other assimilative accounts of the supposed person point to various forms of totalitarianism, whether 'liberal' or non-liberal. We can therefore return to where we left off at the end of the first part of this study: the line of development from Plato to Aquinas – that Mainline Tradition which made substantial advances towards an intelligible account of persons but which remains somewhat leaky and certainly incomplete.

Before going on look at whether other contemporary thinkers may have discovered new ways to advance beyond where Aquinas left off, I will summarize ideas from the period from Scotus to Parfit which have been or might be attached to the original Mainline project. Such cannot be adopted uncritically, because, deriving as they often do from theories which do without both God and the soul, they will be to a greater or lesser extent incompatible with earlier concepts.

There follows, then, a provisional list of 'recyclable' ideas:

1. A more clearly recognized need to distinguish philosophical/psychological descriptions of human beings from assessment of human worth. This has become particularly important since Kant developed a secular theory of human worth and autonomy which challenges the Mainline Tradition – in secularist terms – and however to be defended – in urging an alternative route to the thesis that human beings deserve to be treated as ends and not merely as

means. This question will provide the best point of entry to a treatment of some of the phenomenologists.

2. The emphasis on consciousness and self-awareness which, though present well before Descartes, took on new importance in the early modern period.

3. The emphasis on sympathy and empathy, which became prominent in the eighteenth century and has recently received renewed attention.

4. The widening of our understanding of the moral nature of human beings, especially in the recognition that as possessors of dignity they may be also possessors of rights – or some rights. But of how limited a number?

5. The possible need to revise the older concept of spirit *if* the 'soul' is to be reduced to the mind or brain or self; even, indeed, if it is to be treated as merely offering a way to explain the relationship between our apparently material and non-material 'components' in some neo-Aristotelian version of the thesis that soul is the form of the body – which may leave us unable to account not only for moral but also for aesthetic evaluations, and certainly for the possibility of human worth and so rights.

Beyond these, we can add two other significant themes, largely ignored or too rapidly passed over before the nineteenth or twentieth centuries. The first of these is the difference within the set of persons between males and females. For there are seen to be two 'kinds' of persons, different biologically and therefore, as Aristotle realized, non-reducible to an essentially absolute similarity. Although Aristotle failed to capitalize adequately on what he had observed, it would be absurd, in any current reflection on the individuality of persons, to neglect or misread this most basic distinction, however it is to be accounted for.

The second theme – to which I shall give less specific attention as outside my immediate concern with persons – would be to follow up the social thought of the nineteenth century, but in more ethical mode. Moralists since ancient times (such even as Augustine) have concentrated on educating individuals in virtue, paying less attention to the institutions within which such virtue is perforce developed. More specifically, they have remained largely blind to what is now termed systemic injustice, or, more theologically, 'structures of sin' – and the negative effect of those structures on individual efforts toward moral self-improvement and the care of the self. In reflecting on how personhood might be fleshed out more fully, this purblindness needs to be cured: without, however, falling into the contrary 'progressive' error of supposing *all* vice due to external circumstance.

Of these current concerns and possible supplements to the Mainline Tradition, it is perhaps most helpful to turn immediately to the first: that many modern accounts of the person emphasize especially the connection of 'persons' with the ability both to claim and to recognize moral worth. Crosby has proposed a convenient approach to the problem,[1] listing a number of common 'human' reactions to violations of human rights – or, better, human dignity. As we move through the list, we shall not only recognize why 'dignity' rather than 'rights' is the better term in which to debate, but also that now, as Western thinkers, we commonly *assume* that to be a person is to be the bearer of an ineradicable and Kantian moral standing. As we have constantly urged, this assumption may be merely that: an assumption.

Crosby starts by positing the murder of a member of one racial group by a member of another. The killer escapes and the authorities, in order to avoid rioting, decide to frame an innocent man as perpetrator. 'It is good that one man die for the people', as was said; yet such a policy would commonly provoke dismay, if not horror, that the rights/dignity of an innocent person have been violated.

Crosby's second example concerns the breeding of human beings. That too seems unedifying; it involves treating persons as mere units, reducing them to the level of animals to be bred specifically for some social, economic or political purpose. According to the Mainline Tradition persons are more than a higher species of animal; nor are they part of an organic whole (as legs are a part of the body) but are to be treated (for most purposes) as irreducible individuals.[2]

Crosby's third example is similar: if one man enslaves another, he deprives him of his right to any degree of autonomy, again reducing him to a sub-human level. His fourth and final example, though also apparently straight-forward, is the most revealing: he cites a woman who degrades herself by becoming a prostitute. (We should note that if she has no other means of survival, the matter becomes more complicated.) With

---

[1] Crosby (1996).

[2] I add 'for most purposes' because I follow Plato and Aristotle in holding that membership of any state worthy of the name entails that our uniqueness and individual autonomy have sometimes to be set aside: as in conscription into an army to defend the country against an unjust invader.

that caveat, the example is especially interesting in that although the prostitute allows herself (or himself) to be used merely as the paid means of someone else's gratification, she can hardly claim that her *rights* have been violated, since she decided to take up prostitution. Certainly, her *dignity* has been diminished; words like 'whore', 'putain', 'puttana', etc. hardly indicate respect.

This example confirms that the Mainline Tradition correctly holds dignity to be more basic than rights; that in all cases where it can reasonably be argued that someone's rights have been infringed, it can be pointed out that rights-claims can be re-phrased in terms of dignity, whereas not all infringements on human dignity can be intelligibly considered infringements of human rights. Rights-infringement depends on the improper activity of another person, and yes, another *person*, since only persons as moral agents can infringe on human rights; thus to be able to act immorally, as well as morally, is a mark of an (albeit inadequately developed) human being or person. Animals and events are neither moral nor immoral, though may be in various ways bad for us.

*

We can now turn directly to Crosby's more general challenge, which underlies all his examples – namely that in the phenomenological tradition we have come to recognize either new features of persons or to understand better those features of which the Mainline Tradition down to Aquinas has failed to provide adequate or complete coverage. We should remember, however, that phenomenology offers but one, though perhaps the most philosophically effective, form of 'personalism': that is, a set of theories which developed in reaction to the impersonalizing accounts of human nature that dominated nineteenth- and early twentieth-century European thought. But phenomenology, not being a metaphysic or a theology, can only reinforce the Mainline Tradition if allied with other and earlier modes of thinking. Though in his later works Husserl himself seems to have reverted to some sort of Cartesian or Kantian version of German Idealism,[3] when phenomenology has remained personalist its most frequent ally has been some version of Thomism (usually and necessarily not Thomism 'of strict observance').

---

[3] A number of Husserl's students – especially Roman Ingarden and Edith Stein – believed that Husserl had so reverted. Whether he had or not is less important from our present point of view than that he was widely believed to have done so. For further notice of the dispute see MacIntyre (2006: 65).

Of course, varieties of personalism have existed outside phenomenology; indeed, it is sometimes argued that the history of 'personalism' can
be traced back as far as the late eighteenth century. I shall not attempt to
trace this history since much of it was of only local significance. I limit
myself to comment on three recent centres – apart from the Göttingen of
the school of Husserl itself – in which some form of personalism
developed in the twentieth century: Paris, Munich and Lublin.

In Paris the movement was originally associated especially with
Emmanuel Mounier and the journal *Esprit* which he founded in 1932,
though its most influential representative on the larger canvass was Jac-
ques Maritain, and his influence was as wide in North America as in
Europe. Maritain read personalism in a Thomist spirit, indeed regarded it
as more or less a legitimate development of Aquinas' thought.

Maritain's personalism was affected, and not only for better, by being
largely developed after the Second World War and in reaction to the
totalitarian dictatorships that marred the history of the twentieth century.
As a corrective to that history, he seems to have supposed that the
problem of aggressive nationalisms could be solved by the development
of international rather than national ruling structures, especially the
United Nations, whose Declaration of Human Rights he did much to
promote. But as the name of the Declaration makes plain, it was about
uncritically conceived rights, not about human dignity. In that it reflects
the eclipse of the traditional and more Mainline language and concepts;
and the Declaration and its authors have made no small contribution to
the dubious notion that something like intrinsic value can be accepted
from the decrees of an organization the majority of whose members are
far from democratic, let alone right-thinking, communities – though such
they may claim to be and are too often able to deceive internationalist-
minded observers that that is what they are!

Also problematic is that such cosmopolitan, wide-loyalty 'internationalism' encourages the idea that *liberal* democracy itself is always a toler-
ant and by definition beneficent model for society; this is now proving
increasingly doubtful. More suspect philosophically, however, remains
that the Declaration deludes the uncritical (or of course those who want
to be deluded) into supposing that *qua* international decision-maker the
United Nations by decree can justify human rights as being more than
mere legal enactments. Older rights-theorists such as Locke of course
supposed such rights to be validated by God. Once again, Man has taken
over from God – even referring to his own decrees as 'sacred' – while
remaining incapable of playing the indispensable role God was once

thought to supply. *Capax imperii nisi imperasset* ('Capable of ruling had he not ruled'), as Tacitus put it of a failed Emperor. When the personalism of Maritain and others took this post-Christian and internationalist form, it failed to find a third and binding communitarian path between the ultra-individualisms of the right and the totalitarian, anti-individualist structures built up by both right and left. Maritain's position remained basically Kantian: persons are rational and possess free-will; therefore, they have intrinsic rights. But even if the premises are sound, the conclusion does not follow.

Maritain's overconfidence about international organizations must be put down either to naiveté or a failure to realize that those in charge of such organizations are as liable to misuse their power as are their national counterparts. He was also apparently of the opinion that one could apply modern theories of rights uncritically without thinking through their necessary foundation in human dignity (if any). In defence of him one must admit that since Pope Leo XIII's concern with rights developed in the late nineteenth century, Catholic thinkers have regularly made the same mistake through not recognizing how far is the traditional Christian account of man's creation in God's image from atheist accounts of rights based on theories of autonomy[4] – despite some specious similarities. Which is not to deny that international organizations, whether governmental or NGOs, despite the flimsy nature of their philosophical foundations, can do much good in protecting the vulnerable. And that is perhaps their valid *raison d'être*. But as we shall see in the Appendix, that flimsiness, as in several prominent instances, can easily lead to deviation from an originally right and righteous intent.

It was from the second personalist centre, Munich, that some of the most effective supporters of Husserl's early phenomenology had originated. In later Munich, especially in the person of Robert Spaemann, Maritain's naïve and inadequate political humanism was avoided by a reversal to a more theocentric personalism. Spaemann himself put special weight on anti-Cartesianism and pointed to the Mainline Tradition, not least in its Thomist form, as respecting human dignity. He broke little new

---

[4] A good example of such mistakes can be recognized in Pope John XXIII's encyclical *Pacem in Terris* (paragraph 5); here the thinking is almost certainly influenced by Maritain – and shows it (see Pera 2015: 112–115). But John XXIII's attitude is hardly unique; similar errors are common among Catholic 'liberals' (like Charles Taylor), who, like Maritain, long to reconcile the irreconcilable. For interesting comment (as well as some playing fast and loose with history) see Milbank (2004, 2012).

ground, however, albeit the clear repetition of well-founded principles can but do good.

That brings us to Lublin, the third centre where a new personalism was developed, this time also under the direct auspices of phenomenology which was introduced there by Roman Ingarden, a pupil of Husserl himself. Yet before concentrating on the 'school' of Lublin (and the parallel development of phenomenological thinking continued in Germany by Edith Stein – also a pupil of Husserl, though more independent-minded than many of those who learned with her) it is important to emphasize again that the more accurate *descriptions* of 'persons' we shall discover among phenomenological writers are still descriptions and so contribute nothing to the *evaluation* of persons *sub specie aeternitatis*; nothing, that is, in further support of the claim that persons are not only unique but possess unique *worth*. That phenomenologists have at times been tempted, in the footsteps of Kant, to think that their discoveries are more than descriptive can be recognized if we turn to a recent and excellent book by Sokolowski on the human person.[5]

Sokolowski rephrases the inadequately argued claim of Kant that human beings are of unique value because they are, each and every one, rational beings; more helpfully he calls them 'agents of truth'. That revision helps us avoid misreading Boethius' definition as limiting rational capacity to 'calculation and inference'; rather, in Sokolowski's words (page 1), it is intended to include 'all the forms of understanding, including those that go beyond language'. But although Sokolowski's gloss points to a clearer account of the difference between persons and things, it might seem – though wrongly – to do nothing to help with the question of human *dignity*. Indeed, too quick a reading might suggest that Sokolowski has moved from persons as more complex, more capable in various very interesting and striking ways than other animals, to claiming (with Kant) that it is this rationality (understood in a broader sense) which bestows unique objective *value*: indeed to imply that moral goodness is to be equated with (a wider) rationality as such. As we have repeatedly seen, this is not necessarily the case.

The problem of human worth lurks beneath the surface of the phenomenological movement from the start: less in its precursor Brentano – the teacher of Husserl in Vienna – whose work on the intentionality of consciousness as directed towards an object can readily be added to the

---

[5] Sokolowski (2008: 10).

Aristotelian base from which it stems; the more so in Husserl himself whose apparent return after *Logical Investigations* to a combination of Cartesianism and Kantian Idealism and whose account of the first-person, appearing to be impersonal and would-be 'scientific', cannot be squared with the Mainline Tradition. And nor can his *'epoche'* – neglect of existence and concentration on essence – despite his reformulation of Brentano's project into an investigation of the nature of intentional acts and their objects from a strictly first-person point of view – which implies an undesirable dissociation of consciousness from other conditions of human existence. We need to know much more about what we are conscious of and the physical and metaphysical conditions of consciousness itself if it is be understood as more than mere awareness or feeling. In Kantian terms, we need to know more about the objective status of those 'things in themselves' that lie behind the appearances. Indeed, it was a desire to return 'to the things themselves' that attracted much of Husserl's original student following.

Problems about human worth continued to cause trouble even among more independent members of the phenomenological movement They reappear in Max Scheler's elaborately orchestrated account of the person and his value – and that despite Scheler's emphasis on what he calls love and his advocacy of 'personalism' in preference to Kantian formalism in his account of consciousness. For Scheler's personalism seems to beg basic questions about truth, and to be unable to detach itself from the 'as if' mentality which lies behind Kant's own account of the person and personal worth. For when Kant asks (in the *Critique of Practical Reason*, B 828), 'What is to be done, if the will is free, if there is a God, and if there is a future world'?, he assumes that these if-clauses point to truths that there is no way of demonstrating. Thus they must be taken on faith as given for our consciousness.

According to Scheler, Kant's ethics superseded Aristotle's and hence the Mainline tradition and the metaphysics on which that tradition depends.[6] Phenomenologists should, he argues, work on developing Kant rather than, as I have argued and Husserl originally supposed, demonstrating his inadequacies: not, that is, by abandoning his conclusion that

---

[6] See for example Scheler's comments in the Preface to the third edition of *Formalism in Ethics and Non-Formal Ethics of Values* (1973), where he accuses Hartmann and 'Catholic Scholasticism' of reading non-Aristotelian material into Aristotle. Scheler adds that his own work presupposes Kant's destruction of Aristotelianism, in that remaining a captive of Kant, as of Descartes.

human beings should for moral rather than for prudential reasons be treated as ends and not only as means, but by explaining why his defence of that claim is inadequate, dependent as it is on a wider series of errors about the human person which developed exponentially since Bacon, Descartes and Hobbes: dependent above all on his acceptance of Hume's inadequate account of what is given in perception. For – to recycle an older example – Hume seems to suppose, and Kant to accept, that what we are given in perception is not Plato's wagon but something more like the hundred pieces of wood; the 'impressions' rather than that of which they are impressions.

Scheler claimed that Kant has replaced Aristotle as the starting point for ethics, especially for a just estimate of the person and the possibility of 'values' – or, better, 'goods'. He was thinking in the first instance of Kant's attempt to free the person from a world mechanistically understood, having found, as he supposed, a license to reintroduce human freedom, immortality and God. Were that impossible, by accepting the mechanism without benefit of formal or final causes preached by Bacon and Descartes,[7] human beings, though unique in the universe, had only to concentrate on understanding nature better, then on exercising their seemingly autonomous power over all inanimate forces (including, of course, inferior animals, if they too can be identified as machines).[8]

As we have seen, such themes had been given an ethical turn by Hobbes, and – with inert Cartesian reason replaced by feeling – underlay the 'sentimentalism' of Hutcheson and Hume, besides pointing to the increasingly impersonal utilitarianism to which both Kant himself and Scheler reacted vigorously. Hence Kant's autonomous person satisfies Scheler's demands for some sort of defence against mechanistic nature, at the price – to which Scheler seems to have given inadequate attention – of making the nature of the person and the moral good itself dependent on an unsupportedly optimistic, even 'Promethean' approach.

Kant, as Scheler recognized, had reduced ethics to a formalism: the good is what the autonomous self wills to be right in so far as it is rational; yet the nature of that right and good remain to be identified; hence values too must remain to be identified. And if rationality will offer only a formal

---

[7] Francis Bacon, *The New Organon and Related Writings* (Indianapolis, Bobbs-Merrill, 1960) 129: 'Inquiries into nature have the best result when they begin with physics and end in mathematics'. Similarly, Descartes: 'The entire class of causes which people customarily derive from a thing's 'end', I judge to be utterly useless in Physics' (*Meditation* 4.55).

[8] According to the eighteenth-century atheist and studious libertine Julian Offray de la Mettrie, man too is just a machine. See Thomson (1996).

account of the good – that is, whatever the fallible reason claims it to be – then there will remain only an option suspiciously like the very Humeanism that Kant was trying to undercut. Hence for Scheler values can only be recognized by the emotions: a lame conclusion from the recognizer of 'emotional infection', and who should be asked how, rationality gone, one can distinguish between emotions that are moral and those that are not!

Thus if Scheler was right to criticize Kantian formalism, he was far from right to accept the anti-metaphysical implications easily drawn from Kant's substitution of consciousness for substance in his account of the basic nature of persons. It is in Kantian mode that Scheler can write that 'the person must never be considered a *thing* or a *substance* with faculties and powers, among which [is] the "faculty" or "power" of reason'. The person is, he writes, 'the immediately co-experienced *unity of experiencing*; the person is not a merely thought thing behind and outside what is immediately experienced' (*Formalism in Ethics* 371). To say that is merely to reject Descartes' *misreading* of Aristotle, whereby qualities are piled on the back of substances like baggage on the back of a camel.

Scheler thus repeats Kant's mistake of identifying a particular feature of persons as of the essence; then, making it worse, he assumes that all 'persons must exhibit that feature – predictably identified as some form of consciousness or intentionality – on pain of falling outside the class of persons altogether. Thus he can write (*Formalism in Ethics* 390), 'It belongs to the *essence of the person* to exist and to live solely in the *execution of intentional acts*'.[9] That is to imply that if through illness or accident I cease to be able to perform intentional acts, I cease to be a person. The same criterion disqualifies the immature: '[The word person] is ascribed only to a certain level of development in man. A child manifests ego-ness, possession of soul, and consciousness of self but this does not make him a person in the moral sense'.[10]

Leaving aside the question-begging words 'in the moral sense', we realize that as with non-performers of intentional acts in general, so young children are not yet persons; hence that if value derives from personhood, they can presumably be disposed of if desired – only a step

---

[9] Scheler's unwillingness to identify many groups of persons as 'real' persons or 'persons in the moral sense' is noticed by Ramelow (2013: 600). Needless to say, his discriminatory moves parallel those of many secular ethicists and not a few compliant theologians (now operating outside the framework of the Mainline Tradition).

[10] Ramelow (2013: 600).

beyond what has become practice with the pre-born. A further anomaly only confirms the difficulty. According to Scheler, as already noted, values can only be recognized by the emotions. But unless the emotions are rational (a possibility the Stoics explain), we have no assurance that they indicate more than felt preferences (as much Kantianism as well as much utilitarianism seems to imply). Love, on which Scheler claims to base himself, also turns out to be a feeling.

The case of Scheler serves to indicate that in the end phenomenology without an adequate metaphysic can explain neither persons nor their possible value coherently; further that it is precisely because of the supposed 'supersession' of Aristotelian metaphysics (in this case the distinction between potentiality and actuality) that Scheler and others are drawn to their barbarous conclusion as to how we may treat the young, the severely brain-damaged and the senile. And thus Scheler's view is only a short step away from Heidegger's distinction between those human beings 'capable of dying' and those others (not least all Jews) who can only 'perish'.[11] Had Scheler not discarded Aristotle so prematurely, he could have recognized that there are *no* potential persons; rather that, from the moment of conception, there are persons with more or less potential and whose natural life is directed to a normative mature goal. We neither become persons at some point *after* conception nor cease to be persons at least until death. There is in Scheler's account a curiously Manichaean rejection of the bodily aspect of persons, attached to an attempt to limit personhood to the ability to act intentionally or consciously. German Idealism more broadly is at the root of the trouble.

Phenomenologists (including Scheler) can normally be sorted with reference to their differing attitudes to Kant. Yet despite Sokolowski's use of Kantian language – as we noted earlier – we can recognize that a radical difference between Kant and Sokolowski lies in their approaches to personal agency. As we shall expect from my critique of Scheler, our fundamental concern must ever be with truth. If a person is, in Sokolowski's language, an agent of truth, what it is to be a person will depend upon the *nature* of truth. For all his misleading use of the word 'transcendental', Kant's 'truth' remains at the human level – even in the case of that 'noumenal' life of the real or 'authentic' self. For as we have seen, according to Kant we are specifically persons in that we can separate

---

[11] Discussed on pages 209 above; for further comment on this and other 'Nazi' texts see Rist (2014: 344–348).

ourselves from mechanical 'nature' and live at this higher 'authentic' level of freedom.

Yet if Kant's demolition of traditional metaphysics be accepted, to be an 'authentic' person is still a fact only of the spatio-temporal world; and it could be argued that within that world, although there are persons and they differ from things, yet the world in which they live – and the truth about that world – offers no warrant for attributing to them any unique *value*, only unique qualities such as, perhaps, freedom from mechanistic determinism. For Kant, a person's rational autonomy is what bestows value, yet he can provide no compelling reason why it should: his unwritten message being that God is autonomous, humans are autonomous: therefore humans have worth. But even his claim to human autonomy is chimerical.

Sokolowski, on the other hand, when he writes of a person as an agent of *truth*, knows that the truth to which he alludes must be higher than the Kantian version, and thus potentially be determinant of the worth of persons where Kant's mere distinction of persons and things, so touted by moderns such as Scheler and his successors, is not. In brief, and although Kant and Sokolowski would agree that we 'should' be agents of truth, in respect of that very agency Kant's persons and Sokolowski's are dissimilar. For, in a better sense of 'transcendental' than Kantians deploy, truth may be understood in terms of a metaphysic that points to first principles more dependable than can be recognized in any possible analysis of subjectivity.

*

The problem of how to interpret Kant's view that persons should be treated as ends and never merely as means recurs in others influenced by phenomenology, not least in the version of Scheler himself. Thus commenting on the thought of Karol Wojtyla – Pope John Paul II – who was introduced to phenomenology in general and the thought of Scheler in particular by Ingarden, Maria Wolter notes that 'the moral dignity of the human person, for Wojtyla, lies in the determination of the self through the free choice of what is good'.[12] From that we infer that however much phenomenology may add to our knowledge of the nature of persons, the value and dignity it (as with Kant) claims to attribute to them depends not on phenomenological analysis of the human person but

[12] Wolter (2013: 110).

on the nature of truth – that is, of the good – and, as Wojtyla emphasizes, on the free choice of truth upheld by such persons. Thus, though phenomenology can supplement the Mainline account of the person, it presents no (Kantian-style) substitute for it, needing to be grounded in a metaphysical account of truth. Which truth, being transcendent in the original Platonic (not the Kantian) sense, will have to be theistic (at very least).

Wojtyla observes that 'there is no doubt that Scheler's insufficient objectivism [about values and the substantive person] springs from his phenomenological principles'.[13] Yet for his own part, while his positive attitude towards the sexualized body is a useful corrective to Christian prudishness, in the *Acting Person* and elsewhere he does little to develop the required Mainline *metaphysics* beyond the point where Aquinas left it. His aim, however, is primarily theological rather than philosophical, being to show that it is contrary to Gospel and Pauline Christianity to treat individuals as objects rather than as (phenomenological) subjects.

With a bow to Kant and Scheler, and buttressed by his reading of the Spanish mystic John of the Cross's 'spousal' reflections on the relationship between Christ and the human soul as developed in the Christian tradition at least since Origen's *Commentary* and *Homilies* on the Song of Songs – and doubtless also influenced by Martin Buber's 'I' and 'Thou', in contrast to 'I' and 'It' [14] – Wojtyla wants to emphasize that if persons are subjects, it is illogical as well as un-Christian for us to treat one another simply as objects. If we do that, we damage both others and ourselves; that, Wojtyla believes, is a universal and in theory at least empirically observable truth which is peculiarly pertinent to the relationship between men and women, especially in marriage. On this 'special relevance', however, I leave further comment till the next chapter, here limiting myself to Wojtyla's related concern, especially in his catechetical series on *The Theology of the Body*: that concern is to go beyond the simple acceptance (against Neoplatonists and others) that we are in Augustine's language a 'mixture' of body and soul. Rather we are to pursue further the view which originates with Augustine (though Wojtyla does not explicitly ascribe it to him), namely that we should regard the body neither as a morally and spiritually regrettable associate of the incarnate soul (as typified by Porphyry's *omne corpus est fugiendum*), nor as a

---

[13] Cf. Wojtyla (1980: 109).
[14] For more recent and detailed discussion of the 'second-person' standpoint in the language of the analytic tradition see Darwall (2006).

property to be exploited (as in embryo in Descartes and developed in Locke and many of his successors), but as the instrument through which love and respect for others (especially but not only in the marital relationship) is expressed. The body thus is seen as the soul's outer showing or representative.

Though Wojtyla – to my knowledge – does not cite Augustine's claim (which I discussed earlier) in his work *On the Trinity* that the body is *also* to be viewed as an image of God, or more particularly as an image of the body of Christ, his remarks are entirely concordant with that conclusion. Nevertheless, and like Augustine, he relies for his 'spousal' interpretation of the relationship between the person (or soul/spirit) and the body on some basic texts from the *Song of Songs* and from Paul's letter to the Ephesians, adding in the use those texts were put to by Saint John of the Cross. There are, however, limits to a contemporary appreciation of spousal imagery which Wojtyla does not always observe. While Augustine uses such imagery to describe the relationship between soul and body, it may be less useful than has been traditionally supposed in accounts of marriage, even while it remains important insofar as it helps us to understand marriage sacramentally as indissoluble. The *unequal* relationship of Christ and the Church, as evoked by Paul in Ephesians, fits better with older traditions about marriage as between *unequal* persons than with a modern understanding of marriage as of equal – though essentially far from identical – persons: a theme to which we shall return in the next chapter.

Nevertheless, and given the intense interest in the body (and more especially in its sexuality) in contemporary – post-Freudian – thinking, Wojtyla's writings point to an enrichment (rather than a development) of the Mainline Tradition, and against the pseudo-ascetic denigration of sexuality and of the body more generally in many exuberantly grim ascetic writers, Christian, Manichean, or Neoplatonist. Wojtyla himself, almost inevitably though regrettably, is inclined to limit the term 'Manichaean' to early followers of Mani and other Gnostics, rather than addressing the 'Manichaean' warp which has blighted some 'respectable' ascetic movements within Christianity itself.[15]

Wojtyla also omits to notice the Aristotelian ancestry of his claims about our proper attitude to our bodily selves. According to Aristotle's *De Anima* human beings are differentiated from other animals by the

---

[15] Not least those associated, in recent times, with some of the writings of Adrienne von Speyr, and hence von Balthasar.

possession of reason and the ability to determine (at least to a degree) their own future. Aristotle's levels of capacity in living species – for nutrition, reproduction, motion, sensation and thought – are not just piled on top of one another. The fact that humans are rational affects the way we use our bodily senses; we regard it as sub-human to eat like pigs or to copulate like dogs. This is what gives its pejorative tone to the word 'bitch' when applied to human (or inadequately human) females. Wojtyla's concern to identify the Scriptural roots of his account of the body seems to have encouraged him to downplay the fact that that Scriptural account can be best elucidated (and hence even confirmed) by the work of a pagan philosopher – Aristotle – who has already contributed much to the development of the Mainline Tradition. We have here another example of a phenomenon we have noticed throughout the present study: that new emphases (in this case on subjectivity and consciousness) can lead us to forget or undervalue ancient truths.

*

Reverting to more exclusively metaphysical investigations, I turn now to the writings – especially the last writings – of a more contemporary Carmelite than John of the Cross (but a devotee of his contemporary Teresa of Avila); also another one-time pupil of Husserl: Edith Stein. For in Stein's still too neglected work – she is conspicuously absent from the writings of Wojtyla who as Pope arranged for her canonization – we can at last recognize the prospect of significant continuation of the Mainline Tradition by an 'insider':[16] less, that is, in any ongoing phenomenological account – as desiderated by Wojtyla – of the human subject as revealed in our proper ethical stance, but in those metaphysical underpinnings she supplies to help give that Tradition philosophical as well as theological respectability.

Aquinas began his *Summa Theologiae* with arguments for the existence of God from which, and assuming the validity of those arguments, he develops, among other themes, an account of the nature of human individuals. Although Stein came to accept the Trinitarian God, so that her philosophical approach relies on her theism, an important part of her approach to the human person does not depend immediately on

---

[16] For comment on how Stein confronts phenomenological analysis with Thomist metaphysics before *Finite and Eternal Being* see Bello (2008), especially his comments on her *Structure of the Human Person* on pages 153–154.

arguments for God's existence but on picking up the baton where Aquinas' account of human nature remains incomplete: on, that is, her attempt to explain both our plurality as members of the human set and our unique individual differences. To do that, she must challenge Aquinas specifically about his claim that individuation depends on matter. Hence she notes that she 'has followed the lead of Plato, Augustine and Duns Scotus rather than that of Aristotle and Thomas',[17] though Stein would probably have been more accurate had she invoked Plotinus and his Neoplatonic version of Plato rather than Plato himself. For Plotinus was concerned with possible Forms of individuals as was Scotus with *haecceitas* (though I have argued that he made only limited use of it).

Perhaps, as I have also suggested, Stein recognized that Aristotle's account was more accurate and less Thomistic than Thomas (and others) have believed. For arguing against Plato early in the *Politics* Aristotle maintains that where there are physical differences there must be psychological differences, hence these psychological differences demand explanation. Stein, accepting that, is thus left with the problem of whether the psychological differences *depend* entirely on the physical differences: a position that might look un-Aristotelian, appearing to imply that the soul is little more than an epiphenomenon of the body, rather than that the body is informed by the immaterial soul.

Stein's account of the nature of individuals within the set of human beings is an advance on Aquinas' precisely in that she holds that matter, by itself, cannot explain individual human characteristics and thus our individual nature. There is a strong scientific argument for that claim in that were it not the case, human differences would be entirely dependent on our individual histories; there would be no significant individualizing genetic component: this would be absurd in light of our knowledge of hormonal differences, and beyond that, of our differing DNA. And that

---

[17] References to Edith Stein in this chapter are to her late treatise *Finite and Infinite Being* (volume 9 of her Collected Works, translated by K. F. Reinhardt, Washington, 2002). The comment on Aquinas, Scotus and the rest is in the author's preface, page xxxi. On page 101 she also claims that her concept of 'essential being' is close to Scotus and is ultimately Platonic. It has been suggested (cf. Salas Jr. 2011: 323–340) that it is nearer to Henry of Ghent's *esse essentiae* and as such actually liable to the criticisms that Scotus launched against Henry's thesis. In fact, as Salas allows, Stein probably did not know Henry and perhaps misread Scotus. The whole debate about *esse essentiae* seems to be rooted in a typical vice of much medieval philosophy, that of confusing ontological with logical truth. The notion of 'essential being' is not, however, immediately relevant to Stein's account of individuation, though, as we shall see, that account would be improved if the logic–ontology relationship were given more exact attention.

points to a further conclusion, to be taken as fact: that basic difference between males and females – leaving aside between individual males and females – cannot be explained solely by differences in unspecified human matter; highly individualized human matter is required.

Aristotle concludes that femaleness derives from the inadequate imposition of the form of man – the human soul – on its material associate. That suggests there is a single form (humanity) and different bits of human-making matter. Perhaps he is confused; he appears to be misled by his assumption that since males and females are psychologically as well as physiologically different, one sex must be *superior* to the other.[18] The 'confusion' may be plausible since, as we have noted, his statement 'Man is the father of man but there is no man', would indicate that each 'man' embodies both humanity in general and his own unique particularities: a view that would make good use of Scotus' insights about individuality and offer the more plausible overall account.

Against Aristotle, and certainly against the Thomistic reading of Aristotle, Stein – avowedly dependent *inter alia* on Augustine's *De Trinitate* (so page 448)[19] as well as on Scotus – argues that, contrary to Aquinas' view that the principle of individuation is quantitatively determined matter (*materia signata quantitate*), no theory whereby little bits of prime matter, fashioned in the case of human persons only by the form of humanity, is adequate to explain individual and unique qualitative differences between persons. Indeed, were that the case, Aquinas – we might argue – would come perilously close to a something analogous to the Averroism which he rejected: namely that there is but one common active intellect for all humanity. In fact, the *logical* role of the 'form' of humanity must be to indicate the parameters within which individual variants in the human race will be confined: otherwise they will not be human at all.

According to Stein, each human person is the result of the presence of a uniquely individual human soul informing the qualitatively distinct matter generated at each conception. In modern terms, that would be why DNA, in the vast majority of humans, is unique to each. At conception, the new person is no mere representative of humanity – to cite Aristotle again, 'Man is the father of man, but there is no man, but Peleus

---

[18] For further comment see Rist (2008: especially 23–26).
[19] For Stein's further use of Augustine to show that the 'will' depends on love (and is no separate power as the medievals widely assumed, contrary to Augustine) see *Finite and Eternal Being* 451. For a more detailed introduction to Augustine's treatment of willing, see Rist (2014: 28–32).

is the father of Achilles' – but results from an unique interaction not of two sorts of prime matter, nor of just any matter, but of a particular sperm and a particular egg which fuse. What is then conceived is not an indistinguishable human being, but this particularly qualified (that is, informed) human being, already endowed with unique traits which will be developed as he or she grows in a unique relationship with the world around them, which in the first place is the body of their mother.

The strength of Stein's case – though it might be improved – is clarified if we look at the recent attempt by Sarah Borden to replace it by the older Thomistic theory. Borden offers two sorts of objection. The first is strangely posed: were Stein right, human beings would be hierarchically arranged, some being superior to others (as Thomas thinks the case with angels). That, Borden asserts, is morally unacceptable. There are two objections to that objection: first, that Stein's view demands no such hierarchy, since for Christians it is not human *qualities* which reveal human worth but human existence: God is no respecter of persons (Deut. 10: 17; Acts 10:34). The second objection is that even if Stein's position did demand such a hierarchy – and what Borden regards as its unacceptable moral implications – the truth of the matter, and consequently the moral corollaries, must depend on a correct metaphysic. But, as Augustine pointed out, metaphysics cannot be rewritten to satisfy various (probably erroneous) moral assertions, whatever be the culture, liberal or other, from which these derive.

Borden tries to restate the Thomist alternative which Stein has rejected, and which involves supposing that the common nature is provided by the form, the individuality of each person being derived from the imposition at conception of that common nature on the individual matter. The primary – and serious – objection to this, as already noted, is that it implies – and Borden seems to accept the implication – that individual differences between persons, as distinct from their numerical differentiation, arise solely through the *historical* destiny of the new human after conception, derived, that is, as Borden puts it, *a posteriori*: as the psychologists put it, through nurture not nature. As already noted, that rules out genetic factors in our individuality, thus assuming that our character is formed entirely by our experiences rather than on a basis of an already 'informed' genetic structure. It is plain that both influences are required.[20]

---

[20] A similar point is made by Miller (2011: 343).

Yet there remains a defect in Stein's account of our nature. Stein shows time and again (pp. 166, 478, etc.) that the 'form' of humanity, our common nature, is embedded in the form of the individual. That being the case, there is no need for a *separate* common nature; to posit one is merely to reify a 'formal concept'. An improved version of Stein's account would propose that the individual form, being the form of a particular person, encapsulates the two aspects of each person's character: his or her common and overall humanity and his or her individual characteristics as developing from the genetic framework which passes on our individual membership in the human race. Interestingly, that would shed light on the distinction drawn in traditional Christian theology between original and personal sin. Original sin would be the effect of our flawed genetic inheritance: a moral inadequacy we all display in different ways, like it or not; personal sin would ensue when, genetically ensouled as we are, we set out on our variously erratic paths in life.

If my revised version of Stein's view holds, we have added a further building block to the Mainline account of the person as a conjunction of matter with an individual soul: a specifically human conjunction but uniquely individual as the concretization of a unique person generated by the fusion of an individual sperm and ovum. Such an account can explain not only our plurality as individual members of the human set but also – and from conception – our individuality, we being necessarily more than substitutable units variegated only by differing historical experiences.

Put succinctly, the matter of our individual personhood is matter not merely quantitatively designated, as in Aquinas, but qualitatively, as Aristotle seems to have sensed but to have been, it seems, unable to explain. More than members of the human species, we are individually differentiated *persons*. Plotinus and Scotus both had tried to develop an explanation of this, both inadequately: Plotinus because he thought that the soul is to be identified with the real 'I' – a view which Augustine first accepted and then, rightly as a Christian, rejected – while Scotus seems not to have realized the significance of the difficulties he had thrown up, thus continuing to posit both an individual this-ness and a common nature, though offering no adequate account of the relation between them.

If the above approach to individuality is right, there are two important corollaries which deserve fuller treatment and are not to be entirely passed over now. The first is that there is no such *thing* as 'humanity': this is merely the name we apply to a concept: the collection of characteristics we identify in individual human beings. 'Humanity' is thus the name of the set. If that is what Ockham meant when he read Aristotle as denying the *existence* of some universals – namely those which refer to sets of physical substances – then he was right to do so; and if Aristotle is on this point well interpreted by Ockham, he too is right.

Furthermore, there are moral truths to be derived from that conclusion. For it makes it intelligible to say of someone that he loves humanity but has no time for individual human beings. Dictators can often be categorized under this distinction, but the phenomenon can also be recognized among apparent 'do-gooders'. I heard it said of an erstwhile colleague: 'Oh no, he is no misanthrope! He does not hate the human race; it's just the people he knows'. But the people we know are, in a serious sense, the human race.

A second corollary is even more edifying and may be to many disturbing. A number of contemporary philosophers accuse traditional moralists of speciesism, that is, of over-valuing our own species. If we live in a world where we can merely describe our characteristics and those of every other animal species, this accusation is not absurd. Even though we are different from other animals, and not least in that we can *claim* to be different from other animals, it does not follow – *pace* Kant (as we have seen) and many of his unthinking followers – that we are necessarily more valuable than members of any other species. As Hume observed, you can't derive values from facts about nature. Any value we have must derive not from mere membership in a natural set, but only from a rational account of how we are unique, non-substitutable members of that set, and even then, only if that unrepeatable uniqueness is the dependent image of something *beyond* the natural order. Arguably only a certain type of theist can logically object to being labelled a speciesist; such alone derive our dignity, worth and rights, not from natural phenomena, but by inference from the existence of a God who is transcendent in the strong sense that He is wholly 'above' the natural world: such that His essence cannot be captured in terms of what we denote 'creation'; rather that phenomena of the created order are to be explained in reference to Him. A Christian Aristotelian will think of that approach as indicating the correct focal reference, hence focal meaning, even focal being.

24

God Made Adam and Eve

The human mother will suckle her child with her own milk, but our beloved
Mother, Jesus, feeds us with himself.

Julian of Norwich

I have argued that, broadly speaking, there are in our contemporary
Western society two very different accounts of 'persons': one Catholic
Christian and comparatively stable and straightforward, though still
incomplete; the other secularist and flexible in that it is given to fixing
some arbitrary criterion of personhood and hence allows some apparent
persons to be disqualified on grounds which vary according to the ideological assumptions or desires of the evaluators. Thus, as we have seen,
the unborn, the senile, very young children, Jews and other such 'undesirables' may be excluded, and so deprived of those 'rights' which 'persons'
are assumed to enjoy even in accounts outside that Mainline Tradition
from which they originate.

Such deprivation may be simply ideological, though may pose as
'humanitarian' ('X's life is not worth living'). It may also derive more
generally from an apparent person's inability to satisfy various arbitrarily
posited conditions of personhood. As to this, such a judgment will depend
not only on ideological goals but on cultural assumptions uncritically
taken to be self-evident and of universal application. The matter is complex because, for example, charges of rights-denial might be brought
against anyone who believes that certain persons may properly be
deprived of certain rights because of their behaviour: as a number of
rights are denied to prisoners. But what about the supposed right to bring

up children to be homosexual, or to have simultaneously a collection of wives? In general, such problems are resolved – at least in appearance – by applying social norms: it is socially harmful, we may assert, for a man to be polygamous. All such determinations will depend on the kind of individual human being one assumes to be the perfect (even if unrealizable) exemplar.

In my discussion of Stein, I pointed out that among distinctions between individuals – as also among better or worse individuals – that between males and females is the most obvious. Yet one of the most serious inadequacies in the history of Western moral philosophy and theology has been the scant attention – until comparatively recently – paid to what the French call *la différence*. Normally in primitive (and less primitive) times – at least before the invention of the handgun – men dominate women through a combination of physical strength and women's necessary dependence that is the price of repeated pregnancies. Hence when Greek philosophers, especially Plato and other followers of Socrates, began to think about sexual difference and its social significance, Plato came to believe it strictly physical and that all minds, both of males and of females, are in effect 'male', enabling him to propose that women could and should take prominent roles in intellectual and political life.

It seems that Augustine too thought that sexuality is bodily only and that when women act heroically, as did Perpetua, they reveal the female mind as 'male'. As we shall see, that, combined with Aquinas' acceptance of Aristotle's view that women are defective males, explains, at least in part – there will also be more general cultural reasons – why those developing the Christian account of the person took little interest in the philosophical importance of sexual differentiation. Even Scotus, who took individuality more seriously, passed by *la différence* without comment.

As we have chronicled, neither Plato nor any other Greek philosopher was able to offer anything like a complete concept of the person: that unique member of the human species, whether male or female, which Christianity came to recognize – at least in theory and in heaven – as a spiritual being created 'in the image and likeness of God'. And for all Plato's recognition that sublimated sexual desire could raise men and women to transcendent Beauty and Goodness, his first mistake – in thinking that sexuality is simply bodily – was compounded by a related second: that we are ultimately just our souls (or minds in the non-Cartesian sense he attributes to mind). Furthermore, although human souls are naturally immortal, their possible worth lies not in their mere *existence*, but in their capacity for a godlike moral and spiritual *excellence*. Sometimes – but not always – he suggests that A loves B insofar as he or she is the bearer of noble qualities; that is, that we love not 'persons' but incarnate abstractions (though Plato would have denied that they are merely 'abstract'). Absent a developed concept of persons – not to speak of creation *ex nihilo* – Plato (like other Greek thinkers), as we have noticed at the start of our enquiry, lacked the option to hold that it is not that humans have certain qualities but quite simply that they exist which might be the explanation of their worth. Of course, it would still be legitimate to ask what difference mere existence makes, and why it makes it.

Plato's examination of the differences between males and females and what such differences imply was developed – and also in some respects subverted – by Aristotle and the medieval traditions which followed in what they took to be Aristotle's wake. If bodies are differentiated sexually, thinks Aristotle, so must souls be, and so far so good, but then the disastrous conclusion: if there are both male and female souls, one sort – 'naturally' the male – must be superior to the other. Hence females are incomplete males and should be dominated by 'real' males by being relegated solely to the private sphere. In an analogous version popular among some ancient Christians, women are not *created* in the image and likeness of God, though they can overcome that disadvantage and gain godlike status by asceticism: that is, by renouncing 'female' 'works of the body' and the bodily senses.

It will be informative to examine that culturally-driven conclusion before proceeding to more theoretical questions. Of course, there are theological implications of such an attitude (as also of its rejection) relating to our understanding of the nature of God himself and which cannot be developed here. For if males are in God's image, then they are in the image of a God who is somehow male or intrinsically explanatory of maleness, while if females are in the image they are in the image of a God who is somehow female or explanatory of femaleness: unless, that is, we are to say that God has nothing to do with sexuality at all. That might imply, as some early Christians also thought, that sexuality is ultimately irrelevant to human nature at its best. And if that were true, we might wonder why we are sexually differentiated. As Christians have sometimes supposed, reproduction, if needed, could have occurred otherwise. But if God determined that it occur sexually, then sexuality has a special place in human nature – even human nature at its best.

In early Christian times, some, especially but certainly not only Gregory of Nyssa, supposed that sexuality was God's second-best choice: a view which could only hinder a proper appreciation of the concept of the person. According to Gregory, after the fall death had overcome humanity and if humans were to survive, a means to ensure that had to be found. That God, it seemed, had distinguished males and female in the Garden of Eden could be explained as that he *foresaw* the fall and made plans to circumvent it and thus somehow restore the possibility of human completeness. All despite the fact that this fantasy has no serious grounding, for in the text of *Genesis*[1] Adam and Eve were created not as second-bests, but as in God's image and likeness. But how and in what sense?

The word that the Latin language supplied, 'procreation', should point to the way in which human sexuality, shared by both males and females, is indeed part of the Christian belief that we are all created in the image and likeness of God. No serious Christian can deny that God is the creator, and that the crown of his creation is the human race, formed in his image and likeness. But as *Genesis* teaches, the male Adam is an incomplete representative of that image; for the image to be as good as it could be, he has to have a partner who, with him, can pro-create in his own dependent fashion: dependent because procreation, though creative, is a second-order activity, itself depending on an original creation.

God himself, so this theory runs, is an immaterial being, but human persons are a special combination of spirit, soul and body, and reflect God as image in that combined character. As we have noted, in *De Trinitate* (14.18.24), Augustine concludes that the body (as well as the soul) of human beings is shown to be in the image of God – more specifically in the image of Christ – by the facts of Christ's incarnation and Christ's resurrection. That the body is by its very nature sexed, for Christians, if not for others, should in itself be enough to show, contrary to Gregory

---

[1] On a previous occasion (Rist 2008: 7) I noted how Gregory's fantasy persists in various forms, and how easy it is to bowdlerize the reasons it was contrived: thus Scola's claim (2005: 48) that 'Their [the Cappadocians' especially Gregory of Nyssa's] position ... cannot be confused with fear of sex' is merely politically correct – and importantly fails to ask why and how justifiable was Gregory's fear. For the continuing Gregorian tradition see especially von Balthasar (1991: 99, note 22): 'Sexuality cannot be derived from man's original state as image of God'; also von Balthasar (1990: 318–321): Sexuality, though blessed, 'is removed from God's image'. And Scola again (2005: 32), more moderately if by way of fence-sitting: 'The question of whether or not human sexuality participates in the *imago Dei* is, on many counts, still open'. The question however, is not whether it is still open but whether there are any good reasons why it should be.

and his modern descendants, that human sexuality is an image of divine creativity.

The relationship between procreation and God's creativity needs further consideration, both being connected with theories of love, and love providing the best evidence for the claim that human beings are possessed of dignity, value, and so (in more modern developments) rights. To see this, we need to return once more to the origins in Greek thought of what was eventually to develop into both Christian and post-Christian accounts of the human person.

*

With Plato and other younger followers of Socrates we have recognized a concern that the nature of women was not properly understood. In the *Meno*, Socrates argues that the virtue of men and women is identical; in the *Republic* and *Laws* Plato urges an immensely enhanced role for women in public life, though allowing in the *Laws* that to achieve such a reform a long battle with deeply entrenched prejudice and ignorance would have to be fought. At roughly the same time Aristophanes notices the growing interest in 'the woman-question' and in three plays satirizes the claim that women should be active in public life. Similarly, the tragic poet Euripides emphasizes, especially in the *Trojan Women*, the shocking treatment routinely meted out to women in the slavery (plus rape at best, gang rape more normally) that awaited the defeated in the endless wars which lacerated Greek (as many of our contemporary) societies.

After all this, as we have seen, Aristotle in effect closes the debate down – though with his very reasonable observation that if female bodies substantially differ from those of males, there must be corresponding psychological differences – by, as we have noted, inferring from this apparent truth that women's roles (and presumably women's virtues) must be not only different from those of men but also inferior, women being defective men. Nevertheless, although Aristotle thinks of females as inferior males, an implication of his remarks is that female *souls* (as well as bodies) are not simply inferior but significantly *different* from those of males. That apparently reasonable view of *la différence* – itself needing to be spelled out in more detail than Aristotle himself offered – largely disappeared below the philosophical (but not the cultural) radar among most succeeding Aristotelians: this probably because of the dominant insistence we have noticed that differences between members of the human species are caused not by form but by matter. As we have also noted, Scotus and more recently Edith Stein challenged that interpretation.

Even in antiquity there were protests against the more fantasizing aspects of Aristotle's view as to female 'inferiority': thus the Stoic Zeno, in Cynic and anti-Platonic mode, still urged substantial change in women's lot in his *Republic*, while Epicurus, scandalizing many, not only admitted 'respectable' women to his school – there were many who thought that no respectable woman would come within a mile of any such philosophical establishment – but added *hetairai* to its enrollment. Nevertheless, in antiquity there prevailed a broadly Aristotelian attitude – which certainly reflected popular beliefs, at least among men.

A similar view prevailed among the scholastic philosophers of the Middle Ages – despite Augustine's stated belief that Mary Magdalene exceeded the male Apostles in the primary virtue of love and was thus chosen to be the first witness of the Resurrection.[2] And with the view that women are defective males enthroned, it went without saying that, while women should be respected, whatever excellence they had could only be a defective version of that of the male, more developed human type. Thus, not even the most obvious apparent difference between males and females – that of sexual organs – caused any challenge to the wide assumption that there was no need to think further than Aristotle apparently had done about this basic distinction among individuals.

In the centuries between antiquity and the eighteenth century Enlightenment – and despite the official acceptance of women's inferiority – much in intellectual, and even in ordinary daily life, might be supposed to have the power to disrupt such assumptions; yet and despite the empirical evidence, the 'official' attitudes were too deeply engrained in the Christian cultures of the times – which might have given attention to the attitude to women of the Founder of Christianity himself – to be seriously called in question. By the nineteenth century, John Stuart Mill – surely looking back to views of women's capacities advanced by Plato and thereafter largely ignored – was able to claim (rightly) that those capacities had never been put to the test; and hence that the prejudices against a better understanding of women's nature had rarely been challenged.

Thus England, though well before Mill's time the growing mood of thinking, especially in France and America had thrown up – along with and partly because of the rejection of Christianity itself, together with what passed for proper Christian evaluations of sexuality – the first loud

---

[2] A common theme in sermons (*Sermo Guelf.* 14.1 = 229L; 45.5; 51.3; 232.2, etc.), and elsewhere (*De Trinitate* 4.36; *IoEv.* 121.1 [*fortior affectus*; cf. Borresen 1981: 78]).

claims that the extension of human rights should include an extension of the rights of women. Mary Wollstonecraft, Olympe de Gouges and Tom Paine became the most audible of those calling for change, and thus and ironically it took the advent of atheism to provoke Christians into thinking more about the relationship between women and men. Indeed, atheism may be seen to have been promoted by this defect – though it appears to be a problem for all religions that a necessary conservatism converts into habits of intellectual laziness.

*

But – to revert to the secular tradition – Kant's moves towards advancing our understanding of the differences between males and females are not encouraging. Since for him all rights are based not on human dignity – as the Mainline Tradition at least implied – but on the need to recognize and promote the autonomy of every human agent *qua* human, relationships between human individuals – more particularly that between the sexes in the institution of marriage – are peculiarly problematic. For Kant every autonomous agent is essentially challenged by the autonomy of other agents: an early intimation of Sartre's quip that hell is other people. Kant's concern about this inference can be clearly seen in his voiced objections to polygamy and implied defense of monogamy.

According to Kant the problem of marriage is that the parties forfeit – he seems, predictably, more concerned with the male – some of their autonomy.[3] In the case of monogamy, the dilemma is resolved by the fact that the autonomy I lose to my 'partner' is retrieved by my possession of some part of *her* autonomy. But with polygamy that does not work: by sharing the women, the husband gains more autonomy than he loses, and the women lose more of their own autonomy since they share the retrieved autonomy with the other women (*Metaphysics of Morals* 277–278). Unfortunately, Kant does not recognize such absurd calculations as posing a strong objection to the thesis that all human relationships must be based on the desired autonomy of each free agent.

As we saw in the previous chapter, the account of marriage proposed by Wojtyla is radically opposed to Kant's thesis. From his reflections on the theology of John of the Cross and on the moral philosophy of Scheler,

---

[3] Kant's account of autonomy must always cause problems when autonomies clash: Darwall (2006: 214) seems interestingly to imply that although Kant's morality intends to respect the integrity of others, it is inadequately equipped to account for an 'I–thou' relationship with its concomitant obligations.

Wojtyla derived the idea that the essence of Christian marriage – and therefore by analogy of all properly ordered relations between human beings – depends on the gift of self: in the theology of John of the Cross that gift is to God, in marriage it is in a mutual exchange between the spouses which is the only guarantee that neither will objectify the other: that is, fail to treat them as persons, but rather as objects to be consumed or merely 'possessed'. For Wojtyla the husband wants (or should want) to bestow his desire and affection as a gift and the wife wants to receive that gift as a means to be able to return a parallel gift to her husband.

I do not intend to examine how far Wojtyla's theological schema adequately describes the empirical (as distinct from the ideal) facts of the case, not least in light of the traditional Christian theory of original sin. What I want rather to notice is that the schema itself implies an ultimately similar but initially distinct set of behaviours on the part of husband and wife: that is, that males and females function within ultimately similar (human) parameters but in their own distinctive fashion. Thus Wojtyla's claim is that men and women, though both fully human, are significantly distinct in their behaviours, and that sexual behaviour gives a clear indication of that. And if different in their immediately sexual relations with one another, how could it not be the case that they also differ in less obvious ways too?

But Wojtyla appears to make a false move through anxiety to follow Aquinas's lead. He wants (though the question is evaded rather than determined) to say that sexuality is strictly corporeal; that the *souls* of men and women are not sexually differentiated.[4] But this seems to lead to a version of the very 'Manichaeism' he repeatedly insists we must avoid. Why should not the souls of men and women be both human souls *and* sexually differentiated, thus indicating that the whole human being is a sexual creature, albeit with a sexuality which, like other aspects of our lives, needs to be 'humanized': in theological terms, to be lived sinlessly?

Where Wojtyla draws back, Stein had already pressed boldly on, and in accordance with her belief that sexual differentiation within the human species requires a distinction of form, not merely of matter, proposes that the soul too is sexually differentiated, setting the problem up in a way which curiously reminds us of the debate between Plato and Aristotle; as:

---

[4] I have noted elsewhere (Rist 2008: 94) that Wojtyla (as John Paul II in *Mulieris Dignitatem*) displays a noticeable unwillingness to speak of a female soul. And that Scola (2005: 97) retains the ambiguity uncritically.

'Does the difference between man and woman involve the whole structure of the person' [roughly Aristotle's view – from which he made the false inference about inferiority and superiority] 'or only the body and those psychic functions necessarily related to physical organs? Can the mind be considered unaffected by this difference' [roughly Plato's view]? 'This view is upheld not only by women, but also by many theologians' (183).[5]

Time and again Stein returns to the theme that there are male souls as well as female souls, just as there are male bodies as well as female bodies (44–45, 88–97, 132, 173–174, 181, 183–187). That distinction indicates an important part of the individuality of each of us as unique, revealing the wholeness of human nature with no bow to any radical separation of soul and body; rather a re-enforcement of the genuinely Aristotelian principle that our individual form/soul encapsulates one of the two versions (male or female) of our humanity.

To understand Stein's position, we need to look beyond the obvious reproductive distinctions between males and females to her account of the wider differences between them – without losing sight of the fact that she would have no truck with the notion that 'male' traits are not to a degree – or even substantially – shared with females, and vice versa. In Stein's view masculinity and femininity – albeit dependent on ultimate chromosomal differentiation – are spectra such that, overall, males exhibit 'male' capacities and traits more consistently than do most females, and vice versa, yet the *mulier fortis* will always effectively temper her necessarily feminine virtues with those of the male (80–81) – and vice versa with more 'feminine' males.

Stein insists that whatever the differences between male and female characteristics, they do not affect the fact that the cardinal virtues (and the corresponding vices) are similar for all human beings, even though most men are more prone to some vices and women to others. Thus, while accepting the point made by Socrates in the *Meno* that if we think about *moral goals* there is no substantive difference between males and females, this thesis is not be extended to the point of denying observable differences between the sexes, such as that most men are stronger than most women; it would be merely stupid – or fatuously ideological – to suppose this not so. And Stein does not shrink from stronger claims: thus, 'Among those who have a thoroughly objective formation, there are

[5] I cite Stein's discussions from her *Essays on Woman* (Volume 2 of the *Collected Works*, translated by Freda Mary Oben, Washington DC, ICS Publications, revised edition, 1996).

certainly more men than women. However, in the *small flock* that approaches the goal of full humanity there seem to be more women than men' (257). With Mary Magdalene in view, Augustine might have agreed.

Nor is Stein hesitant about the traits and capacities to which she draws attention, insisting on the connection between the reproductive and nurturing roles of each sex and other male and female capacities (45, 46, 72, 274). She states that 'the species *humanity* is realized perfectly only in the course of world history in which the great individual, humanity, becomes concrete. And the 'species' man and woman are also fully realized only in the total course of historical [– eschatological –] development' (189): Stein thus distinguishes between our general humanity, our sexually differentiated twin natures, and our individuality both as human and as sexually differentiated (49, 178, 182, 254). Moving to the capacities found more typically in one sex than the other, she identifies male behaviour as more focused, more single-minded and more appreciative of the abstract, while women are normally more 'personal' (187, 188, 190, 255), their interests being more 'holistic' in that they have a 'special interest in the living concrete person' (101): 'indeed as much [in] their own personal life as [in] other persons and their personal circumstances' (255, cf. 45).

We are not to assume from Stein's accounts of male and female traits that particular professions or jobs should be reserved for one sex rather than the other (49). In her comments on abstraction she means not that women are incapable of engaging in abstract reasoning – of this she did plenty herself – but that they engage in it from different, ultimately more personal motivations (45). More generally, she thinks that when women engage in a traditionally masculine profession, they perform excellent service in feminizing it, in encouraging it to develop less of the vices typical of male-only institutions – and vice versa. When the sexes do similar jobs, they will do them in different ways, and that difference will help to enrich the jobs undertaken, making each human activity more roundly humane (254).

Stein believes that males, tending to the more abstract and being more inclined to devote themselves to particular studies, have a corresponding tendency to become one-sided, and – since the fall – to domineer (47, 73): sometimes to the extent that woman is reducing to a 'degrading role unsuitable to the dignity of the person' (196). Women, on the other hand, more concerned with the living, the concrete, and a holistic approach, may be led to superficiality, sensuality and a tendency to take things too personally, thus be too liable to take offence (47, 74).[6] Like many of her phenomenological predecessors, Stein puts great emphasis on proper emotional response (96, 102), holding, like Augustine, that women are superior in this regard, as also in their respect for values (78) – while, and unlike Scheler, avoiding any suggestion that it is by the emotions *alone* that values can be recognized.

As we have seen, Stein insists that the differences noticeable between male and female capacities are intimately connected to their different roles in the processes of reproduction and the nurture of the very young (46, 72, 274). She speaks of mothering and fathering – and inevitably that points to the particular suitability of many women for the 'caring' professions. All this may seem very 'politically-incorrect', banal, even archaic, but so to dismiss it is to miss the truth for purely ideological reasons. Stein cannot be faulted over her insistence on the desirability of women in the professions and in public life – making such reactive dismissal of her claims look like mere prejudice.

Overall, Stein concludes that in terms of a full humanity a small number of women exceed the attainments of men (257), alluding to Catherine of Siena, Joan of Arc and 'the great Teresa' of Avila (201, cf. 204). That said, and despite her view that the souls of men and women as well as their bodies are significantly distinct – 'Where the body is so fundamentally different, there must – besides all commonality of human nature – also be present a different kind of soul' – Jesus is the ultimate role model for both males and females: 'Christ embodies the ideal of human perfection; in Him all bias and defects are removed, and the masculine and feminine are united and their weaknesses redeemed' (84, cf. 256–259)). Jesus, that is, is perfectly positioned, as the ideal human being on the spectrum of predominantly male and predominantly female characteristics and capacities. One wonders whether she would have been willing to say that in that respect it would not have mattered whether Christ had come in masculine or feminine form.[7]

If Stein is correct – as I believe she is – in emphasizing that the perfect 'man' is to be viewed as some blend of 'male' and 'female' capacities (56),

---

[6] For more detail see especially Borden (Sharkey) (2006), to whose essay I am much indebted.

[7] Stein's formulation avoids the embarrassing interpretations sometimes put on Paul's statement (Ephesians 4: 13) that we should arrive at full knowledge of the Son of God, unto a perfect male (*aner* not *anthropos*). For patristic attitudes to this passage see Rist (2008: 38–39 and note 42). It may be that Paul was immediately (or exclusively) addressing men.

there are significant social implications, not only in so far as her claims reveal the absurdity of contemporary 'gender-ideology', by which we can merely will – in apparent autonomy – to which sex/gender we belong, ignoring the clear evidence, if not of physique, then of chromosomes.[8] This in extreme forms would, if politically imposed, bring about not merely the disappearance of the remnants of 'patriarchy' (often a code word for European civilization) but replace humanity as we know it with an homogenized, more or less undifferentiated mass of trans-humans at the mercy of their political designers. Stein herself always insists that we are a fallen race (47, 49, 76): that after the fall the relationship between the sexes has been corrupted by male lust to dominate (47, 73–74) and a corresponding female tendency to defeat this by recourse to sensuality. Such failings, however, vary with cultural conditions: in earlier societies where upper-class women lived a life of privileged idleness, they could more easily fall prey to unrealistic, 'romantic' delusions (190, cf. 186) than would or can working women.

*

If the attentive reader should wonder whether Stein's remarks on the differences between the sexes can be dismissed as no more than conventional pre-philosophical thinking, determined largely by the culture in which she grew up, that can be shown to be far from being the case. To understand this, we need to revert both to her phenomenological formation and to her (later) radical rejection of the views of Heidegger on empathy and the person.

Stein's doctoral dissertation, supervised by Husserl and defended in 1916, was on empathy. Husserl himself seems to have thought that she would fill in some of the gaps in his own account of what is given in experience; in effect, her work pointed not merely to an elaboration of Husserl's *Logical Investigations*, but toward a correction of possible readings of his later *Ideas*. Stein had spent the earlier part of 1915 working as a military nurse and as such was able to expand her ideas about how we can become aware (directly, that is, and not by inference, as held – erroneously in her view – by Mill) of other people's feelings and emotions.

---

[8] For a clear and professional introduction to gender-ideology and its combination of ultra-Kantian and sub-Marxist follies with deluded wishful thinking, see Malo (2017). The disease of willing unreality, however, is far from limited to 'gender-ideologists'. The Vatican recently decreed that ex-virgins can become consecrated virgins. Saint Jerome would have loved it.

Thus, we can recognize the pain of another not merely by the appearance of the other's body but simultaneously as a state of their 'soul'. For Stein this helped to confirm her anti-Cartesian view of the person as a combination of soul and body (as the Mainline Tradition had learned to maintain).

But Stein's account of what is given in experience also takes account of the effects of the necessary relationship between oneself and those with whom one has dealings. We are able to correct our first-hand experiences by listening to the descriptions of others of the same phenomena. Someone may point out to me something I have missed in my observation and tell me to look again, thus enabling me to emend my previous awareness. Thus, first-person experience is always also open to correction by third-person experience; indeed, the possibility that we could ever have developed the ability to be aware without simultaneously learning from childhood on to be corrected seems remote. My unique view of myself is partly due to my experience of the (partially unique) views of others. As others can sympathize and empathize with me, so I can sympathize and empathize with them. As a nurse Stein found she had learned that she could empathize with those who were dying, even though she was not dying herself, and this empathy with the dying was one with her ability to recognize and 'feel with' other people's pleasures and pains more generally. To recognize the joy of another is not necessarily to be joyful; to 'understand' at least something of what it means for another to die does not imply that one must be dying oneself.

Thus in Stein's view, whatever the merits of her one-time phenomenological fellow student and former friend Martin Heidegger's account of persons as individuals, it remains one-sided, ignoring the fact that we are necessarily not only unique individuals in our living and dying, but are enabled to be so only insofar as we belong to a community: not, of course, merely the community of the state, let alone the Nazi state on which Heidegger came to rely.

Many years after her dissertation and now a Carmelite nun, Stein felt obliged, while writing her major metaphysical text *Finite and Eternal Being,* to return to what is the proper attitude to death: in particular, it seems, she wanted to distance herself from a Heidegger now become radically 'unhusserlian': Heidegger's view of death is mentioned in a number of her footnotes and more particularly in an Appendix. Perhaps she believed that his views on death best reveal the basic principles of this philosopher who, after the publication of *Sein und Zeit* in 1927, was to have a major, and in the view of many a disastrous effect on subsequent

European thought. If so, she was right to be concerned; the toxic effect is still in evidence so many years after its author's demise.

Stein believed that Heidegger's attitude to death revealed more general and serious weaknesses in his account of persons and of the human condition. According to Heidegger in *Sein und Zeit* (239, p. 282), we cannot experience the dying of other people in a genuine or authentic sense: that is because 'Dying is something that every *Dasein* [real person] itself must take upon itself; hence the only dying that I can experience genuinely [authentically] is my own'. By 'authentically' Heidegger would seem to mean 'being aware of the true nature of what we are experiencing and accepting it for what it is'.

Although Stein obviously agrees that we cannot live the experience of another person's death in the same way as the dying person – and that we need to face the truth, to be 'authentic' at all times on pain of failing to grow up[9] – that citation reveals just how far Heidegger's view is from hers. As we have seen, in her dissertation (deepened by her experiences as a military nurse) Stein had already argued not only that it is possible – in terms of her own account of what is given in awareness – to empathize with the experiences of those who are dying, but also that this capacity is part of our necessary whole development as persons which depends in no small measure on the ability to empathize with the experiences of the others we encounter: in other words, such a capacity – for all the obvious fact that death is our own death and not that of someone else – marks us out as necessarily far from isolated individuals when facing death, as Heidegger supposes us to be. As already noted, just as we can experience the joy of others without experiencing the same joy, so we can accompany someone dying without being in process of dying ourselves.

Heidegger believes that the only way we can avoid our isolation is for the *Dasein* to be assimilated to the state, but at death that assimilation must cease: the state continues; we do not, even if – for good or ill – we be publicly remembered, such as given a state funeral. MacIntyre observed that Heidegger left behind all the friends and acquaintances of his

---

[9] In line with what I noted earlier about Greeks and Germans, Heidegger's account of truthful authenticity may, at least in his view, be 'Greek': we have seen how he could claim at times that the Germans continued the spirit of Greek culture. Aristotle regards Sophocles' *Oedipus the King* as the greatest tragedy, perhaps because it best exacts the due mead of pity and terror. It seems he thought that if you can accept the bleak reality of life as Sophocles – in this typically Greek – portrays it, you are able to face the truth about your own life and death.

Husserlian days:[10] in corollary of his view that friendship does not overcome isolation; only the supra-personal state can do that – and to death the state cannot respond adequately; thus death triumphs.

Stein believes Heidegger's account of facing death to be flawed in assimilating the fear of death to the fear of extinction, whereas the truth of the matter is that while we fear nothingness, we fear also the *loss* of what we have been and have been given. In the Appendix to *Finite and Eternal Being* (p. 110 of volume VI of the *Collected Works* in German), she writes – with a remarkable, though probably unconscious echo of a passage from a sermon of Augustine we looked at earlier – that the human being is such that we 'desire to receive the ever-new gift of Being ... Whatever gives him fullness, he does not want to leave, and he would like to *be* without end' We recall that the passage of Augustine runs as follows (*Sermon* 344.4):

You do not want to die. You would like to pass over from this life to another in such a way that you would not rise again as a dead man, but alive and changed for the better. That is what you would like. This is the nature of human feeling. Somehow the soul itself wishes and desires it ... No one hates his own flesh.

Heidegger's thesis, governed by his views about the necessity of god-lessness, impedes any recognition of Stein's view of what it is to die, even if he might reasonably discount her account of what is given in experience, as that applies to her account of empathy. For not only must he reject her account of life as gift – and a gift not just to someone but to someone who is, in Heidegger's language, 'thrown into being' – but in his account of death he must also reject her conviction that death reveals a basic fact about the human life into which we are 'thrown': namely that we are dependent, and that dependence remains up to the moment of death and affects the account of it. For Heidegger, now that the state is no longer relevant, there is nothing left but the assertion that facing death boldly and honestly is the authentic mark of real humanity of which animals (and many humans) are incapable. For Stein, death should help us realize not the need to assert but the need to recognize our dependence: in humility.

As we saw earlier, empathy became important in accounts of the person with the British sentimentalists, and perhaps most informatively in novels, beginning with those of Richardson. But such portrayals lacked accurate philosophical description – until the appearance, that is, of Edith

---

[10] MacIntyre (2006: 185).

Stein. So here too, as well as in her account of the uniqueness of the individual, she can be recognized as having added important considerations to the possibilities of the Mainline Tradition which was on hand when she realized that her phenomenological studies needed to be set in a more strictly ontological framework.

We conclude that Stein's views – whether on the role of souls of individuals and on the soul's being also, as is the body, sexually differentiated, whether in her examination of empathy as in her rejection of Heideggerian and by implication post-Heideggerian accounts of the 'authentic' death – offer substantial developments of the Mainline Tradition, pointing to much of what Aristotle might have said, but at least in the case of sexual differentiation, will have been too culture-bound to be able to perceive. This she was enabled to do by developing the phenomenology of Husserl metaphysically, while accepting Husserl's refusal to turn metaphysics into logic and psychology – and by facing down the radical challenge to the Mainline Tradition represented by Heidegger.

*

Beside its value in understanding *la différence*, Stein's work contributes to current debates about homosexuality. She believed that humanity is best served if men and women are allowed to complement one another, both reproductively and in social activities more widely, and since to participate in continuing the human race would seem to be a desirable human good and only to be foregone – as she herself forewent it – for good reasons – it follows that choice of a homosexual lifestyle will run counter to the best interests of the individuals concerned and of the human race in general. Leaving aside the possible (though increasingly recognized as uncompelling) genetic factors sometimes evoked to explain choice of such a lifestyle, the encouragement of it for fashionable or ideological reasons becomes entirely undesirable – even apart from the effect upon and possible abuse of children brought up in a homosexual 'family'. On Stein's account homosexuality should be considered a deviation from the right course, deriving from some kind of human malfunction, whether genetic or (more normally) moral, and whether or not accounted for, as Freud plausibly if embarrassingly explained it, by an ongoing state of arrested development. Whatever their other misbehaviours, our first parents (even after the Fall) were not homosexual. For the Mainline Tradition it must remain true that God created Adam and Eve, not Adam and Steve.

Epilogue or Epitaph?

If the salt has lost its savour, wherewith will it be salted?
Matthew 5:13

In this extended essay I have traced the origins of a number of contemporary disputes about the nature of the human person, setting them against what I have identified as the 'Mainline Tradition': that is, what was to become a specifically Christian account of the human person gradually built up from its philosophical origins in Greece and the theology of the Hebrew Bible and through Christian centuries in Europe down to the High Middle Ages. I have argued that a substantial portion of such an account had been developed – though still presented somewhat incoherently – by the time of Thomas Aquinas in the late thirteenth century. I have then gone on to show how although subsequent thinkers right down to our own time have added potentially important material to the tradition – not least by extending accounts of self-awareness and the human powers of imagination – there has also developed what can be seen as an attempt, whether more or less conscious, to demolish the earlier Tradition and substitute something very different: a supposedly more scientifically objective and impersonal 'contemporary' account of human nature that has the effect of calling that nature's ultimate worth ever more into question.

This secondary 'tradition', I have argued, depends on more general metaphysical claims such as arguments against the very existence of God and for the replacement of the animating and determining substance called the soul by a self identified as consciousness and approximating more and more to an epiphenomenon of matter. In this changing environment the older, Christian concept of human dignity, based on the thesis that man was created in the image and likeness of God, has been replaced by a theory about human rights as of purely human origin and legal bestowal, so that in effect – and despite pretentious claims and denials – persons remain with neither dignity nor inalienable rights.

In contrast, therefore, to the concept of man as an image of the divine, there appeared under the new dispensation a set of beliefs whereby we claim no longer to depend on a creator but on our own specious autonomy. Such schemes being no better than castles in the air, recent accounts of the person have pointed less and less ambiguously to the ultimate worthlessness of human beings (as of everything else) and by necessary consequence the disappearance of all those moral and aesthetic values which, under the Mainline Tradition, marked the human person. With the demise of God and the soul, the notion that to be a person implies the possession of any kind of 'spirit' must also fall by the wayside.

Of course, to say that the Mainline Tradition offers a richer account of human nature and human prospects than its rivals is not *ipso facto* to show that its account is true; it too might be a form of wishful thinking. However, that it seems more able to explain the sheer marvels of human culture and creativity indicates its greater plausibility. That said, my own claims are comparatively modest: that the Mainline Tradition points to a coherent account of the human condition, while never denying the particular and scientific truths (insofar as they are truths) which its rivals – often indeed by virtue of their setting side of metaphysical propositions – have uncovered. Beyond that, however, I have further argued that those who reject the Mainline Tradition without offering any persuasive account of human dignity and human worth can only be deceiving the public and, in my earlier phrase, whistling in the humanitarian wind: promoting, that is, a mindless optimism, not least about rights, while claiming, as philosophers – that is, as lovers of wisdom – to expound truth.

*

A reader might object that we have heard very little in earlier chapters about two themes mentioned in the Introduction. First as to the spirit: a valid objection for which redress is due, since the developing Christian concept of the person goes *pari passu* with that specifically Christian concept of the spirit which has played a prominent role in theological speculation since the time of Saint Paul. For while traditions deriving from Greek philosophy tend to divide human beings into soul and body, theologians, as we noted in the Introduction, following the New Testament, have preferred to think of *spirit*, soul and body. Yet though often remaining uncertain whether spirit relates only to man's capacity for the divine and if so how it so relates, when speaking more philosophically, they have tended to assimilate spirit to soul (much as the Greeks tended to assimilate mind): such that when soul disappears one might wonder what happens to spirit.

This is far from the place to embark on a history of the spirit, or of the human spirit; suffice it to say that in as much as the human spirit was thought to refer especially to the human capacity to 'rise' in some metaphysical sense above the human level, with the death of metaphysics that option must seem necessarily closed off. Which would leave spirit to play a more limited, even ghostly role, perhaps indicating the ability of human beings – somehow, and inexplicably – to live more 'heroically', or otherwise amazingly, than one would normally expect of them: as with the phrase 'Spirit of Dunkirk'. Suffice it for now, therefore, to allow spirit in the Mainline Tradition to refer to the apparent ability of human beings to reach beyond the material world, whether in religion, in supererogatory acts of virtue, or in art, literature, music . . .

And the phrase 'Spirit of Dunkirk' should arrest us. In a demythologized, materialist and consumerist world it indicates enduring memory of 'officially' neglected human capacities. As Plato saw, though he has no word for our 'spirit', beauty in all its forms (religious, aesthetic, moral, mathematical) is still – despite the best efforts of those who would homogenize the human race – able to inspire us to rise beyond the level of an evolved animal: giving us, that is, a keener sense of our dignity than any materialism, whether scientistic or consumerist, can offer: provided, that is, we recognize that we are not autonomous but contingent, dependent on others, on our own past, even – as some will conclude, finding it the only available explanation of the phenomena – on God.

*

Our second apparent omission is more philosophical, though it underlay my discussion of utilitarianism. According to a number of philosophers we should overridingly love the entire human race: a thesis I indicated as inclined to hypocrisy. Yet does not the Mainline Tradition introduce the same problems? If all human beings – persons – are of equal dignity in the eyes of God, how could we justify trying to treat some – say members of our own family – differently from others? To answer this brings us back to the particularity of the Christian religion on which that Mainline Tradition about persons is based. According to that religion God knows –

and we need to know – that we are not gods; hence our proper concerns must be limited by our own history and circumstances, and if we ignore that particularity, we risk depriving ourselves of the possibility of living a virtuous life.

The Bible shows God choosing the Jews to perform a particular role in the history of salvation, not expecting them to look after humanity as such – though of course not forbidding them to be concerned with the wider world if proper circumstances arise. As I noted earlier, the Stoics too understood this human dilemma; their theory of *oikeiosis* pointing to our world as of lessening responsibilities: insofar, that is, as we live in the 'real' world. Aristotle too observed that it was pointless – in ancient conditions – for the Athenians to deliberate about what distant Scythians should do. Despite our now greater capacity for outreach to those further from us, the same correction applies to attempts to substitute more distant for more immediate possibilities for honest and humane activity.

*

I have argued that the undermining of the Mainline Tradition has its roots in the fourteenth century; but, as I noted in the Introduction, I have neglected the wider cultural effects of the religious Reformations, limiting myself to the work and role of often 'Reformed' or post-Reformed individuals in observing how the undermining of the person continued with ever-growing rapidity with the coming of seventeenth-century mechanism and constructivism (scientifically with Bacon and Descartes, morally with Machiavelli and Hobbes), and with the shift associated with Locke and Hume from investigation of the nature of persons in their totality to reflection on some single feature – usually consciousness – which could be held to signify that some are not merely human stuff but 'persons' with a claim to special recognition as capable of responsibility.

Then, as clarity about the person, the soul and the supravening 'self' was gradually lost, we saw how following the totalitarian Revolution in France there arose a series of movements either to promote ever more extreme versions of 'Kantian' autonomy or to assimilate the 'person' into some form of totalitarian structure (perhaps under 'democratic' guise) – for where else could any kind of stability be found and alienation 'overcome'? Finally, we observed how nineteenth-century ideology tended to resolve itself into attempts at a post-Nietzschean nihilism. In brief, with the picking over and gradual abandonment of the Mainline Tradition, we concluded that no alternative intelligible account of human persons and their value has been or is likely to be found.

Hence we are left with a choice comparable to that offered by Plato in the *Republic*. After painting portraits of the philosopher-king and the tyrannical man, Plato produces a burlesque argument to show that the former is 729 times happier than the latter. But he also presents options: if you prefer the psychological state of the tyrant (we shall think of Hitler) to that of the philosopher alternative, that is your irrational choice!

We ourselves are, I suggest, in an analogous situation. Either we try to revive the person as presented by the Mainline Tradition, or we settle for a society which is *de facto* totalitarian, hardly even obliged to resort to brute force to keep us 're-educated' enough to suppose ourselves – though now homogenized units – to be autonomous individuals: in a word, soul-destroying. But there is a price to be paid for freedom from such a régime: for starters, we must accept, with the Mainline Tradition, that our dependence is relieved neither by subordination to the state nor by delusive dreams of autonomy; above all that we were mistaken in abandoning the doctrine of original sin, thus claiming to deny a radical flaw in human nature. To admit that, though essential, is at the very least embarrassing!

That said, I close by offering a summary – more elaborate than was available in the time of Aquinas – of the Mainline Tradition as it might now be formulated or even expanded: further refinements are both possible and required. My summary is far from a complete account of what is required, and of what should be recovered. To give one example, it seems to be a necessary part of the nature of the healthy person to possess a sense of shame. That has largely been lost – indeed I have said nothing of it in this essay – but shameless persons are seriously defective and, in traditional language, hence liable to vice: the move in sophisticated Western society, often lauded, from a shame-culture to a guilt culture has been a not unmixed blessing, as the ancient Greeks can teach us.[1]

But now the summary. 'Person' has come to be used in the developing Mainline Tradition to refer to all human beings, both male and female, created in the image and likeness of God and deriving, we now learn, from mitochondrial Eve some 200,000 years ago: all, whether born or unborn, able-bodied or disabled, healthy, gravely ill or senile, each person a unique and ultimately incommunicable combination of body and soul, to a degree capable of independent action whether virtuous or vicious, aware – unless psychologically damaged – of the parameters within which he or she can so act in the passing of historical time: thus, capable of recapturing the past and, to a degree, predicting the future. All can be

[1] For very helpful comment see Scruton (2017: 117–125).

inspired to virtue or *aroused* to vice, their self-awareness enabling them to transcend themselves by reflecting on and modifying instincts in a way not possible to other animals. This 'transcendence' is sometimes called 'spiritual'; it at least refers to a capacity to objectify ourselves without losing sight of our underlying subjective self: I can recognize myself *as* myself, a specific human being, without ceasing to be that specific and unique human being also recognizable by others.

Persons are conceived, not made; albeit conception may be artificially stimulated, and such conception will also generate persons. Each of us is first recognizable as such not by some legal enactment (as was and is often the social reality) but by their mothers in a personal encounter, beginning in her womb. Thus personhood is inalienable from conception to natural death even if subject to legal misdescription. Since the mature person is able to modify his or her behaviour, because more than merely instinctual, we are able to shoulder responsibility for our actions: to be capable of sympathy for our fellows, to put ourselves, to a degree, 'in the shoes' of others and to signal our freedom not least by regretting our failures.

Human persons are capable of self-giving love – whether erotic, parental or more immediately self-sacrificial – inspired by and for goodness itself: also, of creative activity, not only in humanized procreation but in works of literary, artistic or other 'humane' merit. On due reflection, they can understand that *by nature* – before the fall – they were, in contemporary jargon, 'authentic': that is, integrated selves, able to live without contradictions: no mere sum of their qualities; which is why each of them will always remain something of a mysterious substance, including to themselves. They are substantially dependent on their fellow human beings with whom they share the various languages and other means of communication, dependent also, insofar as possessed of intrinsic dignity and therefore certain limited rights, on God. And insofar as they are thus dependent, their lives must have an Aristotelian *telos*: a potential future perfection which only to varying degrees are they capable of recognizing in this present life. That *telos* can be recognized as a possibility in a non-theistic account of humanity; it can only approximate to intelligible specification as the potential completion of a 'narrative' often recognizable only by hindsight, in a theistic context.[2] As Aristotle himself put it, count no man *eudaimon* – his journey approaching a unified completion – until he is dead.

---

[2] For a defence of 'narrative-language' see MacIntyre (2016: 236–242). The 'happy-go-lucky' alternative to narrative, espoused by Galen Strawson (2005), is parasitic on the goodness of others.

For much of the time since the sixteenth century, most defenders of the Mainline Tradition rested on their oars, contenting themselves with damning their opponents as heretics or atheists and in the process forgetting much of the detail and even the *raison d'être* of their own tradition: while the genuine atheists and other post-Christians gradually reconstructed the 'personal' universe to their own model. Not, as we have seen, that nothing new and useful for improving the Mainline Tradition was discovered – a greater understanding of self-awareness, of imagination, sympathy and empathy, perhaps especially of the complex nature and meaning of sexuality – but only in the twentieth century, with the phenomenological movement, if combined with a return to God and the good, did more substantial possibilities for the renewal of the Mainline Tradition appear.

That Tradition had been developed from Graeco-Roman and Jewish roots largely within the culture of a specific institution: the subsequent Catholic Church. Unfortunately, the present leadership of that Church, in a desire to conciliate – even kow-tow to – modernity in its Hegelian account of truth and its neo-Arian characterization of the role of Christ as teacher, seems in process of abandoning it, though still moving slowly and ambiguously to conciliate those of its adherents who have retained trust in its integrity: such 'salami-tactics' were delineated in our earlier discussion of 'How to produce a Virtual Morality'.[3]

That can only increase fears about the likelihood of success for more recent efforts to restore the Mainline Tradition. A few individuals, of course, will carry on trying, as leaven in the lump, though if lacking institutional support their efforts may have only limited effect. Whether they have come too late – whether as Feuerbach and Nietzsche believed and Dostoievsky feared – the stable door has been locked and the horse disappeared without much trace, is the question which underlies the title of this final chapter: Epilogue or Epitaph?

---

[3] In recent times such 'Catholic' kow-towing to political and social pressures is unfortunately not a new phenomenon. Since several pages of this book have been devoted to Edith Stein, I should recall that in 1933 she addressed an appeal to Pope Pius XI complaining that those calling themselves Christians (i.e. the Nazi party in Germany which still retained some pretence of Christianity) were committing atrocities on a daily basis against Jews. Pius's advisers on political matters at the time included pro-fascist Jesuits, members of a once-proud order more recently inclined – whether from an arrogant over-confidence at being able to beat the 'Machiavellians' at their own game or from a *de facto* abandonment of traditionally Christian moral principles – to appease powerful anti-Christian social movements: then of fascism, now of homosexuality and other anti-family features of 'liberal' society. Stein's letter was never answered; as we know, she was later murdered by the appeased.

Appendix
The World of Rights Transformed Again

Rights [but not the right to life] are Trumps.
Ronald Dworkin

Progressing through the history of persons, we have found rights playing an increasingly significant role in the discussion. In recent years their nature and origins have been debated interminably – and inconclusively – in thousands of books and academic articles. This is not the place to launch into a full-scale analysis of this material, nor even to list the major contributions to it. A few largely historical comments about more recent times shall suffice – not least about how the nature of the rights claimed has changed, as have ideas as to how they should be enforced.

But first an urgent preliminary point: rights theory is – admittedly in a limited form – a Christian thesis, in its origins related to the belief that man – the human person – was created in God's image and likeness. We can observe one of its earliest modern versions in the work of Las Casas, who in insisting that the Indians were fully human and not natural slaves – as we have seen – emphasized their right to freedom of religion, apparently even prepared to tolerate their barbarous religious practices: they were to be converted not compelled to worship God more appropriately. Las Casas saw the right specifically to religious freedom as part of the endowment of human persons; that is, they are intended to choose freely to worship the true God.

And in this, despite the persecutions of succeeding centuries, Las Casas was following in the footsteps of several prominent patristic authorities who moved from asking the powers-that-be for toleration of their own religious practices to urging – especially in the cases of Tertullian and

Lactantius (at one stage apparently adviser of the Emperor Constantine) –
that there exists a God-given right (*ius*) to religious freedom (and not
merely for themselves). Unfortunately although Lactantius may have been
partly instrumental in the genesis of the letter of Constantine and Licinius
(in AD 313) demanding freedom of worship throughout the Roman
Empire, this apparent legal and natural right was within a few years
seriously infringed by Constantine himself, not least following several of
his predecessors in longing for uniformity of religion throughout his
domains.[1] Nevertheless since freedom of religion is one of the most
defensible rights, it should be recorded that its origins lie in the history
of Christianity. With one right established, others (as with Las Casas)
could easily (if eventually) follow, but rights in a secular context are very
different from their original versions.

*

Even among opponents of the Mainline Tradition rights have often come
under fire: Hobbes and Bentham were among early attackers. And among
those generally supportive of some version of the Mainline Tradition they
have often also provoked hostility, even contempt. Well known is the
remark of Alasdair MacIntyre that belief in human rights can reasonably be
compared with belief in witches and unicorns.[2] Perhaps what this intends,
however, is that those philosophers – that is, most contemporary philosophers, who assume they deal in a godless universe – are about as entitled to
rights as to witches and unicorns; in that he would be agreeing with
Hobbes and Bentham, not to say with Comte. For in a godless world there
is no human dignity, and rights, being mere legal convenience, are those
desired (and often reified) liberties and opportunities which their owners
are able to claim and exact from society. MacIntyre's concern, of course, is
not only that conflicting rights claims can never be resolved, except by
arbitrary compromise (compare the case of the 'right' to life of an unborn
child versus the 'right' of its mother to kill it), but also with the fact that
such debates, being interminable, invite legal diktat backed by various
forms of force if a term is – however temporarily – to be imposed on them.

---

[1] For evidence for a more generalized claim to religious freedom in early Christian texts
(especially those of Tertullian and Lactantius) see the essays of Shah, Wilken and DePalma
Digeser in Shah and Hertzke (2016).
[2] MacIntyre (1981: 69); repeated with comments on why rights can be used to construct bad
arguments (MacIntyre 2006: 77–78).

We shall return to this when we glance at Hannah Arendt, one of few rights-theorists aware of the problems, practical and theoretical, that honest rights-theorists must face. More immediately, we may revert to in Roman times where the 'dignity' of human beings depended not on their existence but on their status in society, the emperor or king being decked out with 'rights' imposing a high degree of respect while slaves had no rights whatever over their bodies, nor, in the opinion of many, over their 'souls' either.

That Classical account of dignity was modified – at least in theory – with the advent of Christianity which taught – even if spasmodically – that the dignity of all human beings, whatever their social status, depends on and is sustained by the God who has created them in his own image. Yet in the 'Ages of Faith' society – though as yet largely devoid of emphasis on subjective rights – allowed for the gradual growth of the theory that specific groups possessed (and could claim) rights against others: thus, bishops against kings, clergy against barons, guilds against local magnates, etc. All under God against whom no-one claimed rights.

As the medieval world passed into early modernity, the need to trade with or (if possible) conquer new and alien societies brought the need for further clarification. Las Casas was impelled to enquire whether Indians were just 'natural slaves' or whether, like other humans – even though their practices were cruel and their religion often vicious – they too were creatures in God's image and thus possessed of an inherent dignity which could and should be cashed out in terms of rights. In similar mode Grotius held that even if (the Christian) God did not exist, some sort of natural law did and conveniently indicated that we can all find mutually agreeable principles – whether or not backed by metaphysical truths – in accordance with which trade and general commercial transactions can be profitably concluded.

In Europe itself more radical change was at hand, with the Reformation and the Renaissance bringing challenges to traditional accounts of both Church and State. The time had come not merely to castigate vice but to propose basic changes in the structures of society: the 'rights' of (some) individuals might be asserted against the real or imagined despotism of both Church and State, whether in terms of religious reform or of constitutional reconstruction and revolution. The first unambiguous example of such movement in England involved attacks on both the religious establishment (already to a degree 'reformed') and on the monarchy with which that establishment seemed inextricably entangled. The 'Army Debates' of the late 1640s contained the seeds not only of enlarged demands for subjective rights against authoritarian governance but also a thorough reconstruction of the entire religio-political context, summed up by a revival of an earlier medieval slogan of the politically disenfranchised and oppressed: When Adam delved and Eve span who was then the gentleman?

But the extreme views of Levellers such as Lilburne or Overton or the Diggers of Gerard Winstanley were ahead of their time. Most rights-claims were as yet for the lifting of what was seen as religious intolerance (often to be replaced by an intolerance of its own, especially against the few remaining Catholics) or for a royal or aristocratic tyranny to be modified or even replaced by more 'republican' and 'popular' structures whereby the rising commercial class – the new 'middle class' – could claim and grasp its 'fair' share of the political cake. For such claims, presented in the name of the people of England and designated the 'rights of man', were primarily the concern and advantage of commercial middle-class groups: a scenario which obtained regularly in later 'revolutionary' (or less obviously revolutionary) movements ostensibly on behalf of humanity focussed not least on the poor. In many cases the poor were expected or compelled to accept the rights determined for them, as much later in tsarist Russia.

In more mainstream English circles – and later among European admirers of the 'Glorious Revolution' of 1688 – a more modest, godly version of subjective rights was claimed, the guiding spirit being Locke, and certainly not Hobbes who vigorously protested that the very term 'rights' was only a blatant manifestation of an outdated religious way of thinking and that in the real world so-called rights were mere 'liberties', that is, the satisfaction of desires which powerful individuals could miscall as 'rights'.

Though Locke still proclaimed rights as the gift of a 'voluntarist' God to human beings, Hobbes was the voice of a future where seventeenth-century rights claims were to be urged for privileged English males, even for all Protestants, yet where – absent God or a Nature the laws of which would be of God's ordering – a master was required to wield the big stick as enforcer. Earlier (however ineffectively) that role had been played by God, the awarder of dignity and hence rights; now it must be some human being or legalized institution: either state or dictator. For the mature Hobbes religion should be entirely under the control of the state, which would also decide who was a legal person, and as a presage of things to come Hobbes could hardly have failed to notice that the Army Debates about rights turned out to be the preamble to the rise of Cromwell, the regicide though still godly dictator – or in official vanguard-style, the 'Protector'.

Yet Cromwell, godly dictator and Protestant hero, was also the rare military genius who recognized his own limitations. (Franco was something of a more recent parallel.) Urged by Protestant co-religionists to cross the Channel, pass through a potentially Protestant France, invade Italy and kick out the 'anti-Christ of Rome', he declined such an undertaking – in intent unlike Napoleon, or later Hitler. Thus far rights claims, backed by competent force and consequent power to enforce, were to be imposed in one's own godly country (Cromwell made an exception for Catholic Ireland); there was no compelling motivation – let alone existential necessity – to universalize them. Christian godly power was available but as yet knew its limits; Christians had always placed due emphasis on what it is possible for a man to achieve – as that he cannot create himself – but a time was coming when power would be no longer Christian: rather, and vehemently, anti-Christian.

Then would also come the time in which freedom would be sought not only from various forms of political and ecclesiastical tyranny; desires (Hobbesian 'liberties') might be directed not only in immediate political action to change one's rulers, but also to a radical modification of the morality and civil principles which (after the end of the Wars of Religion in the mid-seventeenth century) seemed either to replace the moral authority of the ever more discredited Christian churches or to claim recognition as the essence of religion itself. Nor need claims about rights and freedoms now be fitted into the conventions of particular nation-states which might for a while be their bulwark; they could take on a more demanding and universalizing role – prompted above all by an extreme interpretation of the dogma that 'All men are equal' (of which nothing can more effectively reduce persons to mere human units), hence promoting theories about the need for a 'revised' human nature to replace what had been proposed by a disintegrating Mainline Tradition.

It is needless to enlarge on the philosophy that inspired the French Revolution to an active contempt and hatred for Christianity already well developed in eighteenth-century France; a hostility fed not by the atheism and scepticism of David Hume but by the corrosive anti-Christian (and hence anti-Judaic) rhetoric of Voltaire, as also by Rousseau's emphasis on a new education in 'autonomy'. The latter mingled sentimental notions of empathy (as in the cult of the mother with babe at breast) with a totalitarian programme of education governed by a General Will to which (and apparently in whatsoever respects) our individual wills are to be subordinated: less (as in the Greek *polis*) for the good of the whole as for the fulfilment of the parts, than (of course) for our good as supposedly autonomous agents in a democratic (understood as crudely egalitarian) society.

Thus well before Robespierre, the roots of 'totalitarian' democracy with its claims about the rights of man (i.e. mankind, sometimes even including females) had become well established and needed only a catalyst to burst into flame. That was supplied by the well-intentioned (or at least prudential) reformist politics of Louis XVI, setting the scene for a revolutionary dynamic of ever-increasing ferocity which more moderate reformers failed to understand and consequently had no hope of controlling. For it is an entailment of any revolutionary dynamic that the more ruthless – led by those prepared to kill – will come out on top, at least in the short run. Dante had put into a killer's mouth the ominous words: *Cosa fatta, capo ha* ('What is done is done').

Edmund Burke was one of the earliest to recognize, as early as 1790, that the terror was in sight. Whatever the motives of Mirabeau and the other popular leaders, they understood the fire with which they played no more than had the king and his reformist counsellors. As Burke realized, the ever-expanding claims about the rights of man, now proposed within the confines of a *revolutionary* state, could not be met within the boundaries of that state (the Cromwellian model), but as universal must be imposed by the ungodly but now 'righteous' state on the world, at least on the political world of Europe. If a new Cromwell were to arise, his ambition would necessarily be less moderated. As Burke put it, probably with Caesar or Augustus as well as Cromwell in mind:[3]

> Some general, who understands the art of conciliating the soldiery, and who possesses the true spirit of command, shall draw the eyes of all men upon himself.

Burke recognized that the totalitarian features of Jacobin claims about the rights of man featured a variety of new (or reinforced) threats: they would aim to destroy national sovereignty (except, as yet, the sovereignty of the righteous state, France); and where earlier rights-talk normally took the form of protest against specific real or supposed abuses perpetrated by Church or State, the new version would be far less restricted. Potentially (as Hobbes would have put it) any claim (to a 'liberty') could be

---

[3] Burke (2003: 193).

reclassified as a claim to extend the rights of man.[4] Thus, and whereas the potential for rights-claims implicit in earlier Christian teaching on mankind's dignity as created in the image and likeness of God (in more voluntarist theology as willed by God) was restricted, the 1789 revolutionary version would admit no theoretical limits to what might be claimed.

Earlier *Christian* limits would have been implied by the love of a God who would not wish his image to be deformed by wicked human desires, but rather that our autonomy be controlled and restricted by the bonds of morality and a loving spirituality; nor should we strive to be equal but only in basic respects *similarly* human. Now, the only limit to our liberties (barring that our proposed 'equality' will require that those desires be homogenized by the state) was to be imposed by anti-godly France or – in the future, as we might add – by some supra-national entity with the power (and immense potential for its abuse) which larger, necessarily more bureaucratic bodies could provide, these in accordance with whatever criterion, rational or emotional, would make their determinations. As Hobbes (again) had proclaimed, only the 'commonwealth' would (or perhaps should) have the power to determine not only who are persons but also what rights those persons will be allowed to claim.

It has sometimes been said (not least by Burke) that views of this kind imply a politics dominated by morality. The reality is more complicated, as is apparent in our own time: when new lobby groups arise to claim rights for themselves or their paymasters which go far beyond those of seventeenth-century theorists of the rights of man, and are made by immediately *political* groups – operating, of course, under the common revolutionary banner that the same equal rights should be available to all. This may involve changing the meanings of key words in various languages: thus, marriage as a union between a man and a woman is taken to imply a discrimination against people of the same sex who want an optionally permanent sexual relationship, so 'marriage' has to refer to *any* kind of 'sexual' union, whatever its nature and purpose – in the extreme case bestiality need not be excluded if you want to 'marry' your dog.

---

[4] Though Kant's treatise on perpetual peace – with its cosmopolitan and universal-government implications – appeared only in 1795, his emphasis on equal autonomy as a democratic reality (as he leaned from Rousseau) should not be forgotten in any account of the nature of the rights-demands of 1789. With a naiveté often characteristic of *ben pensanti* philosophers and their admirers, Kant seems to have been largely unaware of the relationship between his claims about autonomy and a top-down organization of perpetual peace and the likelihood of revolutionary violence (implicit or explicit).

Whereas the Hobbesian state of nature leads to deals between warring individuals (and ultimately to the Leviathan), so in contemporary debate about rights the deals made are the result of strictly political activity by competing lobby groups. Those neo-Hobbesian assemblages of individuals fight for what they can contract to get for themselves: in the process generating the need for legal arbitration of their conflicting claims, preferably according to the terms of a written Constitution and Bill of Rights (as in the United States and the dream of Eurocrats) by almost unrestricted exposition of which all-powerful and unelected judges determine the outcome.

Quis custodiet ipsos custodes? ('Who shall control the controllers?'), as the Roman poet Juvenal put it. And the answer is, Whatever lobby group or collection of ideologists can control the political acts whereby the *custodes* are appointed. Who supposed that rights-theories diminish rather than merely deform strictly political processes? And ultimately (as the universalizing and cosmopolitanizing of power develops), as the Macedonian kings emasculated the Greek city- states (whether or not 'democratic'), so Cromwell, Robespierre, Napoleon, Hitler, Stalin, Mao and other potentates yet unborn will attempt to subvert smaller and arguably more democratic régimes. Is this, we may ask with Burke, the future for a world controlled by some revamped United Nations, or more nationally by a Fourth Reich of the European 'project'? And in such bodies who will eventually be a new Hitler or new Stalin?

But that cannot happen, can it? Not many Europeans are advocates of a bureau-tyranny oiled by limitless human-rights claims, nor obsessed by the myth of human equalization. But nor were all eighteenth-century Frenchmen sans-culottes, nor were all twentieth-century Germans guards at Belsen or Auschwitz nor even volunteers in the SS (albeit thirteen million of them had voted more or less democratically for Hitler), nor were all twentieth-century Russians would-be Communist apparatchiks or commissars. It is not numbers that 'count' but the power of the élites of whatever stripe, whether desirous of retaining more 'traditional' human rights or of securing more specifically anti-Christian and by extension 'anti-person' demands.

Of course, to criticize the abuses of contemporary rights-theorists (whether or not proposed by the heirs of 1789) is not to reject human rights – even, within limits, subjective rights – it is merely not to turn them into supreme and uncontrollable idols. Burke himself defended the rights of Irish Catholics, of British dissenters, of American 'patriots' (in his view grossly mistreated by the English government) and of Indian subjects of the East India Company, as seen in his vigorous support for the impeach-ment of Governor Warren Hastings. His concern about the French Revo-lution was of a piece with those rights-based stances. And as we noticed, he recognized, almost from the beginning of the Revolution in 1789, that it would end in terror and military dictatorship. And though his own claims about rights are nostalgic and pragmatic, lacking metaphysical defence – he fails to explain why we are entitled to rights at all – he was able to recognize the coming French terror and militarism as the first fruits of an egalitarianism which could only be imposed by force (unless – as perhaps in a later day – by fraud):[5]

Whatever each man can separately do without trespassing upon others, he has a right to do for himself; and he has a right to a fair proportion of all which society, with all its combinations of skill and force, can do in his favour. In this partnership all men have equal rights; but not to equal things. He that has but five shillings in the partnership has as good a right to it as he that has five hundred pounds has to his larger proportion; but he has not a right to an equal dividend in the product of the joint stock. And as to the share of power, authority ... It is a thing to be settled by convention.

To claim equal right across the board, according to Burke, is to reveal oneself as merely envious.[6] – and he has no time for a politics of envy, whether or not masquerading under fine-sounding phrases. Such an equality can only be achieved in defiance of the nature of man and society, leaving nothing between the 'naked' individual and the rights-enforcing state. Note that when presenting his own view of rights Burke discusses not the rights of man (in the abstract and thus open to ideological reasoning) but of men. In accordance with Aristotle's tag which has played so vital a role in all our present discussion, he disbelieved in the existence of Man, preferring to concentrate on the particular rather than the politically dangerous abstract: aware that it has proved easy to sacrifice individual persons to 'love of Humanity'. Indeed, even when individuals are viewed as persons, 'equality' can be read as equal worth-lessness – entailing an equal likelihood of being sacrificed for the 'good' of the whole.

Yet Burke skates over a major difficulty in assuming that rights could and so should be protected within the boundaries of individual

---

[5] Burke (2003: 52).
[6] For comment see LaCroix and Pranchère (2018: 78) – and a comparison with the view of the early Marx that human rights claims depend on the egotism of the possessors (157–158).

nation-states so long as these are not corrupted by ideological fervour. That ideological fervour was the reason he believed war against the French revolutionaries a moral duty. Yet one of the problems of going to war, however well prepared, is that you may not win; a conundrum for more honourable régimes as for their more disreputable counterparts. Hence so long as human rights are protected – or not – only within national boundaries, foreign critics are normally unlikely to go to war in order to enforce improvement.

*

Although during most of the nineteenth century rights claims were less prominent than earlier – not least because of the growth of more 'social' philosophizing, whether the utilitarianism of Bentham (he who considered rights nonsense upon stilts), or the positivism of Comte (who took a rather similar view), or in the first-fruits of Marxism (though some will claim that Marx was not 'really' opposed to human rights) – the situation began to change again with the Dreyfus case in France, where fear of a racist barbarism to come was beginning to be felt.

Thus in the twentieth century such misgivings began to demand international solution. In particular, Nazi atrocities before and during the Second World War made international action seem imperative: hence the Nuremburg Tribunals and the 'determination' of 'crimes against humanity' as a category. The problem often remained unresolved, since only in cases where the powerful of the earth were willing to act was there much chance of the new international agreements (the UN Declaration on Human Rights of 1948 or the European Convention on Human Rights of 1950 or the Helsinki Final Act of 1975) being implemented outside the borders of those compliant nation-states where they were least needed. In many cases this has meant the 'International Community' regularly lamenting atrocities but only able to bring the perpetrators to justice when the United States (primarily) has been willing to sacrifice its soldiers to enforce international law.

Nevertheless, and despite such grotesque United Nations failures as in Rwanda and Srebrenica, politically impractical (if not grossly naïve) demands for world government still emerge from time to time. Yet who could seriously expect Putin – let alone the successors of Chairman Mao – to bow to toothless tigers, whether Europe or the United Nations? The current debacle in the Ukraine well illumines the prevailing state of power-politics and the impotence of such tigers. Still, one must admit that even to put the new rules on to the table offers a chance of future and better enforcement.

*

It has sometimes been argued that the real explanation of the increased importance currently attributed to human rights lies not with the atrocities of the Second World War but with the political, social and especially sexual Revolutions of the nineteen-sixties.[7] More or less accompanying the development of the 'pill' came the civil rights movement in the United States, decolonization of much of Asia and Africa, and the Soviet invasion of Czechoslovakia which ended the dalliance of many Western intellectuals with Marxism (or at least Stalinism). Those who taught in Universities at that time will recall the proliferation of courses on Sartre, Heidegger (in more 'respectable' circles Kierkegaard), and (as pop-psychology posing as philosophy) on 'Psycho-sexual Experience'.

Samuel Moyn's view that rights only really took off again in the 1970s has been largely rejected; not least his account of the late 'reception' of the Nazi atrocities is seriously flawed. Nevertheless, the 'sixties' (and 'seventies' following) were a watershed. Up until then, from the seventeenth century through the French Revolution down to the UN Declaration, rights claimed were 'political' rights. Claimants demanded freedom from the more obvious features of political oppression represented by the murder, rape and torture of victims, or, in the particular case of decolonization, by governance from beyond their own borders. We too, they said, want our own nation-state: a significant example of this being Jews who had concluded that to be certain of survival they needed again a national home.

Such rights were certainly 'subjective', in that each claimant wanted them for himself and beyond that for equity in the state in which he lived. Though occasional exceptions can be found, they were not yet claims for an absolute *moral* 'freedom' contradictory to what could be tolerated within the Mainline Tradition. Yet such untraditional rights might be seen as necessary corollary of newly fashionable accounts of autonomy (whatever Kant and others may have supposed). In this particular the importance of the so-called sexual revolution cannot be downplayed, for whatever the status of sexual sins in the catalogue of sins in general, all changes in sexual morality will have effects more far reaching than most

---

[7] The most influential exponent of this type is Moyn (2014).

(not all) of their advocates may anticipate. To demand relief from the fear of torture and execution at the will of overweening political power is a very different matter from claiming that what once had been damned as the sin of buggery should now be accepted as the right to engage in it.

As already noted, this ideological change began in the 1960s and 1970s, but as is often the case, the transformation of radical ideas into legal documents published by recognized institutions took time. One of the more helpful guides to what happened may be recognized in the change in the content of declarations issued by the United Nations about the rights of women. Before the 1990s these treat almost exclusively of the removal of discrimination in voting, pay equality, etc.; there then appear with growing frequency references to gender, reproductive rights (especially the claimed 'right' to abortion) and 'sexual orientation': all reflect both the sexual revolution of the 1960s and the so-called third-wave feminism of such as Judith Butler, Kate Millett and Christina Hoff Sommers. These in turn rely on a blend of neo-Marxist theory (deriving ultimately, as we have seen, from Engels via De Beauvoir) with postmodern dogma formulated by Foucault and Derrida about the disappearance of the author and the (Nietzschean) denial of truth; leaving only socially-based perspectives.[8]

The Platform of Action of the United Nations Conference on Woman in Beijing (1995) is a striking example of the adoption of gender ideology, sexual orientation and reproductive rights by an official international organization. As for the NGOs, a peculiarly informative instance of the developing change at about the same time can be seen in the shifting mission of Amnesty International.[9] Founded in 1961 to work on behalf of political prisoners and distinguished for its campaigns against torture, Amnesty suddenly redirected much of its attention from these its original goals to the new and fashionable area of 'reproductive rights' (especially abortion), thus in no small degree shifting from being a humanitarian organization advocating for the humane treatment of captives of various sorts – in the wake of internationalist bodies such as the UN itself and the EU – to becoming another powerful pressure group for butchering the unborn, again following the big international organizations in tending to impose 'reproductive rights' of the mothers, not of their yet unborn children, as the price of help and support.

---

[8] For a brief but lucid summary see Malo (2017: 27–35); see also Donert (2014: especially 85–87).

[9] For brief comment in a monumental work see Eckel (2014: 356–357).

How this came about is beyond the scope of the present book. Part of the explanation was a shift in Amnesty's attitude to homosexuals: a slide from an original concern that they not be maltreated, especially in the Third World, to a conscious adoption of the LGBT political and social agenda, which in turn, and in a characteristically modern dynamic, pushed Amnesty towards anti-life and anti-person causes. The shift was further not unconnected with the huge increase in Amnesty's membership after the disillusion with Communism that began with the Prague Spring and continued until the fall of the Berlin Wall, leaving many younger rebels without a cause. Be that as it may, Amnesty's activists increasingly picked up much of the mentality and aims of organizations like Planned Parenthood International (and of governments such as that of the United States under Clinton and Obama which largely funded them), more formally adopting reproductive rights as part of its mission early in the twenty-first century. In international affairs, as national, we need to beware of the company we keep.

Obviously, the advocacy of claims to the right to abort or to engage in buggery will be anathema to those still holding with the Mainline Trad-ition about persons, but fortunately the new wave of such claims has not entirely obliterated (though it has certainly damaged the credibility of) older views of how to promote human rights. Yet, absent the theological notion of an inborn human dignity, those views will lack foundation even when shifted from reforming activity *within* nation-states to the wider stage of demands for the restriction of obvious 'crimes against humanity' *by* nation-states driven by Nazi-style ideologies.

*

Hannah Arendt is probably the contemporary thinker who best under-stood the difficulties with both nation-based and internationalist guaran-tees of human rights. That she yet remained deeply committed to secular versions of rights theory is clear in the following passage from *The Burden of the Time* (chapter 13):[10]

The concept of human rights can again be meaningful only if they are redefined as a right to the human condition itself,[11] which depends upon belonging to some human community, the right never to be dependent on some human community, the right never to be dependent on some inborn human community which *de facto*, aside from its guarantee by fellow men, not only does not exist but is the last

---

[10] Arendt (1951).   [11] Elsewhere she refers to this as 'the right to have rights'.

and most arrogant myth we have invented in all our long history. The Rights of Man can be implemented only if they become the prepolitical foundation of a new polity, the prelegal basis of a new legal structure, the, so to speak, prehistorical fundament from which the history of mankind will derive its essential meaning in much the same way Western Civilization did from its own fundamental origin myths.

In this passage (and elsewhere) Arendt makes the following claims:

1   That claims resembling the Mainline Tradition about human dignity are arrogant myths and cannot therefore be used as basis for theories of rights.
2   Therefore, and in place of God's dignity, we must establish a *'prepolitical'* basis for rights claims, not by trusting that nation-states as currently structured will correct their own abuses – these normally will only protect *citizens* – but something more international or at least internationally recognized. This new version of internationalism must be the product of connections between individuals willing to recognize one another as equals.

Arendt's interest in human rights arose primarily from her concern for stateless persons: refugees of the interwar period and in massively increased numbers generated by the displacements that followed the end of the Second World War. She became aware that in current political terms stateless persons or persons deprived of statehood but compelled to rely on their mere humanity had *de facto* no legal – let alone supra-legal – rights at all. In her words: 'the abstract nakedness of being nothing but human was their [viz. the inmates of concentration camps] greatest danger'.[12] She also regularly observed that Jews were unable to judge crimes against Jews *until* and unless they had their own state. Yet she also recognized, along with many contemporaries, the failure of nation-states to protect the stateless, while being far too sophisticated, too little naïve, to suppose that organizations like the United Nations will ever be fit for this purpose; that body's actions, as I have already noted, being entirely dependent on the willingness of powerful states not to veto even humanitarian proposals and on their willingness to impose penalties on the guilty – at a possible cost of warfare in which many of their own nationals would be killed.

Unsurprisingly, Arendt is clear-headed enough to recognize that her new proposed 'community' can be little more than a dream. It is certainly

---

[12] Arendt (1951: 455).

quite implausible – just as in such matters the United Nations has so often been found implausible – that agreement within any possible new community will be reached, for the community itself will be composed of the more or less good, the decidedly wicked, the wise, the cynical and the gullible. In Arendt's pre-political framework, the good will vote for the good one day only to find – when troubles or demagogues have arisen – that the vicious or gullible have voted it down the next. International organizations are better at voicing a righteous indignation than at doing anything effective to end the atrocities they go through the motions of lamenting – and Arendt's hypothetical community would be equally ineffective. Consciences would be massaged, victims would die.

My own conclusion is thus disappointingly limited. Whatever practical difficulties the option Arendt has rejected as arrogant myth shares with her desired alternative, it at least has the metaphysical strength to justify, to those willing to think, that there *are* indeed inalienable human rights, but only if god-given. Arendt's notion that rights are generated by political action by the dispossessed – though sometimes (as with the foundation of Israel) historically verified – awards 'rights' so conceived no more validity than does any other preferred option. Hence, and inevitably, at least at the theoretical level, it must be the Mainline Tradition – at least its 'spirit' – or nothing. The choice is again between intelligibility, framed by humility, and Cloud-cuckoo-land. Or, in modern myth, 'La-La- Land': that land so accurately – though ironically – designated in view of Hollywood's massive financial support for the virtue-signalling, anti-person fantasies of our times.

Bibliography

Albritton, R. 1957. 'Forms of Particular Substances in Aristotle's *Metaphysics*', *JP* 54: 699–708.

Anscombe, E. 1953. 'The Principle of Individuation', *Proceedings of the Aristotelian Society* 27(suppl.): 83–96 [= J. Barnes, *Essays on Aristotle* 3 (1979) 88–95].

Arendt, H. 1951. *The Burden of Our Time*. London, Secker and Warburg.
1958. *The Origins of Totalitarianism*. New York, Meridian Books.

Armstrong, A. H. 1960. 'The Background of the Doctrine that Intelligibles are not outside the Intellect', in E. R. Dodds (ed.) *Entretiens Hardt 5: Les Sources de Plotin*. Vandoeuvres, Geneva, pp. 391–425.

Arnou, R. 1967. *Le désir de Dieu dans la philosophie de Plotin*, 2nd edition. Rome.

Aubry, G. 2008 'Individuation, particularisation et détermination selon Plotin', *Phronesis* 53: 271–289.

Balthasar, H. von. 1990. *Theo-Drama II* (trans. G. Harrison). San Francisco, Ignatius.
1991. *The Glory of the Lord VI* (trans. B McNeil and E. Leiva-Merikakis). Edinburgh, T. and T, Clark.

Banateanu, A. 2001. *La téorie stoicienne de l'amitié: essai de reconstruction*. Fribourg.

Beckett, L. 2006. *In the Light of Christ*. San Francisco, Ignatius.

Beiser, F. 1992. 'Kant's Intellectual Development 1746–1781', in P. Guyer (ed.) *The Cambridge Companion to Kant*. Cambridge, Cambridge University Press, pp. 26–61.

Bello, A. A. 2008. 'Edmund Husserl and Edith Stein: The Question of the Human Subject', *ACPQ* 82: 163–176.

Bett, R. 2012. 'Did the Stoics Invent Human Rights', in R. Kamtekar (ed.) *Virtue and Happiness: Essays in Honour of Julia Annas*, pp. 149–169.

Blackburn, S. 1994. *Spreading the Word*. Oxford, Oxford University Press.
1998. *Ruling Passions*. Oxford, Oxford University Press.
2004. *Lust*. Oxford, Oxford University Press.

Boersma, G. P. 2016. *Augustine's Theory of Image: A Study in the Development of Pro-Nicene Theology*. Cambridge, Cambridge University Press.

Borden Sharkey, S. 2006. 'Edith Stein's Understanding of Women', *IPQ* 46: 171–191.

Borden (Sharkey), S. 2010. *Thine own Self: Individuation in Edith Stein's Later Writings*. Washington, DC, CUA Press.

Børresen, K. E. 1981. *Subordination and Equivalence: The Nature and Role of Women in Augustine and Thomas Aquinas* (English translation). Washington, DC, CUA Press.

Burke E. 2003. *Reflections on the Revolution in France*. Indianapolis/Cambridge, Hackett.

Burnell, P. 2005. *The Augustinian Person*. Washington, DC, CUA Press.

Cameron, M. 2012. *Christ meets us Everywhere*. Oxford, Oxford University Press.

Cavadini, J. C. 2005. 'Feeling Right: Augustine on the Passions and Sexual Desire', *AS* 36, pp. 195–217.

Chappell, T. J. D. 2004. 'Absolutes and Particulars', in A. O'Hear (ed.) *Modern Moral Philosophy*. Cambridge, Cambridge University Press, pp. 99–117.

Chiaradonna, R. 2000. 'La teoria dell' individuo Porfiriano dell'idiōs poion stoico', *Elenchus* 21: 303–331.

Clayton, L. A. 2012. *Bartolomé de las Casas: A Biography*. New York, Cambridge University Press.

Connor, R. A. 1990. 'Relation, the Thomistic *Esse* and American Culture: Towards a Metaphor of Sanctity', *Communio* 17: 455–464.

Cory, T. S. 2012. 'Diachronically Unified Consciousness in Augustine and Aquinas', *Vivarium* 50: 354–381.

2014. *Aquinas on Human Self-Knowledge*. Cambridge, Cambridge University Press.

Crosby, J. 1996. *The Selfhood of the Human Person*. Washington, DC, CUA Press.

Daley, B. E. 1984. 'Boethius's' Theological Tracts and Early Byzantine Scholasticism', *Medieval Studies* 46: 158–191.

Darwall, S. 2006. *The Second-Person Standpoint*. Cambridge, MA, Harvard University Press.

De Koninck, T. 1999. 'Persons and Things', in T. Hibbs and J. O'Callaghan (eds), *Recovering Nature: Essays in Natural Philosophy, Ethics and Metaphysics in Honor of Ralph McInerny*. South Bend, Notre Dame University Press, pp. 53–67.

De Libera, A. 2007. *L'Archéologie du sujet 1*. Paris, Vrin.

2008. 'When did the modern subject emerge?', *ACPQ* 82: 337–354.

De Lubac, H. 1995. *The Drama of Atheistic Humanism* (trans. E.M. Riley). San Francisco, Ignatius.

Denyer, N. 2001. *Plato: Alcibiades*. Cambridge, Cambridge University Press.

Dörrie, H. 1959. *Porphyrios' 'Symmikta Zetemata': ihre Stellung in System und Geschichte des Neuplatonismus nebst einem Kommentar zu den Fragmenten*. Munich, Beck.

Dodds, E. R. 1959. *Plato's Gorgias*. Oxford, Oxford University Press.

Donert, C. 2014. 'Whose Utopia? Gender, Ideology and Human Rights at the 1975 World Congress of Women in East Berlin', in J. Eckel and S. Moyn (eds.) *The Breakthrough: Human Rights in the 1970s*. Philadelphia, University of Pennsylvania Press, pp. 68–87.

Dworkin, R. 1993. *Life's Dominion*. Knopf, New York.

Eckel, J. 2014, *Die Ambivalenz des Gutes: Menschenrechte in der internationalen Politik seit des 1940ens*. Göttingen, Vanderhoeck und Ruprect.

Finnis, J. 2005. '"The thing that I am": Personal Identity in Aquinas and Shakespeare', in E. F. Paul, F. D. Miller Jr. and J. Paul (eds.) *Personal Identity*. Cambridge, Cambridge University Press, pp. 250–282.

Fortin, E. L. 1959. *Christianisme et culture philosophique au cinquième siècle*. Paris. Vrin.

Gill, C. H. 1988. 'Personhood and Personality: The Four-persona Theory in Cicero, *De Officiis I*,' *OSAP* 6: 169–199.

1994. 'Peace of mind and being Yourself: Panaetius to Plutarch', *ANRW* 36.7. pp. 4599–4640.

Gioia, L. 2008. *The Theological Epistemology of Augustine's De Trinitate*. Oxford, Oxford University Press.

Gracia, J. J. E. 1988. *Introduction to the Problem of Individuation in the Early Middle Ages*, 2nd revised edition. Munich and Vienna, Philosophia Verlag.

1996. 'Individuality and the Individuating Entity in Scotus's Ordinatio. An Ontological Characterization', in L. Honnefelder, R. Wood and M. Dreyer (eds) *Individuality and the Individuating Entity in Scotus's Ordinatio: An Ontological Characterization*. Leiden, Brill, pp. 229–249.

Gregory, B. 2012. *The Unintended Reformation*. Cambridge, MA, Harvard University Press.

Guardini, R. 1965. *The World and the Person* (trans. S. Lange). Chicago, Regnery Press.

Hadot, P. 1992. *La citadelle intérieure: introduction aux Pensées de Marc Aurèle*. Paris, Vrin.

1995. *Philosophy as a Way of Life* (trans. By M. Chase). Oxford, Blackwell.

Haji, L. 1999. 'On being Morally Responsible in a Dream', in G. B. Matthews (ed.) *The Augustinian Tradition*. London, Los Angeles, San Francisco, University of California Press, pp. 166–182.

Halper, E. 2005. *One and Many in Aristotle's Metaphysics: The Central Books*. Las Vegas, Parmenides Publishing.

Harper, K. 2016, 'Christianity and the Roots of Human Dignity in Late Antiquity', in *Christianity and Freedom, Vol. 1*. New York, Cambridge University Press, pp. 123–148.

Hill, C. 1958. *Puritanism and Revolution*. Harmondsworth, Penguin.

Hill Jr., T. H. 1992. *Dignity and Practical Reason in Kant's Moral Theory*. Ithaca, Cornell University Press.

Honoré, T. 2002. *Ulpian: Pioneer of Human Rights*, 2nd edition. Oxford, Oxford University Press.

Hunt, L. 2000. 'The Paradoxical Origins of Human Rights', in J. N. Wasserstrom, L. Hunt and M. B. Young (eds) *Human Rights and Revolutions*. Lanham, Rowman and Littlefield.

Hunter, D. G. 2011. 'Augustine on the Body', in M. Vessey (ed.) *A Companion to Augustine*. Oxford, Blackwell, pp. 353–364.

Irwin, T. H. 1996. 'Stoic Individuals', in *Philosophical Perspectives in Metaphysics*. Naples, Bibliopolis, pp. 459–480.

   1998. 'Mill and the Classical World', in J. Skorupski (ed.) *The Cambridge Companion to Mill*. Cambridge, Cambridge University Press, pp. 423–463.

Kaufmann, W. 1974. *Nietzsche: Philosopher, Psychologist, Anti-Christ*, 4th edition. Princeton, Princeton University Press.

Koterski, J. 2004. 'Boethius and the theological Origins of the Concept of Person', *ACPQ* 78: 203–224.

Lacroix J. and J.-Y. Pranchère, 2018. *Human Rights on Trial: A Genealogy of the Critique of Human Rights*. Cambridge, Cambridge University Press.

Laing, J. A. 2004. 'Law, Liberalism and the Common Good', in D. S. Oderberg and T. J. D. Chappell (eds.) *Human Value: New Essays in Ethics and Natural Law*. London/New York, Palgrave MacMillan, pp. 184–216.

Lamont, J. 2011. 'In Defence of Villey on Objective Right', in H. Ramsey (ed.) *Truth and Faith in Ethics*. Exeter, Imprint Academic, pp. 177–198.

Lantigua, D. M. 2016. 'Faith, Liberty and the Defense of the Poor: Bishop Las Cass in the History of Human Rights', in T. S. Shah and A. D. Hertzke (eds.) *Christianity and Freedom, Vol. 1*. New York, Cambridge University Press, pp. 176–209.

Lewis, E. 1995. 'The Stoics on Identity and Individuation', *Phronesis* 40: 89–108.

Lloyd, A. C. 1970. 'Aristotle's Principle of Individuation' *Mind* 79: 519–529.

Long, A. A. 2006a. 'Stoic Philosophers on Persons, Property-Ownership, and Community', in *From Epicurus to Epictetus: Studies in Hellenistic and Roman Philosophy*. Oxford, Oxford University Press, pp. 335–359.

   2006b. 'Seneca on the Self', in *From Epicurus to Epictetus: Studies in Hellenistic and Roman Philosophy*. Oxford, Oxford University Press.

MacIntyre, A. 1981. *After Virtue: A Study in Moral Theory*. South Bend, Notre Dame University Press.

   1999. *Dependent Rational Animals*. London, Duckworth.

   2006. *Edith Stein: A Philosophical Prologue: 1913–1922*. Lanham, Rowman and Littlefield.

   2016. *Ethics in the Conflicts of Modernity: An Essay on Desire, Practical Reasoning and Narrative*. Cambridge, Cambridge University Press.

Malo, A. 2017. *Uomo o Donna; Una Differenza che Conta*. Milan, Vita e Pensiero.

Mann, W. 1983. 'Dreams of Immorality', *Philosophy* 58: 378–385.

   1999. 'Inner Life Ethics', in G.B. Matthews (ed.) *The Augustinian Tradition*. London, Los Angeles, San Francisco, University of California Press, pp. 140–165.

Manning, C. E. 1986 'Stoicism and Slavery in the Roman Empire', *ANRW* 36(3), 1518–1543.

Markus, R. 1964. '"Imago" and "Similitudo" in Saint Augustine', *Revue des études augustiniennes* 10: 125–143.

Martin, R. and J. Barresi 2000. *Naturalization of the Self: Self and Personal Identity in the Eighteenth Century*. London/New York, Routledge.

Martin R. and J. Barresi 2001. *Authority and Estrangement: An Essay on Self-Knowledge*. Princeton University Press.

Matthews, G. B. 1981. 'On being Immoral in a Dream', *Philosophy* 56: 47–54.

Mautner, T. 1989. 'Pufendorf and the Correlativity theory of Rights', in S. Lindstrom and W. Rabinowicz (eds.) *'In So Many Words': Philosophical Essays Dedicated to Sven Danielsson on the Occasion of his Fiftieth Brithday*. Uppsala, Uppsala University Press, pp. 37–57.

Meconi, D. 1996. 'Augustine's Early Theory of Participation', *Augustinian Studies* 27: 79–96.

Menn, S. 1998. *Descartes and Augustine*. Cambridge, Cambridge University Press.

Milbank, J. 2004. 'The Gift of Ruling: Secularization and Political Authority', *New Blackfriars* 85, pp. 212–238.

    2012. 'Against Human Rights: Liberty in the Western Tradition', *Oxford Journal of Law and Religion*, pp. 1–32.

Miller, J. 2011. 'Review of S. Borden Sharkey, *Thine own Self: Individuation in Edith Stein's Later Writings*', *ACPQ* 85: 341–343.

Motta, B. 2004. *La Mediazione Esterna*. Padova, Il Poligrafo.

    2010. 'Nemesius', in L. P. Gerson (ed.) *The Cambridge History of Philosophy in Late Antiquity*. Cambridge, Cambridge University Press, pp. 509–519.

Moyn, S. 2014. *The Meaning of Rights. The Philosophy and Social Theory of Human Rights*. Cambridge, Cambridge University Press.

Nagel, T. 1986. *The View from Nowhere*. New York, Oxford University Press.

Nédoncelle, M. 1948. 'Prosopon et persona dans l'antiquité classique', *Revue des sciences religieuses* 22: 278–299.

Noone, T. B. 2003. 'Universals and Individuation', in T. Williams (ed.) *The Cambridge Companion to Duns Scotus*. Cambridge, Cambridge University Press, pp. 102–128.

Nota, J. 1987. 'Edith Stein and Martin Heidegger', *Carmelite Studies* 4: 50–73.

Nozick, R. 1974. *Anarchy, State and Utopia*. New York, Basic Books.

O'Callaghan, J. P. 2007. 'Imago Dei: A Test Case for St Thomas' Augustinianism', in M. Dauphinais, B. David and M. Levering (eds.) *Aquinas the Augustinian*. Washington, DC, Catholic University of America Press, pp. 100–144.

Oderberg, D. 2005. 'Hylomorphic Dualism', in E. F. Paul, F. D. Miller Jr. and Jeffrey Paul (eds.) *Personal Identity*. Cambridge, Cambridge University Press, pp. 70–91.

    2007. *Real Essentialism*. New York, London, Routledge and Kegan Paul.

O'Daly, G. 1987. *Augustine's Philosophy of Mind*. London, Duckworth.

O'Donovan, O. 1984. *Begotten or Made?* Oxford, Oxford University Press.

O'Meara, D. 2010. 'Plotinus', in L. P. Gerson (ed.) *The Cambridge History of Philosophy in Late Antiquity* 1. Cambridge, Cambridge University Press, pp. 301–324.

Parfit, D. 1986. *Reasons and Persons*. Oxford, Oxford University Press.

2011. *On What Matters*. Oxford, Oxford University Press.

Pembroke, S. G. 1996. 'Oikeiosis', in A. A. Long (ed.) *Problems in Stoicism*. London, Athlone Press, pp. 114–149.

Pera, M. 2015. *Diritti umani e cristianesimo*. Venice, Marsilio Editor.

Ramelow, A. 2013. 'The Person in the Abrahamic Tradition', *ACPQ* 87: 593–610.

Ratzinger, J. 1990. 'Concerning the Notion of Person in Theology', *Communio* 17: 438–454.

Rauschning, H. 1939. *The Revolution of Nihilism*. London/New York, William Heinemann.

Renaud, F. and H. Tarrant. 2015. *The Platonic Alcibiades 1: The Dialogue and its Ancient Setting*. Cambridge, Cambridge University Press.

Riley, P. 1986. *The General Will before Rousseau: The Transformation of the Divine into the Civic*. Princeton University Press.

Rist, J. M. 1963. 'Forms of individuals in Plotinus', *Classical Quarterly* 13: 223–231.

1973. 'Forms of Individuals in Plotinus: A Reply to Dr. Blumenthal', *Revue Internationale de Philosophie* 24: 298–303.

1982. *Human Value: A Study of Ancient Philosophical Ethics (Philosophia Antiqua* 40). Leiden, Brill.

1988. 'Ps-Ammonius and the Soul/Body Problem in Late Antiquity', *AJP* 109: 402–415.

1989. *The Mind of Aristotle*. Toronto, University of Toronto Press.

1993/1996. 'Is Plotinus' Account of the Body too Etherialized?', in K. Lee, C. Mackie and H. Tarrant (ed.) *Multarum Artium Scientia: Festschrift for Godfrey Tanner (Prudentia Suppl.)*. Auckland, University of Auckland, 1993 [reprinted as Essay XV in *Mind, Soul and Body: Essays from Plato to Dionysius*. London, Ashgate, 1996].

1994. *Augustine: Ancient Thought Baptized*. Cambridge, Cambridge University Press.

1998. 'Plotinian Soul, Aristotelian Form and Christian Person', in A. Baumgarten, J. Assman, G. G. Stroumsa (ed.) *Self, Soul and Person in Religious Experience*. Leiden, Brill, pp. 347–362.

2000. 'What will I be like tomorrow? Augustine vs Hume', *ACPQ* 74: 95–114.

2007. 'On the Original Nature of Christian Philosophy', in R. E. Houser (ed.) *Laudemus Viros Gloriosos: Essays in Honor of Armand Maurer, CSB*. South Bend, University of Notre Dame Press, pp. 13–37.

2008. *What is Truth: From the Academy to the Vatican*. Cambridge, Cambridge University Press.

2012. 'On the Nature and Worth of Christian Philosophy: Evidence from the *City of God*', in J. Wetzel (ed.) *Augustine's City of God: A Critical Guide*. Cambridge, Cambridge University Press, pp. 205–224.

2014. *Augustine Deformed: Love, Sin and Freedom in the Western Moral Tradition*. Cambridge, Cambridge University Press.

2016. 'Augustine and Religious Freedom', in T. S. Shah and A. D. Hertzke (ed.) *Christianity and Freedom, Vol. 1*. New York, Cambridge University Press, pp. 103–122.

Robinson, R. 1948, 'The emotive theory of ethics', *ASPS* 22:79–106.
Rosen, M. 2012. *Dignity: Its History and Meaning.* Cambridge, MA, Harvard University Press.
Salas Jr., V. M. 2011. 'Edith Stein and Medieval Metaphysics', *ACPQ* 85: 323–340.
Schacht, R. 1984. 'Nietzsche: Art and Artists', in T. Honderich (ed.) *Philosophy though its Past.* Harmondsworth, Pelican, pp. 399–432.
Scheler, M. 1973. *Formalism in Ethics and the Formal Ethics of Value* (English trans.), 3rd edition. Chicago, Northwestern University Press.
Schneewind, J. R. 1998. *The Invention of Autonomy.* Cambridge, Cambridge University Press.
Schrenk, R. 1991. 'Athroisma in Didaskalikos 4.7', *Hermes* 119: 497–500.
Scola, A. 2005. *The Nuptial Mystery* (trans. M. K. Borras). Grand Rapids/ Cambridge, Fortress.
Scruton, R. 2017. *On Human Nature.* Princeton and Oxford, Princeton University Press.
Sedley, D. 1982. 'The Stoic Category of Identity', *Phronesis* 27: 255–275.
Seigel, J. 2005. *The Idea of the Self.* Cambridge, Cambridge University Press.
Shah, T. S. and A. D. Hertzke (eds) 2016. *Christianity and Freedom, Vol. 1: Historical Perspectives.* New York, Cambridge University Press.
Shklar, N. 2001. 'Rousseau's Images of Authority, especially in *La nouvelle Héloise*', in P. Riley (ed.) *The Cambridge Companion to Rousseau.* Cambridge, Cambridge University Press, pp. 154–192.
Smilansky, S. 2000. *Free Will and Illusion.* Oxford, Oxford University Press.
  2002. 'Free Will, Fundamental Dualism and the Centrality of Illusion', in R. Kane (ed.) *The Oxford Handbook of Free Will.* Oxford, Oxford University Press, pp. 489–505.
Smith, S. D. 2010. *The Disenchantment of Secular Discourse.* Cambridge, MA, Harvard University Press.
Sokolowski, R. 1985. *Moral Action: A Phenomenological Study.* Bloomington, Indiana University Press.
  2003. 'Language, the Human Person and Christian Faith', *PACPA* 76: 27–38.
  2008. *Phenomenology of the Human Person.* Cambridge, Cambridge University Press.
Sorabji, R. 1988. *Matter, Space and Motion.* London, Duckworth.
Spaemann, R. 2012. *Persons: The Difference between 'Someone' and 'Something'* (trans. O. O'Donovan). Oxford, Oxford University Press.
Starobinski, J. 1978. '"Se mettre à sa place"; la mutation de la critique, de l'âge classique à Diderot', *Cahiers Vilfredo Pareto* 38: 363–378.
  1988. *Jean-Jacques Rousseau: Transparency and Obstruction* (trans. A. Goldhammer). Chicago University Press.
Stock, B. 2017. *The Integrated Self.* Philadelphia, University of Pennsylvania Press.
Strawson, G. 2005. 'Against Narrativity', in G. Strawson (ed.) *The Self.* Oxford, Blackwell, pp. 63–86.
Strawson, P. A. 1959. *Individuals: An Essay in Descriptive Metaphysics.* London, Methuen.

Strawson, P. F. 1974. 'Freedom and Resentment', in Freedom and Resentment and other Essays. London, Methuen, pp. 1–28.

Tassi, H. 1993. 'Persona as the Mark of Being', Philosophy Today 37: 201–210.

Taylor, C. 1989. Sources of the Self. Cambridge, MA, Harvard University Press.

Teske, R. 1990. 'The image and likeness of God in St. Augustine's De Genesi ad Litteram liber imperfectus', Augustinianum 30: 441–451.

Thomson, A. (ed.) 1996. Julian Offray de la Mettrie, Man the Machine and Other Writing. Cambridge, Cambridge University Press.

Tierney, B. 1989. 'The Origin of Natural Rights Language', HPT 10: 615–646.

1997. The Idea of Natural Rights: Studies in Natural Rights, Natural Law and Church Law 1150–1625. Atlanta, Scholars Press.

Tornau, C. 2009. 'Qu'est-ce qu'un individu ? Unité, individualité et conscience de soi dans la métaphysique plotinienne de l'âme', Les Etudes Philosophiques 90: 333–360.

Tristram Engelhardt Jr., H. 1986. The Foundations of Ethics. Oxford, Oxford University Press.

Tuck, R. 1979. Natural Rights Theories: Their Origin and Development. Cambridge, Cambridge University Press.

Tullius, W. E. 2013. 'Haecceitas as Value and as Moral Horizon: A Scotist Contribution to the Project of Phenomenological Ethics', ACPQ 87: 459–480.

Vimercati, E. 2007. 'Tre studi recenti sull'oikeiosis e sul fondamento del morale stoico', Rivista di Filosofia Neoscolastica 99: 573–608.

2014. 'Panaetius on Self-Knowledge and Moral Responsibility', in P. Destrée, R. Salles and M. Zingano (eds.) What is up to Us? Studies in Agency and Responsibility in Ancient Philosophy. Sankt Augustin, Akademia, pp. 151–167.

Voitle, R. 1874. The Third Earl of Shaftesbury 1671–1713. Baton Rouge.

Watt, I. 1957. The Rise of the Novel. London, Chatto and Windus.

West, J. L. A. 2007. 'The Real Distinction between Supposit and Nature', in P.A. Kwasniewski (ed.) Wisdom's Apprentice: Thomistic Essays in Honor of Lawrence Dewan O.P. Washington, DC, CUA Press, pp. 85–106.

Whiting, J. 1986. 'Form and Individuation in Aristotle', HPQ 3: 359–377.

Williams, B. A. O. 1973. 'Consequentialism and Beyond', in B. A. O. Williams and J. J. Smart (eds) Utilitarianism: For and Against. Cambridge, Cambridge University Press.

Wippel, J. 2000. The Metaphysical Thought of Thomas Aquinas. Washington, DC, CUA Press.

Wojtyla, K. 1978. 'Subjectivity and the Irreducible in Man', Analecta Husserliana VII. Dordrecht, Reidel, pp. 107–114.

1980 Uber die Möglichkeit eine christliche Ethik in Anlehnung an Max Scheler zu schaffen. Stuttgart-Degerloch, Seewald.

Wolter, M. M. 2013. 'Karol Wojtyla's Ethical Personalism', ACPQ 87: 97–115.

Wood, R. E. 2010.'Art and Truth; From Plato through Nietzsche to Heidegger', in K. Pritzl (ed.) Truth: Studies of a Robust Presence. Washington, DC, Catholic University of America Press, pp. 232–276.

Woods, M. J. 1968. 'Problems in Metaphysics Z, chapter 13', in J. M. E. Moravcsik (ed.) *Aristotle: A Collection of Critical Essays*. South Bend, Notre Dame University Press, pp. 215–238.

Yolton, J. 1970. *Locke and the Compass of Human Understanding*. Cambridge, Cambridge University Press.

Young, F. 2013. *God's Presence: A Contemporary Reappraisal of Early Christianity*. Cambridge, Cambridge University Press.

Zarka, Y.-C. 1993. 'Identité et ipseité chez Hobbes et Locke', *Philosophie* 37: 5–19.

Zuckert, M. 2000. 'Natural Rights in the American Revolution: An American Amalgam', in R. Wasserstrom, L. Hunt and M. B. Young (eds) *Human Rights and Revolutions*. Lanham, Rowman and Littlefield, pp. 59–76.

Index